THE
EDUCATION
OF
BRETT
KAVANAUGH

PORTFOLIO / PENGUIN

THE
EDUCATION
OF
BRETT
KAVANAUGH

AN INVESTIGATION

ROBIN POGREBIN
and **KATE KELLY**

PORTFOLIO / PENGUIN
An imprint of Penguin Random House LLC
penguinrandomhouse.com

Library of Congress Cataloging-in-Publication Data
Names: Pogrebin, Robin, author. | Kelly, Kate, 1975–, author.
Title: The education of Brett Kavanaugh / Robin Pogrebin, Kate Kelly.
Description: New York : Portfolio/Penguin, 2019. | Includes bibliographical references.
Identifiers: LCCN 2019027621 (print) | LCCN 2019027622 (ebook) |
ISBN 9780593084397 (hardcover) | ISBN 9780593084403 (ebook)
Subjects: LCSH: Kavanaugh, Brett Michael, 1965– | United States. Supreme Court—Officials
and employees—Biography. | Judges—United States—Biography.
Classification: LCC KF8745.K38 P64 2019 (print) | LCC KF8745.K38 (ebook) |
DDC 347.73/263 [B]—dc23
LC record available at https://lccn.loc.gov/2019027621
LC ebook record available at https://lccn.loc.gov/2019027622

Printed in the United States of America
1   3   5   7   9   10   8   6   4   2

BOOK DESIGN BY MEIGHAN CAVANAUGH

To our families

CONTENTS

AUTHORS' NOTE

On September 28, 2018, after a wrenching Senate hearing in which a California professor accused the Supreme Court nominee Judge Brett M. Kavanaugh of sexually assaulting her as a teenager, the Federal Bureau of Investigation opened an inquiry into the matter. Ten people were interviewed. Kavanaugh and his accuser, Christine Blasey Ford, were not among them.

Six days later, members of the Senate Judiciary Committee gathered in a secure facility to review the FBI's report on the allegations. It was inconclusive. Armed with two deeply conflicting accounts and little else but contextual details, the committee voted to confirm Kavanaugh to the high court on October 6. Later that day, he took the oath of office.

During that same period, dozens of people from Kavanaugh's past clamored to be heard. The FBI, Senate offices, and newsrooms had been overwhelmed with messages from friends, former classmates, and acquaintances of the judge, offering a range of perspectives on his life and work. Some had known Kavanaugh as a youth. Others knew him at different points in his career. The vast majority were never able to reach the FBI to have their input considered.

With so many loose ends dangling, much of the country had a sense of unfinished business—and so did we. Thanks to unexpected news tips and our shared backgrounds with the judge, we had been pulled off our regular beats at *The New York Times*—Robin culture and Kate business—to join the team covering Kavanaugh's confirmation. Robin was in Kavanaugh's class at Yale, just a few doors away from him in the freshman dorm. Like Kavanaugh, Kate grew up in the Washington, D.C., area and attended a girls' high school in the network of his high school, Georgetown Prep.

After Kavanaugh was confirmed, we put away our notebooks and moved on to other stories. But we continued to think about the leads that had come to light during the confirmation process and the questions that remained unanswered.

Did Brett Kavanaugh assault one or several women during his youth? Should he be on the Supreme Court, where he is poised to be a swing vote on matters of security, social justice, and personal freedom? How do we dispassionately examine these questions when the allegations are so emotionally resonant for so many people? And what did we learn about Justice Kavanaugh, our country, and ourselves from the polarizing confirmation process?

We set out to complete the investigation. Over a ten-month period, we read thousands of pages of media accounts and public documents; studied high school and college writings from the 1980s; watched video of Kavanaugh's past speeches and testimony; and conducted hundreds of interviews.

In the course of our efforts, we spoke to Ford, Deborah Ramirez, Leland Keyser, and, briefly, to Mark Judge. Kavanaugh himself declined to be interviewed.

We are grateful to the scores of other people who informed our work, many of whom are on the record and are referenced in the text. Because of the heated nature of the Kavanaugh confirmation debate and the harassment and death threats endured by Kavanaugh, Ford, and others involved, many of our sources declined to be identified by name. Their recollections are embedded in this book but not cited individually.

Some of our published sources are referred to directly in the text of the book. In places where sources are not noted in the main body of the text, or where further reading could be informative, we have referenced our sources in the notes. Information that is not explicitly noted in either place comes from source interviews or documents that are not publicly available and have been reviewed by the authors with the understanding that the source would not be named.

For Kavanaugh—and for our country—the confirmation was an education in the political partisanship and cultural sensitivities of the current moment two years after a polarizing presidential election and one year into the galvanizing #MeToo movement. It was also a cautionary tale of how past behavior can impact future prospects—a heightened reality in the age of social media, when so much is now recorded.

We realize that our readers will evaluate the results of our investigation through their own perspectives. In the course of our reporting, we saw how easy it was for observers to project onto the confirmation process whatever they wanted to believe. Even without a fuller sense of the facts, many had already made up their minds.

It is hard—maybe impossible—to set aside personal history or political orientation when considering the questions about Kavanaugh. If Kavanaugh mistreated Ford and Ramirez but has conducted himself honorably in the past thirty-six years, does he deserve to be on the court? If there is not dispositive proof that Kavanaugh engaged in such misbehavior, were the accusations enough to eliminate him from consideration? Was his temperament during the last day of testimony in itself disqualifying?

We leave those conclusions to our readers. No doubt they will be debated for many years to come.

DRAMATIS PERSONAE

BRETT M. KAVANAUGH, judge on the U.S. Circuit Court of Appeals

ASHLEY ESTES KAVANAUGH, his wife

MARTHA KAVANAUGH, his mother

EDWARD KAVANAUGH, his father

FROM KAVANAUGH'S TIME AT GEORGETOWN PREP

MARK JUDGE, journalist and author, former classmate

PATRICK J. SMYTH, managing director at accounting firm, former classmate

CHRIS GARRETT, teacher and former classmate

DONALD J. URGO, former classmate and close friend

TOM DOWNEY, former classmate

WILLIAM FISHBURNE, former classmate

PAUL RENDÓN, teacher and former classmate

DRAMATIS PERSONAE

MICHAEL BIDWILL, football team president and friend

GREGORY PAPPAJOHN, former classmate

JOE CONAGHAN, former classmate

RENATE SCHROEDER DOLPHIN, high school friend

FROM KAVANAUGH'S TIME AT YALE COLLEGE

DAVID WHITE, former suitemate and friend of Kavanaugh

KEVIN GENDA, former classmate and friend of Kavanaugh

KAREN YARASAVAGE, former classmate and friend of Kavanaugh

DAVID TODD, former classmate and friend of Kavanaugh

MARK KRASBERG, professor and former classmate

KENNETH APPOLD, religious historian and former classmate

JAMES ROCHE, tech company executive, former roommate

TRACY HARMON JOYCE, former classmate

RICHARD OH, emergency-room doctor and former classmate

KERRY BERCHEM, lawyer and former schoolmate (class of 1988)

CHAD LUDINGTON, former classmate

MALCOLM FRANK, former schoolmate (class of 1988)

FROM KAVANAUGH'S TIME AT YALE LAW SCHOOL

JAMES E. "JEB" BOASBERG, federal appeals court judge and close friend

RICHARD ROBERTS, real estate investor and former classmate

KENNETH CHRISTMAS, entertainment executive and former classmate

DRAMATIS PERSONAE

ON CAPITOL HILL

CHARLES GRASSLEY, Republican senator from Iowa, chairman of the Judiciary Committee

DIANNE FEINSTEIN, Democratic senator from California, ranking member of the Judiciary Committee

MIKE DAVIS, chief nominations counsel to the committee

JENNIFER DUCK, Democratic staff director for the committee, Feinstein's former chief of staff

LINDSEY GRAHAM, Republican senator from South Carolina, committee member

AMY KLOBUCHAR, Democratic senator from Minnesota, committee member

SHELDON WHITEHOUSE, Democratic senator from Rhode Island, committee member

CHRISTOPHER COONS, Democratic senator from Delaware, committee member

JEFF FLAKE, Republican senator from Arizona, committee member

MITCH MCCONNELL, Senate majority leader

IN SILICON VALLEY

CHRISTINE BLASEY FORD, psychology professor

RUSSELL FORD, her husband

ANNA ESHOO, Democratic congresswoman from California's Eighteenth District

KAREN CHAPMAN, Eshoo's district chief of staff

KEITH KOEGLER, friend of Ford

JAY BACKSTRAND, friend of Ford

KIRSTEN LEIMROTH, friend of Ford

REID HOFFMAN, entrepreneur

MARK PINCUS, entrepreneur

IN COLORADO

DEBORAH RAMIREZ, volunteer coordinator and Kavanaugh's classmate

VIKRAM SHAH, her husband

STAN GARNETT, lawyer to Ramirez

JOHN CLUNE, lawyer to Ramirez

IN THE WHITE HOUSE

DONALD J. TRUMP, president

DONALD F. MCGAHN II, chief counsel

KERRI KUPEC, spokeswoman

IN WASHINGTON

ANTHONY KENNEDY, retiring Supreme Court justice

CHERYL AMITAY, former schoolmate and supporter of Ford

LISA BANKS, lawyer to Ford

ZINA BASH, lawyer and former clerk to Kavanaugh

MICHAEL BROMWICH, lawyer to Ford

WILLIAM A. BURCK, lawyer and friend of Kavanaugh

MERRICK GARLAND, chief judge of the D.C. Circuit Court and colleague to Kavanaugh

NEIL M. GORSUCH, Supreme Court justice, former Georgetown Prep schoolmate to Kavanaugh

DEBRA KATZ, lawyer to Ford

LELAND INGHAM KEYSER, former classmate and friend of Ford

ROMAN MARTINEZ, lawyer and former clerk to Kavanaugh

MONICA MCLEAN, former classmate and friend of Ford

TRAVIS LENKNER, lawyer and former clerk to Kavanaugh

LARRY ROBBINS, lawyer to Ford

RICKI SEIDMAN, adviser to Ford

KENNETH W. STARR, independent counsel during the Whitewater investigation, 1994–1998

HOWARD WALSH, lawyer to Leland Ingham Keyser and fellow parishioner

PORTER WILKINSON, chief of staff to institutional board, former clerk to Kavanaugh

CHRISTOPHER WRAY, FBI director and Yale schoolmate of Kavanaugh

ELSEWHERE

ALEX KOZINSKI, retired federal judge and mentor to Kavanaugh

REBECCA TAIBLESON, federal prosecutor and former clerk to Kavanaugh

Nostos

Homecoming

I t was cold for October, with evening temperatures dropping into the forties as alumni poured onto Georgetown Preparatory School's leafy campus in suburban Maryland for their thirty-fifth-year high school reunion. It had been a tumultuous day for the country. A Florida man had been arrested for sending package bombs to more than a dozen prominent Democrats, including former president Barack Obama and former secretary of state Hillary Clinton. Despite the serious threat, President Donald Trump was focused on the upcoming midterm congressional elections and wanted his party to do the same. The "'Bomb' stuff," as Trump put it in a tweet, risked slowing Republican momentum at a critical time.

On the Georgetown Prep campus, hundreds of former students were gathering in the George Center, a large brick building adjacent to the football stadium where the school store and snack bar were located. Nicknamed "Stag Night" because significant others were not invited, the Friday evening cocktail gathering was the traditional start to Reunion Weekend. There would be welcome speeches from school officials; wisecracks about thickening waists and thinning hair; beer and finger food.

The next day, about four hundred people would gather to watch the school's football team, the Hoyas, play the homecoming game against Episcopal High School, despite the chilly, wet afternoon. During the years when it was still part of Georgetown University, Prep had at some point dubbed its teams the "Hoyas," which derived from the Latin cheer *"Hoya Saxa!"* (translation: "What Rocks!"). After this particular homecoming game—during which the Hoyas trounced their Episcopal High rivals, 24–6—classmates, spouses, and friends would toast over cocktails and trade stories at nearby Pinstripes, a bistro/bowling-and-bocce venue in North Bethesda.

Brett Kavanaugh typically welcomed these rare opportunities to reconnect and reminisce with old friends. But this year, he had seriously considered opting out. Three weeks had passed since his confirmation as the newest associate justice of the United States Supreme Court, about six since the devastating accusation that almost derailed it. So when he arrived on campus for his reunion, Kavanaugh was steeled for awkward interactions.

At the same time, he appeared resolutely upbeat, in keeping with his often articulated philosophy to "live on the sunrise side of the mountain."

As a justice on America's highest court, Kavanaugh now had a security detail that followed him to public places, particularly since, during the confirmation process, his wife had been targeted by vicious emails and his family had received death threats. Many of Kavanaugh's fellow Georgetown Prep alumni had been supportive. Nearly two hundred had signed a letter endorsing his Supreme Court candidacy when he was nominated. Some had even gone on TV to praise his character. But given the polarizing nature of the hearings, he knew that not everyone stood behind him.

The reunion was likely to be particularly fraught because the Georgetown Prep campus had been central to the drama. The friendships Kavanaugh built at the all-boys high school, the sports he played, and the hallways where he bantered with classmates had all featured prominently in his very public interrogation. Here was the lawn outside Boland Hall, where on Monday mornings before first period he and his friends recounted their weekend adventures. There was the football field, festooned with blue-and-gray Hoya signs, where he endured years of grueling drills and played cornerback and wide receiver. On the edge of the school's golf course, next to the dormitories, was the gilded chapel where he and his fellow students gathered for scheduled prayer during the week and before games on Saturdays.

At Stag Night, Kavanaugh walked in and scanned the sea of suits, blazers and khakis, taking in the steady thrum of conversation. He was noticed immediately. Those who hadn't known Kavanaugh as a student at Georgetown Prep recognized his face from the weeks of continual news coverage. Those who had followed him more closely noted that Kavanaugh was dressed in the same type of dark suit, white shirt, and royal-blue tie he had worn to his contentious final confirmation hearing on September 27.

One by one, alumni began approaching him, saying hello, shaking hands, expressing their good wishes. Kavanaugh smiled. "How are you? Good to see you!" he said jovially. The more recent graduates came forward first, while those from his own class hung back. Kavanaugh posed for pictures with some of the alums, as well as several of the kitchen staff.

Every conversation—including those Kavanaugh was not part

of—seemed to circle back to the Senate confirmation process. During the hearings, Christine Blasey Ford, a psychology professor at Palo Alto University and a research psychologist at the Stanford University School of Medicine, accused Kavanaugh of sexually assaulting her when they were teenagers. Her claims had been volcanic, precipitating additional misconduct reports and a late-stage FBI inquiry. In forceful public testimony, Kavanaugh had denied the Ford story and others, insisting he had never assaulted anyone.

Some of the guys at Stag Night poked fun at Kavanaugh's testimony among themselves and even playfully to his face, saying he had embellished his image and those of his high school friends—for example, describing Tobin Finizio, former co-captain of the varsity football team, as a "great quarterback" when they remembered it differently. Others, standing in smaller groups and away from the main crowd, speculated that the sexual assault allegations could well have been true. Still others avoided the topic entirely.

Among those in the crowd was Patrick J. Smyth, the amiable former football player whom Ford remembered being present at the gathering on the night she was allegedly attacked. Talking with his friends, Smyth, now a tall man, wearing casual pants and glasses, disputed the characterizations of Kavanaugh and his brethren that had dogged the justice's confirmation.

Although Ford had described Smyth in her testimony as a nice person who might have come to her aid if he had heard her cries for help, he had nonetheless endured uncomfortable public scrutiny and been one of the classmates interviewed by the FBI as part of an extended investigation.

Smyth said at the reunion that, as a longtime friend of Kavanaugh's, he had worried about being hurt professionally through "guilt by association," particularly since he had become the subject of unwanted media attention. Still, Smyth said that the substance of Ford's allegations had not worried him, because there was "nothing here."

The alumni talked about how difficult it was to remember incidents that had occurred decades ago, how everyone had embarrassing moments from high school, and how poisonous the political atmosphere had become. No one appeared to recall the scenario Ford had described. In other side conversations, however, several alumni questioned her character.

Smyth's group discussed a 1983 letter Kavanaugh had written to organize their attendance at Beach Week—an annual citywide seven days of partying in Ocean City, Maryland—that had been leaked to the press. By turns persnickety and salacious, the letter laid out Kavanaugh's travel schedule, the need to chip in for a $398 deposit on a condominium rental, and the fact that they should warn the neighbors about their disruptive drinking habits.

There was a general consensus that the letter rang true.

"It looked like classic Brett," said one of the classmates.

Yes, said another in agreement: "Classic Brett."

THE
EDUCATION
OF
BRETT
KAVANAUGH

ONE

Alea Iacta Est

The Die Has Been Cast

At nine o'clock on the evening of July 9, 2018, President Donald J. Trump gathered an audience in the White House's East Room to nominate Brett Kavanaugh to the Supreme Court. The judge, wearing a dark suit and crisp white shirt, was flanked by his two young daughters, Margaret and Liza, and his wife, Ashley, who stood smiling beside him.

A showman who relished his moments on camera, Trump joked about how he had rarely seen an East Room reception as warm as the one that Kavanaugh had received. Otherwise, the president was uncharacteristically disciplined as he read his speech from the teleprompter. "Judge Kavanaugh has impeccable credentials, unsurpassed qualifications, and a proven commitment to equal justice under the law," Trump said, clasping the podium with both hands. "He's a brilliant jurist, with a clear and effective writing style, universally regarded as one of the finest and sharpest legal minds of our time."

Kavanaugh then switched places with Trump, taking in the room as the crowd enthusiastically applauded. His parents were in the front row, seated next to First Lady Melania Trump. Nearby was Father John Enzler, the local Catholic Charities president, for whom Kavanaugh had once served as an altar boy. Zina Bash, one of Kavanaugh's favorite former law clerks, was in the second row, not far from his friend Roman Martinez, another former clerk, now a Supreme Court litigator, who caught Kavanaugh's eye and flashed him a quick thumbs-up.

Kavanaugh thanked the president for his warm remarks and said he was "deeply honored" to have been named to replace Justice Anthony M. Kennedy, for whom he had once clerked. He recognized his parents, his wife, and their children, brushing back what appeared to be tears of joy.

"Margaret loves sports, and she loves to read," he said of his older daughter, a tall, blond-haired basketball player. "Liza loves sports, and she loves to talk," he added, exchanging a grin and a quick hand slap with his younger daughter, a smaller brunette. He poked fun at his own nickname among the girls on his daughter's basketball team, "Coach K," implying with a furrowed brow and faux grimace that he was unworthy of the name most commonly attached to Mike Krzyzewski, the famed Duke University men's basketball coach.

Finally, he turned to the nomination process about to commence.

"Tomorrow, I begin meeting with members of the Senate, which plays an essential role in this process," Kavanaugh said. "I will tell each senator that I revere the Constitution. I believe that an independent judiciary is the crown jewel of our constitutional republic. If confirmed by the Senate, I will keep an open mind in every case, and I will always strive to preserve the Constitution of the United States and the American rule of law."

The moment was understandably heady. Kavanaugh had worked his whole life toward a Supreme Court nomination. He had studied at prestigious schools, apprenticed himself to powerful mentors, mastered Washington politics. He had also remembered his origins, staying true to old friends and maintaining his Catholic traditions. But nothing had prepared him for the perils he would face in the next few weeks. Those would be an education of a very different kind.

ON JUNE 27, JUSTICE KENNEDY had abruptly announced his retirement from the Supreme Court. The Missouri Democratic senator Claire McCaskill, one of the many politicians whose careers would be impacted by the process that followed, would later describe it as her "'oh shit' moment."

"Everybody in my office knew this was going to be a challenge," McCaskill, who learned of the news from a staffer yelling expletives at a computer screen telegraphing the news, told *The Daily* podcast. "Because it was going to bring to the forefront issues that divide us."

Kennedy's departure meant that Trump could replace him with a more reliable conservative, cementing a right-leaning majority on the court. That opportunity meant the White House—together with Majority Leader Mitch McConnell—would need to move quickly to get its nominee confirmed by the Republican-led Senate before the midterm elections, which threatened to upend their majority.

The stakes were also high for the Democrats, who had experienced a series of heartaches over the makeup of the court. The sudden death of conservative justice Antonin Scalia, in February 2016, had led to Obama's nomination of Merrick Garland, the respected chief judge on the D.C. Circuit Court. But McConnell and his caucus had effectively scuttled Garland's chances by refusing to grant him a

Senate hearing on the grounds that the incoming president should be the one to name Scalia's replacement.

A year later, when Trump took office, he named the conservative Tenth Circuit judge Neil Gorsuch to the court. Gorsuch's confirmation was practically assured by McConnell's implementation of the so-called nuclear option, which adapted the Senate rules governing federal court nominees so that a simple majority vote of 51 out of 100, rather than a supermajority of 60, would confirm a Supreme Court nominee. Democrats were fuming.

They were also worried about the future of landmark decisions, in particular *Roe v. Wade*. Despite the nation's deep divisions over the right to abortion, the 1973 *Roe* decision had, for forty-five years, withstood a number of court challenges, including the 1992 *Planned Parenthood of Southeastern Pennsylvania v. Casey*, which upheld all but one of several state restrictions on abortion.

The Affordable Care Act, President Barack Obama's legislation that aimed to broaden Americans' access to affordable health care, was also at risk. Over the years since its 2010 enactment, the law had been protected by the high court, even though repealing and replacing the act had been a centerpiece of Trump's presidential agenda. A 5–4 conservative majority on the high court would make defending the law considerably harder.

Kavanaugh shared history with both Gorsuch and Garland. Gorsuch had attended Georgetown Prep at the same time, starring in *The Odd Couple* along with some of Kavanaugh's classmates and graduating two years behind Kavanaugh. Garland was the chief justice on Kavanaugh's circuit court, and Kavanaugh deeply respected him. When Garland was nominated, Kavanaugh said he was "supremely qualified by the objective characteristics of experience, temperament, writing ability, scholarly ability for the Supreme Court." He described Garland as a role model and had voted with him 93 percent of the time while they were on the D.C. Circuit together.

That was precisely the reason Kavanaugh was not considered a top contender among Republicans now leading the effort to replace Justice Kennedy: he wasn't conservative enough.

Kavanaugh only grudgingly made the short list originally circulated among leading conservatives, which was generated by the Federalist Society, the originalist legal group that had become central to Trump's judicial nominations. He had disappointed them with his 2011 opinion on a case that challenged the legal basis of the Affordable Care Act. (Kavanaugh might have pleased conservatives by dissenting from the 2–1 ruling in Obamacare's favor, but he muddied the picture by saying judges had no jurisdiction to resolve the dispute over the legislation.)

The political right wanted a dependable conservative vote on the court to secure their majority. But they also wanted court candidates to come from outside the Washington establishment—ridiculed by Trump as the "swamp." The Federalist Society list was long on judges from the Midwest and the South, focused on red states like Indiana, Michigan, and Georgia that Trump carried in 2016 and might need again in 2020. Blue coastal states and Washington itself—which had minuscule bearing on the presidential election—were largely unrepresented.

In addition, Kavanaugh was closely associated with George W. Bush, having worked for several years in his White House. Trump was ill-disposed toward the Bush family, having bitterly clashed with Jeb Bush in the primary, during which he called Jeb the "low-energy" candidate in the GOP race.

Senator Charles E. Grassley's aide Mike Davis often summed up these Kavanaugh caveats to his colleagues in three words: "Bushy. Swampy. Chiefy."

Davis, a plain-speaking lawyer who had worked in the Bush 43 administration, thought Kavanaugh too much of an inside-the-Beltway creature who was more akin to the establishment George W. than the ideological Trump and therefore less likely to fire up the right-wing base. Davis also believed that Kavanaugh, much like the sitting chief justice, John Roberts, was far too concerned about the high court's legitimacy and his own legacy than about seizing a historic opportunity to shift decisions firmly to the right.

And Davis mattered: as chief counsel for nominations, he was the staff lead on the Senate Judiciary Committee for vetting and approving important federal judicial candidates. With a tight head of red hair, compact build, and caustic wit, Davis had a puckish aspect that belied his ruthless political acumen. He had grown up in Iowa and gone to work for Grassley right out of college, opening the senator's mail for six months before joining the Bush 43 administration. He had clerked for Gorsuch and helped the justice land in Scalia's seat in 2017.

Unapologetically unvarnished, Davis had also developed into an unflappable political operative and, as a redhead, often referred to himself as "a honey badger," in reference to the relentless, indestructible creature who became a YouTube sensation in 2011 and the motto of the conservative Breitbart News Network ("Honey badger don't give a shit"). Now and for the next several months, Davis would be one of the most powerful staff members on Capitol Hill.

In spring 2017, Grassley, chairman of the Judiciary Committee, saw a potentially formidable ally in that honey badger, given that Davis had helped shepherd eighty-four of the eighty-five federal judges who had been appointed under Trump, including Gorsuch. Davis and his allies in the White House thought the Gorsuch confirmation process had been challenging. But after Kavanaugh's confirmation process, Gorsuch's would come to look like a layup.

When Davis saw Richard L. Hasen's article in *Slate* on June 26 headlined "Did Justice Anthony Kennedy Just Signal His Retirement?," he immediately set to work preparing a statement for Grassley. Then, on the morning of June 27, Davis received a cryptic message from a friend "to be ready after 1 pm . . . something is coming."

Once the news of Kennedy's retirement began filtering out in the media, Davis sent a message to Republican staffers on the Judiciary Committee who handle nominations with the subject line "Kennedy is retiring." As chaos broke loose, Davis received an email from Kavanaugh's personal lawyer, Beth Wilkinson: "Here we go my friend."

Davis sent back his response: "Pumped."

But Davis wasn't pumped about Kavanaugh. He wanted Trump to nominate a candidate with the best chance of winning, shoring up the court's conservative contingent. In his view, either Amy Coney Barrett, the conservative Chicago Circuit Court judge who had taught at Notre Dame Law School, or Raymond M. Kethledge, a judge on Cincinnati's federal appeals court, was a better bet. In fact, Davis also could have been happy with many of the twenty-three other candidates on the list who had been vetted by the Federalist Society. The bottom line, which Davis voiced freely, was essentially that anyone would have been better than Kavanaugh.

Even before his divisive testimony in late September, Kavanaugh was found by two polls to have relatively low initial support for confirmation among recent Supreme Court nominees. This put him in a category with the infamous Robert Bork, who in 1987 was denied a seat on the court after Democrats like Senator Edward M. Kennedy of

Massachusetts warned of "a land in which women would be forced into back-alley abortions, blacks would sit at segregated lunch counters, rogue police could break down citizens' doors in midnight raids."

McConnell and Grassley were concerned about Kavanaugh's voluminous paper trail from his years in the White House Counsel's Office, and later as staff secretary to George W. Bush, when he was the guardian of the president's in and out box. Bush's senior political adviser, Karl Rove, shortly after Kavanaugh's nomination, described the latter position: "Literally every document that goes to the president on a policy issue has to pass through the hands of the staff secretary," Rove said on Fox. "He has to be the person who asks people tough questions about what they are trying to say in that document and helps edit it."

Because of all that correspondence—in which he was directly involved or cc'd—Kavanaugh was drowning in documents, any number of which could contain fodder for Democrats.

In Kavanaugh's last two rounds of confirmation hearings for the D.C. Circuit—in 2004 and 2006—Democratic senators had gone hard at the records from his Bush years. In particular, Kavanaugh was asked whether he knew that Judge Jay Bybee of the Ninth Circuit had written the infamous memo permitting the president to ignore the law that makes torture a crime. (Kavanaugh said he learned about the memo from the media.) Similarly, Kavanaugh testified in 2006 that he was "not involved in the questions about the rules governing detention of combatants." But reports later surfaced about a heated meeting in 2002 at which Bush's lawyers, including Kavanaugh, debated whether detainees should have legal counsel.

Senator Patrick J. Leahy, Democrat of Vermont, who was then chairman of the Judiciary Committee, subsequently asked Alberto R.

Gonzales, the attorney general at the time, to investigate this "possibly false testimony," which "played a critical role in many Senators' consideration of Mr. Kavanaugh's nomination." Gonzales's office ultimately determined there was insufficient basis for such an investigation.

Given this potential baggage and Kavanaugh's lack of a clear political constituency beyond D.C.'s borders, Davis kept telling people that Kavanaugh would be "the hardest one to confirm."

Kavanaugh was more a product of the Washington swamp, Davis argued, than he was a red-meat Republican who could transform the Supreme Court. He was popular with Bush White House alumni, prominent Republican lawyers in private practice, and the Washington-area country club crowd, which ranged from some of the city's political power brokers to the basketball moms who watched Kavanaugh's daughters play theirs courtside.

Many considered Gorsuch the more talented and confident writer. And while Gorsuch was largely uncontroversial, Kavanaugh was a known "bro," a highly social animal whose proximity to powerful men had raised uncomfortable questions about his connection to their own controversial policies. During Kavanaugh's previous confirmation hearings in the mid-aughts, a picture had made the rounds that showed him smiling as Karl Rove slung his arm around his shoulders— suggesting that Kavanaugh's judgeship was a political favor. It exemplified Kavanaugh's place in the GOP fraternity.

Even more potentially radioactive, some thought, was Kavanaugh's long association with Judge Alex Kozinski, who in December 2017 had retired after six women accused him of sexual harassment, a number that eventually grew to fifteen. Had Kavanaugh continued to direct law clerks to Kozinski, despite knowing about his misconduct, essentially, as one GOP aide put it, "sending lambs to slaughter"? Or had Kavanaugh really not known of the senior judge's harassment of women, as he would later claim?

McConnell wasn't enthusiastic about Kavanaugh, either. The seventy-six-year-old Kentuckian initially argued for his own pick: Amul Thapar of the Sixth Circuit, who had previously served as a federal judge in Lexington, in McConnell's home state. Most important to McConnell, however, was not blowing this opportunity to appoint a conservative justice. As one GOP staffer summarized McConnell's stance: "If we fail, we lose the senate, we lose the court, we lose the country."

As a result, McConnell was all over the nomination. Every day after Kennedy announced his retirement, McConnell was on the phone to Trump, White House counsel Donald F. McGahn II, or both. He counseled them "that there is no margin of error," *The New York Times* reported, "because the timing of the Senate's court vote is so close to an election that could hand control of the chamber to Democrats."

Other Republicans pushed for Barrett, a recent Trump appointee to the Seventh Circuit, who had an army of social conservatives behind her. They appreciated her accessible, non–Ivy League background, her legal reputation as a strict constructionist, and her strong Catholicism. Among Barrett's skeptics, there was concern over her ties to a Christian group called People of Praise, which dictates that the husband is the head of a family and that women be guided by oaths of loyalty to personal advisers formerly referred to as "handmaids." Also of concern was a 1998 law review article in which Barrett argued that in certain cases, Catholic judges should recuse themselves from decisions that involved the death penalty, a position upon which she later cast doubt.

Broadly, Barrett was viewed as a judge in the tradition of Scalia, for whom she had served as a law clerk. Kavanaugh was closely associated with Kennedy, who had proved a less reliable vote for social conservatives on several abortion and gay rights cases. Davis and some of the lawyers in McGahn's office feared that Kavanaugh would be similarly unpredictable.

On these grounds and others, Davis made no secret of his desire to eliminate Kavanaugh—to, as he later put it to colleagues, "take him out."

Stories soon showed up in the *Daily Caller*, a conservative news and opinion website, that Kavanaugh was "the low-energy Jeb Bush pick," invoking the epithet Trump had used to denigrate Jeb during the 2016 election. Republicans who opposed choosing Kavanaugh planted the story in the hopes that it would help push the president, who had a printout from the *Daily Caller* delivered to his desk every day, toward choosing a different Supreme Court nominee.

But Kavanaugh skeptics had a powerful force working against them: McGahn, who had counted Kavanaugh as a good friend and party loyalist since their days working for Bush. "Brett's always been a team player," McGahn would tell his colleagues.

As White House counsel, McGahn was responsible for vetting potential nominees on behalf of the president. A seemingly self-contained Republican stalwart who often wore his hair long and his mouth turned down, he never really clicked with Trump. But the president knew what he didn't know when it came to picking judges, so he had delegated that process to McGahn, along with McConnell and the Federalist Society.

As a result, Kavanaugh came to be regarded inside the White House as one of the top two contenders for the newly open seat, ultimately vying only with Barrett.

McGahn's White House staff had been working toward this moment for more than a year. In the aftermath of the Gorsuch confirmation, in April 2017, a collection of staffers had thoroughly researched another half dozen or so leading conservatives as possible nominees.

Kavanaugh's more than three hundred judicial opinions were read closely and marked with color codes indicating their future implications: green for reliably conservative, red for a potentially divisive break with traditional thinking, and yellow for something in between.

During that period, Kennedy had signaled that he might be leaving the court soon, hiring clerks for the October term but suggesting that he may not stay. When Kennedy made no moves to depart, however, he was assumed to be staying put for a while. Then came his surprise announcement, after Kennedy was privately assured by the White House that Trump would strive to preserve the justice's Supreme Court legacy and that he was leaning toward replacing Kennedy with the justice's former clerk Kavanaugh.

McGahn immediately sprang into action, calling Kavanaugh just a few hours after the Kennedy news broke and meeting with him in person two days later. McGahn was present on July 2, when Kavanaugh was interviewed by Trump, and two days later when the judge met with Vice President Mike Pence. On the morning of Sunday, July 8, Kavanaugh spoke again with Trump, this time by phone, and that evening he sat down with the president and his wife, Melania, at the White House. During that meeting, Trump offered Kavanaugh the nomination and he accepted, speaking later that evening with McGahn.

McGahn was on his way out of the White House, having clashed with Trump and cooperated with the investigation of the president by special counsel Robert S. Mueller III. Kavanaugh's confirmation would be McGahn's last push—for Trump's legacy as well as his own. He planned to leave the job as soon as his friend's place on the bench was assured. "He wanted to steer that process in a good and principled direction—he was Kavanaugh's sherpa," said Akhil Reed Amar, a prominent constitutional law professor at Yale Law School. "He persuaded Trump to go with Kavanaugh, and he persuaded Trump to stick with Kavanaugh after Ford. Kavanaugh is McGahn's greatest accomplishment."

Many assumed that Leonard A. Leo, the Federalist Society's executive vice president, was also pulling the strings, but—having been cut out of the Gorsuch nomination process because he was viewed by GOP staffers as hoarding credit—Leo accepted more of a backseat as one of McGahn's soldiers.

With McGahn in charge, Davis was forced to stand down in his opposition to Kavanaugh. And then he stepped up: if Kavanaugh was going to be the nominee, Davis was going to do whatever it took to get him confirmed. What mattered, in the end, was filling Kennedy's seat with a conservative, and doing so before the midterm elections could potentially upset the power structure in Congress.

And Team Kavanaugh had another force working in their favor: Justice Kennedy himself. With Kavanaugh as his clerk in 1993 and then as one of the two judges he trusted to vet his future clerks (along with Judge Alex Kozinski), Kennedy had developed a fatherly relationship with Kavanaugh over the years. Trump was also likely to take Kennedy's preference for Kavanaugh into consideration, since the president was kindly disposed toward the justice. Kennedy's son Justin, who had been Deutsche Bank's global head of real estate capital, had worked closely with Trump's son Donald Jr.

CHARLES SCHUMER, the New York Democrat who was the Senate's minority leader, immediately announced his strong opposition to

Kavanaugh. Schumer, a gray-haired political street fighter who people joked was at his most dangerous when something came between him and a microphone, said he'd fight the candidacy with everything he had. In a press conference held outside the high court the day after Kavanaugh's nomination, Schumer, along with California Democrat Kamala Harris and Connecticut senator Richard Blumenthal, inveighed against Kavanaugh's past decisions on abortion, gun control, and presidential powers.

Republicans pounced on these pronouncements as canned invective. "They wrote statements of opposition only to fill in the name later," said Mitch McConnell in a press release that day.

Though Democrats tried to paint Kavanaugh as an evil threat, he wasn't easy to demonize. The judge had an impressive résumé as a public servant. He had forged important connections throughout his career, as a law clerk to Walter Stapleton of the U.S. Court of Appeals for the Third Circuit, then to the influential Kozinski on the Court of Appeals for the Ninth Circuit, and ultimately to Justice Kennedy on the Supreme Court.

The private sector seemed to hold little appeal for Kavanaugh, despite the multimillion-dollar paychecks that an attorney of his experience could have pulled in at a prestigious Washington law practice. Kavanaugh had spent just a few years total—a stint interrupted by government jobs—at the law firm Kirkland & Ellis. He had earned the loyalty, trust, and admiration of a U.S. president, working for George W. Bush as associate counsel, senior associate counsel, assistant to the president, and staff secretary. He had been an associate counsel in the office of independent counsel Kenneth W. Starr, where he led the investigation into the death of President Bill Clinton's aide Vince Foster and was a principal author of the Starr Report to Congress on the Monica Lewinsky scandal.

Kavanaugh was a lifelong Republican and an observant Catholic. If his GOP connections had recently grown more pronounced, that likely seemed to him a necessary strategy, signaling to Republicans that they could count on him if appointed to the Supreme Court. And Kavanaugh had the conservative establishment behind him—influential voices that included the Heritage Foundation, the Federalist Society, the senior D.C. Circuit Court judge Laurence Silberman, and an array of conservative lawyers across the country. J. D. Vance, author of the bestselling memoir *Hillbilly Elegy*—who took Kavanaugh's law school class at Yale and whose wife, Usha, had clerked for Kavanaugh— argued the case for Kavanaugh in an op-ed.

"His judicial record spans just about every important area of the law," Vance wrote, citing the fact that Kavanaugh's opinions had been adopted by the Supreme Court eleven times, "and conservatives should be happy with the results."

Akhil Reed Amar, who had taught Kavanaugh at Yale Law School, wrote in a *New York Times* op-ed, headlined "A Liberal's Case for Brett Kavanaugh," that he was "a superb nominee."

"More important, he is an avid consumer of legal scholarship," Amar continued. "He reads and learns. And he reads scholars from across the political spectrum."

But not all of the Yale community was united behind Kavanaugh. On July 10, Yale Law students, alumni, and educators issued an open letter, taking Dean Heather K. Gerken and the Yale Law School leadership to task for issuing a press release that touted Kavanaugh's qualifications, saying they were "ashamed of our alma mater."

"Judge Kavanaugh's nomination presents an emergency—for democratic life, for our safety and freedom, for the future of our country," the letter said. "Support for Judge Kavanaugh is not apolitical. It is a political choice about the meaning of the constitution and our vision of democracy, a choice with real consequences for real people. Without a doubt, Judge Kavanaugh is a threat to the most vulnerable. He is a threat to many of us, despite the privilege bestowed by our education, simply because of who we are."

The institution where Kavanaugh had happily spent his undergraduate and graduate school years—and to which he had eagerly returned for reunions and football games—would soon become a cauldron of debate due to the allegations against him, a campus where he might never feel entirely welcome again.

TWO

Hoya Saxa

What Rocks

Kavanaugh had barely stepped away from the podium in the White House East Room on July 9, after accepting the Supreme Court nomination in front of his family and political supporters, when another critical support base mobilized: his high school classmates. Less than an hour after the nomination's announcement, a letter signed by nearly two hundred Georgetown Prep alumni was released, praising Kavanaugh's strong character and intellect.

An elite Jesuit boys' school on the outskirts of Washington that was founded in 1789, Georgetown Prep educates the sons of affluent religious families, with an emphasis on faith, academics, and athletics. Over the years, Prep's graduates have gone on to chair the Federal Reserve Bank, preside over prominent federal courtrooms, and run major league sports teams. Now many of its alumni were delighted to see another one of their own make it to the very top of his profession.

Kavanaugh came from an upper-middle-class household in which both his parents worked. In 1974, when Brett was nine years old, his father, Edward, started working for the Cosmetic, Toiletry, and Fragrance Association. The trade group had recently moved its head-quarters to Washington, where over time, Edward—known as Ed—grew comfortable on Capitol Hill, lobbying members of Congress to reduce regulatory burdens on his hundreds of constituent companies.

Ed had a passion for sports that he imparted to his son. In 1972, Brett and Ed attended the National Football Conference championship game—during which their home team, the Washington Redskins, beat its nemesis, the Dallas Cowboys, 26–3. Nearly five decades later, Brett would still remember the exact location of their seats. He had been seven years old at the time.

Kavanaugh's mother, Martha, started as a teacher in 1968. While Brett attended a Catholic all-boys school in Bethesda, Mater Dei, Martha taught history at two Washington public high schools, H.D. Woodson and McKinley Technology, whose students were largely black. Brett would later proudly recall visiting his mother's classrooms as a child, encountering students of color who were born before the landmark 1954 school-integration cases *Brown v. Board of Education* and *Bolling v. Sharpe.* Those experiences, he later said, helped build a foundational sense of the importance of equal opportunity.

Partway through Brett's years at Mater Dei, both Ed and Martha began attending law school. Martha graduated from American University's law school in 1978 and became a prosecutor in Montgomery County, Maryland, where the Kavanaughs lived. She introduced Brett to law at the family dinner table, practicing her closing arguments and honing her trademark line: "Use your common sense. What rings true? What rings false?" Later, she would become a judge.

At Mater Dei, an emerging school for grades one through eight that was founded in 1960, there was an emphasis on becoming men. The upper-grade teachers were all male. There was a sense among the students in the school's first two decades that they needed to become tough, traditional men. Over the years, the school adopted a contemporary-sounding motto: "Work hard, play hard, pray hard. But most of all, be a good guy!"

Mater Dei emphasized the scholar-athlete, which fueled a jock-centered ethos at a relatively early age. During the 1970s, one social studies course was taught by an Olympic-level discus thrower who had set records in Maryland. Another was taught by a noted high jumper.

Kavanaugh excelled—studying hard, playing sports, and becoming close to some of the boys who would continue on with him to Georgetown Prep. As a seventh grader, he won the prestigious Headmaster's Award, which recognized both academic excellence and personal integrity. The prize, which had in the past been presented by Redskins quarterback Joe Theismann (the team was owned by Ed Williams, the defense attorney and school board trustee), waived the winner's tuition for the eighth and final year at Mater Dei, regardless of need.

In 1979, Kavanaugh matriculated at Prep, the nearly two-centuries-old high school that was favored by many of the area's Catholic families—including a large contingent from Mater Dei. Located in Rockville, Maryland, a slightly less fashionable spot up the road from where many of the students, including Kavanaugh, lived in Bethesda, the school was spread out over ninety acres. It featured a nine-hole golf course, elegant colonial-style academic buildings, a swimming pool, and a modern football stadium.

Prep's priorities were similar to Mater Dei's. Catholic traditions were foundational. Athleticism was strongly encouraged. Academics were rigorous. For many students—especially those coming from public or less demanding private schools—it was a daunting place.

To organize the boys and keep them focused, Prep's teachers emphasized structure and discipline. "Tighten the diaper, gentlemen," was how one teacher exhorted students to improve their behavior. Students said prayers before every class and football game. Weekly attendance at mass was also required. The boys undertook service projects—teaching disabled kids to swim, preparing food in soup kitchens—as part of an increasingly popular Jesuit ethos of educating "men for others," in other words, developing young people who cared about social justice and the poor. The faculty enforced a strict dress code: jackets, collared shirts, neckties, short hair, and a clean-shaven face. They punished infractions with after-school detention—known as JUG, for Justice Under God.

Religion, Latin, math, art, English, history, and speech were required courses. Students also took advanced classes, including math and a history course in which students were asked to re-create the Civil War battle of Ball's Bluff using documents from the National Archives. A compulsory religion course spent a day on the topic of exorcism, taught by a priest who played tapes of a possessed child speaking in an ancient tongue after which he would bless the Prep boys to protect them from being influenced by the devil.

Kavanaugh was not a regular in JUG; he was not one to start fights or grow his hair long. The spiritual and academic facets of Prep were familiar to him. Sunday mass and prayer were part of his family traditions, and he had developed diligent study habits at Mater Dei.

To his teachers and coaches, he was respectful and reliable. He excelled in his coursework, joining advanced-track academic sections and playing varsity sports as an underclassman. He vied for top ranking in his class, landing one of the top three spots most of the time.

Culturally, he was also a good fit. Kavanaugh's family was financially comfortable, able to afford Prep's tuition of $3,000 to $4,000 per year (fees that rose during the course of Kavanaugh's time there; reaching $38,330 for a day student in 2019). His family lived in a three-bedroom brick house in a tranquil cul-de-sac of Bethesda, not far from the Washington line. The Kavanaughs also owned a second home in St. Michaels, on Maryland's Eastern Shore, where Brett sometimes brought friends for the weekend.

Still, amid the wealthy circles of Georgetown Prep, the Kavanaughs didn't stand out. Martha Kavanaugh worked, whereas many other Prep mothers were homemakers in the 1970s and '80s. Brett didn't have a car and depended upon friends to spare him the bus ride to school. P. J. Smyth, one of the football players who regularly drove Kavanaugh, lived about a half mile away in a large colonial-style house with a semicircular driveway. Other friends lived on expansive properties with tennis courts and pools. Some even had private planes.

Kavanaugh's parents, while on track to become part of the Washington elite, weren't well-known figures then. Prep was populated by the sons of senior Catholic senators and of the Kennedy and Shriver families. It graduated the sons of Ed Williams, the lawyer and Redskins owner, and John Sears, who had managed Ronald Reagan's campaign. The sons of diplomats and foreign leaders were also enrolled.

Despite the structure and high expectations, however, Prep, like most high schools, also had its seamy side. Students could be cruel and combative, and competitive. Tensions sometimes became inflamed on the weekends because of excessive drinking. Many of the Prep boys were also ill-equipped for socializing with girls. An environment with limited sex education, no female students, and just a handful of female educators, some alumni say, became a breeding ground in the early 1980s for a casual brand of misogyny.

Among Prep's alpha males, there was a sense of entitlement—over girls, younger students, smaller boys, public school graduates, and non-athletes. A military-style social hierarchy was immediately evident to freshmen. First-years were treated like plebes, to be picked on and pushed around by the upperclassmen, some of whom had suffered the same hazing rituals. The more diminutive students were sometimes deposited into campus trash cans or stuffed into lockers. The bigger boys and those who had standing because of older brothers or ties to Mater Dei were inoculated.

Tom Downey, who was a larger kid but had a smart mouth, was taped to the front of a locker his freshman year after telling members of the wrestling team that their practice room smelled bad. William Fishburne, a petite boy who had come from public schools, was shoved from behind into one of the full-height gym lockers. He still remembers the sense of claustrophobia inside.

The upperclassmen knew better than to harass freshmen when faculty members were around, given the threat of JUG, calls to their parents, and stern lectures from the dean of students or their coach. But in the more private corners of Prep's campus, bullying was common.

"Violence in general was part of the culture," said a member of the class of 1984, adding that faculty looked the other way. At one point, the alumnus said, a sophomore repeatedly put him into headlocks. "At first it was fun, then annoying," the former student recalled. "I asked him to stop. He would not. The faculty and staff knew what was happening, and did nothing. It was understood that you had to 'sort it out yourself.'

"So I did," he continued. "The next time he tried to grab me, I connected with his nose, which exploded in blood. I was in tears, convinced I would be expelled. The next day, a teacher close to me said, 'I understand you took care of something.' Everyone knew, and nobody said a word. It was completely acceptable." (Georgetown Prep did not respond to requests for comment on this account or any others in this book.)

Anthony Desir, who graduated in 1977, also punched out a classmate who provoked him, but he was punished for it. Desir, a Trinidad native, was moving into his dorm room during the fall of his freshman year when a white student began calling him names and moving his belongings around. Then, when the student used the n-word, Desir hit him.

Shortly after that, Desir was summoned before the dean of students, who asked if punching the other freshman had been the proper response.

"Yes," said Desir.

The dean asked Desir what color he was.

"I'm brown!" said Desir.

"What color are you going to be for the rest of your life?" asked the dean.

"Brown," said Desir.

The dean replied that Desir was going to have to find a better response than physical assault to deal with people's reactions to his skin color. Then he assigned both Desir and the student who provoked him to JUG. The student never messed with Desir again.

During the 1970s, the party scene was kept largely in check. "We had very strict guidelines in terms of what we were allowed to do," said Desir. "We were severely punished if it was ever identified that we were crossing the line." Policing the boys was a community effort. Not only did parents and faculty members try to keep kids in line; the owners of Hank Dietle's, the store up the road from Georgetown Prep on Rockville Pike, would occasionally report back to school officials if they suspected underaged Prep students of coming in for beer.

To boys who graduated in the late 1970s, just as Kavanaugh was arriving, acting out meant embracing a Holden Caulfield version of challenging authority—following through on Senior Skip Day, for instance, when most of the other students chickened out, and being forced to pick up cigarette butts off the golf course as punishment. But worse things occasionally happened. Football players caught smoking pot on the bus home from a losing game during those years were publicly balled out by their coach, Jim Fegan; the entire team was penalized. There were suspensions and expulsions, too.

Sometime between the 1970s and the early '80s, the social behavior within Prep's in-crowd seemed to change. With national messaging focused on the war on drugs, the perils of alcohol were less emphasized among teenagers. Many private-school families, even those with traditional values, took a hands-off approach to parenting. In the wake of the feminist movement, popular culture had generated movies like *Animal House*, a glorification of fraternity binge drinking; *Porky's*, about a group of boys trying to help one of their friends lose his virginity; and *Fast Times at Ridgemont High*, a coming-of-age story featuring the stoner Jeff Spicoli. Catholic teachings reminded teenagers to stay in line, but the Jesuits were fighting an increasingly bold cultural sanctioning of booze and sex.

In July 1982, the summer before Kavanaugh's senior year, Maryland's drinking age was raised from eighteen to twenty-one. Kids who had turned eighteen before the law took effect could still drink legally. But others—including Kavanaugh, who would be seventeen until February of 1983—could not.

Still, both adults and kids seemed to shrug off teenage alcohol use.

"You didn't really think about it," said Pam Burns, who graduated from the Connelly School of the Holy Child in 1985 and attended parties with Kavanaugh and other Georgetown Prep boys when she was an underclassman. "It was like, 'So-and-so's having a keg party. Big deal.'"

Kavanaugh was by that time a powerful figure in the student body. As a senior, he would captain the basketball team after scoring an average of eight points per game. He played defensive back for the football team, wearing the number 23 on his jersey. He was named to the National Honor Society and recognized with a National Merit Scholarship after scoring highly on the PSAT, a precursor to the SAT college entrance exam. His senior fall, he applied to Yale, Brown, Princeton, and the University of Pennsylvania. He planned to study English or history.

"I busted my butt in academics," Kavanaugh later recalled. "I always tried to do the best I could. As I recall, I finished one in the class, first in—you know, freshman and junior year."

Toward the end of his junior year, Kavanaugh lost the popular vote for student body president—a position known at Prep as "president of the yard." But among the athletes who ruled the school, Kavanaugh's footing was solid. He was friends with the football players Tobin Finizio, who would quarterback the varsity team their senior year; J. C. del Real, who would play tight end; Mark Judge (who played his first and only football season senior year); as well as Chris Garrett, Don Urgo, Tim Gaudette, and P. J. Smyth. They'd bond over their teeth-gnashing loss to crosstown rival Gonzaga College High School that fall, noting it on their yearbook pages: "Gonzaga, you're lucky!" They'd cheer the Redskins and its star players—Theismann and the beloved running back John Riggins—all the way to a Super Bowl victory. They'd drink beers together and trade anecdotes about scoring with girls.

They existed in their own bubble, which alienated some of their fellow students. "There was animosity between the majority of those who played football and a large group of the ones who didn't," wrote Jim Sears, a 1981 Prep graduate, in a 1980 opinion column in the school paper. "To members of that large group it seemed the football players thought they were of a different breed—a breed that should be treated specially."

In many settings, Kavanaugh was kind and well mannered. His extracurricular activities were frequently of the more wholesome variety—albeit with an elite Washington twist. He saw Washington's NBA team, the Bullets, at the Capital Centre, and the Kemper Open golf tournament at the Congressional Country Club; went to the beach with friends; played tennis with his mother; talked to his female friends on the phone; and went out to see movies. He went to the prom and dated girls, sometimes going to great lengths to impress them—one time walking a couple of miles through the snow to visit a girl whose father wouldn't let her outdoors in such inclement weather.

But when drinking beer or palling around with his teammates, Kavanaugh often showed a cocky, dismissive side. While not typically the instigator of bad behavior, he often readily participated in it. He made fun of Fishburne, the diminutive football team manager who was active on the forensics team, as a "master debater," implying that Fishburne masturbated a lot. He sang a chant about Renate Schroeder, a neighboring schoolgirl, about how she was a good person to call if someone wanted to get laid, recalls classmate Paul Rendón, who has a "very clear memory" of it. He boasted about his drunken adventures.

On Monday mornings before class, Kavanaugh and his friends

would often gather outside one of the main academic buildings and debrief one another on the weekend's exploits. They'd tick off the number of kegs consumed and sexual conquests achieved (though most classmates assumed the stories were exaggerated or false). They would talk about Schroeder, a buxom girl whom many of the boys found attractive, and sing the chant about her. (Schroeder, now Renate Dolphin, has called the boasts "horrible, hurtful," and has denied—as has Kavanaugh—that there was sexual contact in high school between her and those boys.)

Many Prep students of that time possessed "a collective sort of jocular disdain for women," said Joe Conaghan, who was in Kavanaugh's class. "It was not a good tie that binded. We all thought it was sort of a funny thing to do, or be, which was to be disrespectful toward women."

"We had a good saying that we've held firm to to this day," Kavanaugh would say in a 2015 speech to the Columbus School of Law at the Catholic University of America, "which is 'What happens at Georgetown Prep stays at Georgetown Prep.' That's been a good thing for all of us."

Like many high school teenagers, Kavanaugh attended some raucous parties, and by senior year, these gatherings frequently veered out of control. Kavanaugh and some of his friends had vowed to drink a hundred kegs of beer by the time they graduated. They established a "100 Keg Club," writing of their high jinks in the school's underground newspaper and, later, in their yearbook. The drunken folklore included sports games watched but not remembered, copious vomiting, the breaking of household furniture, epic cleanup efforts, and getting grounded.

Though smaller gatherings happened, the big blowout parties

defined the social culture. Opulent homes, like Urgo's, near Falls Road in Potomac, or Finizio's, farther north, were the favored spots, because outdoor space was considered ideal for large get-togethers with overflowing kegs and minimal home damage. In addition to the host's friends from Prep, those typically in attendance included girls from the local sister schools, including Stone Ridge, Holy Child, and Georgetown Visitation; friends or siblings from neighboring schools like Holton-Arms and Landon; and occasionally students from area public schools such as Walt Whitman and Churchill.

Some of the parties were overseen by parents. Finizio's mother was quoted in the school's newspaper, *The Little Hoya*, his senior year, saying she preferred to have kids drinking at home rather than out and about. But the parents also left town from time to time, which was when the real debauchery went down. If a boy was going to be on his own over the weekend, word would quickly spread that he was "popping," or planning to hold a party. And even a gathering that started modestly could soon become a sprawling mess, with strings of cars lined up for blocks and unfamiliar friends of friends passing out from drinking.

As a junior, Judge, hoping to host a smallish party, unintentionally held one of these ragers. Before the festivities began in earnest, he and a few friends moved the family china and the best furniture into sealed-off rooms.

"Despite our precautions," he later wrote, "I had a feeling I was in for an apocalyptic evening."

The party went well until a friend climbed into Judge's attic, looking for a stash of booze, and got trapped in the dark, resulting in his kicking a large hole through the second-story ceiling below. Judge writes that he was both drunk and furious, almost starting two fistfights in anger over the damage before he cut off the keg and sent everybody home.

As senior year progressed, Kavanaugh and his friends kept tabs on where they were in the hundred-keg challenge. The school's underground newspaper, *The Unknown Hoya*, started by Judge and two friends, tallied the number of kegs that had been consumed so far at various locations: four at Donny's, five at Tobin's, and so on. The competition grew more challenging during the winter months, when the weather made outdoor parties impossible and people were less interested in consuming cold beer. Nonetheless, a few individual house parties were held to watch the Redskins' Super Bowl bid on a Sunday in January 1983. When the beloved team prevailed over Miami, the after-parties spilled into the bars of Georgetown and, eventually, into the following school day.

During the winter of Kavanaugh and Judge's senior year, the initiation of a classmate who had reportedly never drunk before was chronicled in *The Unknown Hoya*. The account, positioned below a picture of a teenage boy resting his cheek on the seat of an open toilet, was laced with inside jokes and ironies. It even included a reference to Schroeder:

"Several weeks ago, the senior class at Prep was doubting the party ability of a few members. Among the specific outcasts was Reilly Dolan. However, on January 14, Reilly Dolan silenced the critics; he became a party animal. At approximately 9:55 p.m., Reilly Dolan consumed his first alcoholic beverage in the form of a Bud. After the first cold one, there was no way to stop this machine, for he was destined to get wasted. After downing 3 more, Reilly headed for Tobin's party a la the Party Van. On the trip over, the party hound put down 6 oz. of vodka, straight. Upon staggering in to Tobin's modest home, Reilly grabbed Renate and yelled, 'Where's the keg?' After taking a seat in front of the keg, Reilly indulged for two straight hours. Within minutes, he found himself leaning in front of a toilet and asking, 'Where are my glasses?' After waking the next morning, Old Reilly Dolan could only remember one thing, that he fell madly in love with Elizabeth Malia. Reilly, you really are a party animal!!!!"

The event happened largely as described, said classmates, including two who attended. The "party van" belonged to one of the football players and was often used as weekend transportation with boys drinking in the back, while Malia was a student at a neighboring school. In any case, the upshot of the column was clear: Dolan, a bespectacled cross-country runner and swimmer, had earned the jock clique's grudging respect by getting fantastically drunk and sick at a classmate's house.

Heavy drinking, of course, was not unusual at this time and place; rich teenagers in suburbs around the country were guzzling beer and pushing boundaries.

But parents at Prep and other Washington-area private schools were starting to get concerned. Early in Kavanaugh's senior year, some complained about the size and unpredictability of the house parties, given that uninvited kids from other area schools would often show up, and parents felt responsible for kids who drank and then drove home. A front-page story in the October 9, 1982, edition of *The Little Hoya*, written by Kavanaugh's friend and fellow football player J. C. del Real, summarized the debate:

"Parents have become alarmed over the size of the parties and the beverages which have been served. 'We couldn't believe the size of the party. . . . I didn't know there were 600 people at Prep,' said one parent. . . .

"The consensus is that beer and parties go hand in hand. Parties are better with beer. 'I don't mind the kids having beer if they enjoy it,' says one parent, 'as long as they take care of one another and control the drinking.'"

Prep's board of trustees planned to address the party issue in a subsequent meeting, del Real wrote, and scheduled a follow-up discussion on "adolescent behavior," to be attended by the Montgomery County police.

Kavanaugh wasn't known for hosting parties. He was known for attending them, getting drunk, and throwing up. In Judge's autobiographical book *Wasted: Tales of a Gen X Drunk*, he writes about a classmate named Bart O'Kavanaugh who passed out on his way home from a party and puked in someone's car one year at Beach Week. (Bart was Kavanaugh's nickname in high school and is still used by some Prep friends today; the "O" in front of "Kavanaugh" appeared to be a thin disguise of his surname.)

In a 1983 letter to plan Beach Week, Kavanaugh made light of his weak stomach. "It would probably be a good idea on Sat. the 18th," the planned day of arrival, "to warn the neighbors that we're loud, obnoxious drunks with prolific pukers among us," he wrote. The note was signed "Bart."

It would be one of the last times so many classmates were together before Kavanaugh packed up for Yale College at the end of the summer.

By 2018, Kavanaugh's former classmates from Georgetown Prep had become sports executives, lawyers, government officials, nonprofit advocates, and entrepreneurs—many of whom united behind him.

Among the prominent signatories to the letter of support from Prep alums were Michael Bidwill, a Prep trustee and president of the

Arizona Cardinals football team; Brian Cashman, general manager of the New York Yankees; Urgo, the hotel company executive who remained one of Kavanaugh's closest friends; and Smyth, now an accountant at PricewaterhouseCoopers. Gorsuch's Georgetown Prep classmates had undertaken a similar effort when he was nominated, and Kavanaugh's cohort felt that he deserved no less.

The letter had been organized days after Kennedy's retirement, by Urgo, Bidwill, and three other classmates from 1983. Thanks to Kavanaugh's long-standing friendships with fellow Prep alumni and the conservative inclinations of others, about half their class—some fifty men—were immediately on board. Those who might have reservations about Kavanaugh—because of concerns about the possible overturning of court precedents or doubts about the judge himself—received a more tailored pitch.

Tom Downey, a lawyer in private practice in Denver, Colorado, thought hard about whether to sign the letter. A father of three with progressive values, Downey had served under a Democratic governor and attorney general in Colorado. He was worried about the future of *Roe* as well as about LGBTQ rights; the idea of a justice who was über-conservative on such issues made him nervous. Downey was going to disagree with anyone Donald Trump selected, he thought on July 2, when he received an initial email from Urgo and the others. But he thought that Kavanaugh, at the very least, would be methodical and open-minded in rendering decisions.

Downey, a former theater geek, had never been close to Kavanaugh in high school. But he remembered the future judge as an upstanding person who had always been bright. Kavanaugh had treated Downey well, Downey remembered, in spite of the rude joshing that others recalled. Downey had also read some of Kavanaugh's judicial opinions and been impressed. Downey had even clerked for a judge on the same Maryland circuit court where Martha Kavanaugh had worked as a judge after her stint as a prosecutor. He'd been impressed with her, too.

Downey and two classmates, Tim Gaudette and William Fishburne, began exchanging emails and texts about what a Justice Kavanaugh might mean for the country. Fishburne suggested that he himself might want to write amicus (or "friend of the court") briefs on matters important to him—in the style of Justice Scalia, a strict interpreter of the Constitution—as a way of communicating with Kavanaugh.

Fishburne was less impressed with Kavanaugh than were Downey and Gaudette. Fishburne had often felt like a loner in school, thanks in part to the behavior of Kavanaugh and his friends. As manager of the football team, he had been responsible for logistics—keeping track of equipment, carrying water to the sidelines, taping up injured ankles on the field—but was never fully accepted by the players. And Fishburne, now a government contractor, had concerns about Kavanaugh's jurisprudence.

So as Georgetown Prep alumni were canvassing their fellow graduates for support, Fishburne declined to sign the letter, even when his former classmate Paul Murray called, asking him to reconsider. "I don't think Brett would make a good Supreme Court justice," Fishburne said to Murray.

Murray pushed back, arguing that even if Fishburne didn't like Republican candidates, Kavanaugh was still a good choice. (Murray disputed this account of their interactions over the letter but declined to elaborate.)

Fishburne was unbending.

After gathering the signatures, Bidwill, who was among the most prominent of the group, worked the media circuit. As far back as thirty-seven years earlier, when they met in high school, Bidwill had respected Kavanaugh, predicting he would go on to big things.

"We all knew Brett was pretty special," Bidwill said.

Some criticized Bidwill for taking what they regarded as a political stand. The flap made him among the first to get heat for publicly supporting Kavanaugh. He would hardly be the last.

THREE

Inveniam Viam aut Faciam

I Will Find a Way
or Make One

A s Kavanaugh's childhood friends were sharing warm memories, a fifty-one-year-old psychology professor named Christine Blasey Ford was wrestling with what to do about a much darker recollection.

In 1982, when she was just fifteen, Ford remembered a time when Kavanaugh had pressed her to a bed at a beer-fueled house party, covered her mouth to prevent her from screaming—making it difficult for her to breathe—ground his body over hers, and tried to remove her clothes. Ford hadn't told anyone about the incident at the time—not her parents, nor her two brothers, nor any of her close friends. Instead she had buried the experience, unsure how to process it or articulate it to others.

Now, thirty-six years later, she finally felt compelled to report what had happened.

. . .

THE SUMMER OF 1982 started off as a pretty typical one for Kavanaugh and Ford, then Christine Blasey.

Kavanaugh, who had turned seventeen in February 1982, was a rising senior with high aspirations. Already he had interviews set up with recruiters for Yale and Brown scheduled for July. In late June, to help kick off his summer athletic training, he attended a weeklong basketball camp in Honesdale, Pennsylvania, with a few friends. He also played summer league basketball to maintain his scoring ability and to stay fit—sometimes three games in a row on a weekday—lifted weights twice a week in Prep's gymnasium, and ran drills in the sprawling backyard belonging to Tobin Finizio, the burly classmate who would be named starting quarterback of their football team that fall.

Those practice sessions started in the evening after Finizio, who had a construction job that summer, and his father, an oral surgeon, returned home from work. This was important preparation for the end of August, when the boys would enter a rigorous preseason football camp run by Prep's uncompromising coach, Jim Fegan.

Kavanaugh had worked construction the summer before. But this year, he mowed lawns around his suburban Bethesda neighborhood.

Despite these commitments, Kavanaugh did plenty of socializing. He spent the second week of June at a rented beach condominium on the Eastern Shore with a group of friends, part of the Washington-area Beach Week tradition. Kavanaugh also hung out with his buddies at his family's beach house in St. Michaels, a two-hour drive from Bethesda across the Chesapeake Bay Bridge. He saw new releases at the movie theater, including *Poltergeist*, *Rocky III*, and *Grease II*, and went for beers—referred to as "skis," for "brewskis"—at the homes of his friends Tim Gaudette, Anne Dougherty, and Chris Garrett.

It was a freewheeling time for many of the boys. "Because we were going to be seniors, our parents gave us tremendous slack," wrote Judge. "We were pretty much left alone to do what we wanted, when we wanted." For Judge, this meant an opportunity to drink heavily in the evening and show up hungover to his job at a local Safeway grocery store the next morning.

Chris Garrett featured prominently on Kavanaugh's summer calendar, which Kavanaugh used as both datebook and diary, a habit inspired by his father. A friend since their shared years at Mater Dei, Garrett, tall and broad-shouldered, was known as "Squi," because his voluminous head of hair resembled that of Ramin Oskoui, an upperclassman whose surname was pronounced "Os-squee."

"When I was in town, I spent much of my time working, working out, lifting weights, playing basketball, or hanging out and having some beers with friends as we talked about life and football and school and girls," Kavanaugh later recalled of his teenage summers.

Don Urgo, part of a large and wealthy family that ran a hotel management company, was a particularly close friend. Buff, with deep, serious eyes, Urgo liked to hang out shirtless, standing with his friends at the beach or goofing around in a cowboy hat during poker games. Also close to Kavanaugh was Judge, a garrulous class-clown type who would wax poetic about the musical talents of the Who or U2. Judge, the youngest in a family of four kids, was full of nervous energy and liked to horse around with games of "chicken," in which two people fight each other while on friends' shoulders. He had a staccato laugh and a toothy smile that looked a little forced in photographs, as if he was masking a sense of discomfort.

Christine Blasey at that time was in a separate, if overlapping, world. The youngest of three children, she was also the only girl, and her parents were particularly protective of her. As a fifteen-year-old rising junior, she couldn't yet drive. She also had one of the earliest curfews of anyone in her close group of more than a dozen friends at Holton-Arms, the girls' school she attended in a tony section of Bethesda.

Blasey's father, Ralph Blasey Jr., was an entrepreneur who ran a business leasing furniture and computers to local companies. He was outgoing and had a politician's knack for connecting with other people. Blasey's mother, Paula, was the quieter of the two. Like many affluent moms in Montgomery County, she stayed at home, raising her children and overseeing their activities.

The Blaseys lived in a comfortable two-story home in the southern portion of Potomac, Maryland, not far from the Potomac River. Both Ralph and Paula played golf at the Columbia Country Club, a historic recreational and social club on Connecticut Avenue in Chevy Chase. Established in 1898, the Columbia club was known for its grooming of skilled amateur golfers, and its membership included prominent business executives, journalists, and politicians.

The Blaseys were Republican and Protestant. They weren't regular churchgoers, though they did attend an Episcopal service at the National Cathedral on Easter and the occasional Sunday service at a neighborhood church. Both Ralph Blasey and Ed Kavanaugh were golfers and would eventually belong to the same men-only golf club, Burning Tree, where Ralph served a stint as president.

As a child, Christine attended Carderock Springs Elementary School, a public school in Rockville. But for middle and high school, the Blaseys opted for a more competitive environment and switched her out of the public-school system and over to the private school Holton-Arms.

Founded by two Washington women in 1901, Holton was imag-

INVENIAM VIAM AUT FACIAM

ined as a place to educate the city's elite girls. During the school's early years, students learned French and music in a borrowed home on Hillyer Place in Washington before moving to a larger facility on S Street, where Jacqueline Bouvier, the future first lady, briefly attended the school. In 1963, Holton moved to the suburbs, where it occupied a more expansive tract on River Road, at the end of a winding driveway. Holton's motto was "Inveniam viam aut faciam," Latin for "I will find a way or make one." Its crest featured an ancient-style oil lamp representing the light of knowledge.

During the late 1970s and early '80s, Holton took advantage of the school's proximity to power, with frequent field trips to Washington's historic sites: the Supreme Court, Capitol Hill, the National Cathedral, and Ford's Theatre, where Abraham Lincoln was shot. Good behavior was required. "We'd be prepped before we went in there," Christine recalled in an interview later. "If anyone speaks within the halls of Congress, there'll be consequences." The trips instilled in her a sense of reverence for American history. (On Martin Luther King Jr. Day, she would often post on Facebook the passages from Lincoln's speeches that are carved in the memorial's walls.)

Blasey, who was tall and dressed conventionally and wore her shoulder-length blond hair in feathered bangs, was a bright but aimless student. Within the curriculum, she had her likes (Homer, Kafka, geometry) and her dislikes (James Joyce). She was fond of some of the school's more popular faculty members, like the anthropology teacher John "Jack" Caussin—whose students wrote term papers on topics like the caste system in Sri Lanka and memorized the name of every African country—and Thomas F. N. Gilbert, the ninth- and tenth-grade English teacher who could singlehandedly reenact entire scenes from Shakespeare plays.

"In class, she always contributed," Caussin, now eighty-four and retired, later told *The Washington Post* of Blasey. "I could always count on her for a wise crack or two to make me laugh."

But while other girls in her class had their eyes on Ivy League admissions and defined career tracks, Blasey had no idea what she wanted to do when she grew up.

She was, however, outgoing and popular, running with a cliquish crowd of about fifteen girls. Her close friends included Leland Ingham, a sports prodigy with a Princess Diana–style blond bob and a thousand-watt grin; Monica McLean, a preppy girl with a spirited sense of humor who often volunteered to lead school tours or undertake other projects at Holton; and Lulu Ward, an accomplished gymnast with a kind smile.

The group hung out regularly, developing their own language and inside jokes. An ad placed by a bunch of the girls that was published in the back pages of their senior yearbook, issued in 1984, reflected memorable moments and phrases, among them "mange-moi," "pass out in John," "Barf on wall," "slug in underpants," and "Kill Dick." The references were decipherable only to the group—which was identified by cryptic nicknames like "Blas" for Blasey and "Inga" for Ingham. But the ribaldry underlying these terms was clear.

One of the phrases, tucked in the middle of the list, would have ironic resonance many years later: "That's what he-she said."

At Holton, appearances were important. Morning assemblies were held in a majestic room with parquet floors, oil paintings, and Persian rugs; the graduating seniors wore white dresses and carried red roses. Many families lived in expensive homes and gave their daughters their own cars. Among Holton's students around this time were Princess Aisha bint Hussein, daughter of King Hussein of Jordan; the daughters of the hotel company executive J. W. "Bill" Marriott Jr.; and

Julia Louis-Dreyfus, the daughter of a prominent commodity trader, who went on to become a well-known comedic actress. Tuition was in line with Prep's: between $4,000 and $4,500 in 1981, when Blasey started her freshman year.

Students wore school uniforms—slacks or navy skirts in a particular Holton plaid—so shoes and jewelry were the only options for fashionable expression. Pearl necklaces, gold jewelry, and add-a-bead necklaces were commonplace. Cheerleaders like Blasey wore saddle shoes. The insides of lockers were decorated with magazine covers featuring popular 1980s supermodels like Christie Brinkley. Most girls carried their books around in canvas tote bags from L.L.Bean rather than backpacks. During their free time between or after classes, they would often lie in the grass and sun themselves, drinking cans of Tab diet cola.

"People seemed very Barbie-ish. Perfect lives. Superficial," recalled Cheryl Amitay, who had come to Holton in tenth grade after years in Rockville public schools. "No one seemed concerned with issues of the day."

Holton was a nonreligious school, and its girls did not always move in the same circles as Prep boys. Their brother institution was Landon, a nonreligious boys' school attended by Blasey's brothers, Tom and Ralph III. Many of her schoolmates' brothers had gone there, too. When Blasey cheered, it was sometimes at Landon games.

Still, Holton girls frequently mixed with—and sometimes dated— Prep guys. And, like Renate Schroeder, some of those girls were subjected to mean-spirited lampooning. During Kavanaugh's senior year, a column in the underground paper *The Unknown Hoya*, written by Judge and two classmates, mocked the Holton girls of the early 1980s in a column titled "The Truth About Holton."

"We do know that Holton is the home of the most worthless

excuse for an underground newspaper. In fact, it is also the home of the most worthless excuses for human females," the column said, adding that "all it takes to have a good time with any H.H. (Holton Hosebag)" is a Montgomery County library card.

Such jokes were part of the thoughtless chauvinism that existed among many of the Prep boys, which also inspired the sneering Renate ditty and the Noël Coward quote found on Judge's yearbook page: "Certain women should be struck regularly, like gongs."

During her sophomore year at Holton, Blasey briefly dated Chris Garrett, Kavanaugh's football friend with the famously full hair. She had met him at the Columbia Country Club, where both his family and hers were members, and their romance lasted a couple of months.

During the fall of 1981, Blasey accompanied Garrett to several Prep parties, meeting some of his friends, including Kavanaugh and Smyth. Smyth, a tall, dark-haired football player, struck her as affable and magnetic. Blasey was not memorable to Smyth—at least, not decades later, when her name resurfaced publicly.

Summers allowed Blasey to indulge one of her biggest passions: swimming. From about age six, she'd been on the team at the Columbia Country Club—where kids clapped their hands over their ears when the coach's whistle blew—and had taken lessons at a local community center during the cooler months. Eventually, Blasey took a swim course at the American University pool, in northwest Washington, and moved from swimming laps to diving at the country club. But with the usual adolescent distractions, Blasey found it increasingly hard to find time for the team.

Still, in the summer of 1982, Christine spent most days at the country club, swimming and practicing diving. The club was a mecca for teenagers, where they could mix with kids from various schools in the area, hang by the pool, and order fries—all on the family account. It was considered a safe space, so familial that members and their friends would walk easily in and out. "Sometimes my mom would drop me off in the morning," Blasey later said, "and not pick me up until the pool closed."

Garrett, Blasey's romantic interest from the previous school year, was a regular at the club. By this point the two were no longer dating, but another Holton–Prep romantic interest had emerged, this time between Kavanaugh's hard-partying friend Mark Judge and Blasey's friend Leland Ingham.

Ingham was a jock with a sunny personality. Her sports included field hockey, basketball, and tennis; during high school, she played on no fewer than eight varsity teams. At one point, the tennis star Arthur Ashe, whose manager's children attended the school, came to Holton's campus to give Ingham a private tennis lesson; her mother had placed the winning bid on a session with Ashe at the annual school auction. Though Ingham had her own car by that summer, her parents kept a close eye on her. She was straitlaced, which often made her the designated driver.

Judge was tall and lean, with floppy hair, an angular jaw, and, often, an antsy, searching expression. Dressed in his regulation sports jacket and necktie, he looked every bit the smart but insouciant schoolboy—a little too insouciant, in fact, for Ingham's parents, who were traditional when it came to boys courting their daughter. The first time Judge came to pick Ingham up for a date, her parents insisted he come to the front door and introduce himself. The second time, Judge refused to come to the door, and her parents wouldn't let her leave with him.

Ingham liked Judge but recalled later that his "sloppy" behavior also made her nervous, particularly when he was at the wheel of a car. "I just had to pay attention to him," she said, "and make sure he didn't run off the road."

Much of that June and July, Blasey and Ingham were both home in Maryland. Ingham, who was developing a passion for golf, worked in the pro shop at the nearby Congressional Country Club, practicing with the club's coaches after her shift ended. Many weeks, she said in an interview later, she spent as much as seventy or more hours on the club's property. But she remembers occasionally stopping by the Columbia Country Club early in the morning, before work, to give diving pointers to her friend Blasey at the pool.

One evening after a day at the Columbia Country Club, as Christine recalls it, she and Ingham went over to an unfamiliar house in the area, where they met up with a handful of boys from Prep. Kavanaugh was there, along with Judge, Smyth, and a fourth boy whose name Christine can't remember.

Christine cannot reconstruct the exact details of how the gathering came together. She suspects she ended up there because Ingham was in contact with Judge, and that Ingham probably drove her there, since she already had her license and often gave Christine a ride. The house was located somewhere between the Columbia club and the Blasey home, in Potomac; Christine cannot remember a more specific location.

She does have a visual memory of the house—two stories high and sparsely furnished. It could have been a bachelor pad for one or more single men, or a family home that was undergoing renovations or was the site of a recent move. It was not warmly decorated with photographs or collectibles, she recalls, and it lacked a lived-in feel. She recalls there were cans of beer, and that she drank one.

Christine doesn't remember who the house belonged to, but she recalls that Judge seemed particularly possessive of it, urging people not to damage anything and appearing preoccupied with the amount of time they spent there, as if they had to be gone by a certain hour. Judge struck Christine as nervous, as if he was responsible for the space and anything that might happen to it.

At some point, Christine says, she went upstairs to use the bathroom, which was located at the top of a short, narrow staircase with walls on both sides. At the top of the stairs, she was pushed into a bedroom, whose door was swiftly closed and locked by Kavanaugh and Judge, who were in the room with her. What happened next, she says, changed her forever.

Here is how she describes it: There was music playing in the bedroom, and it was turned up louder by either Kavanaugh or Judge. She was pushed onto a bed, and Kavanaugh climbed on top of her. He began running his hands over her body and grinding into her.

She yelled for help and tried to scramble away, but Kavanaugh was too heavy. He groped her and tried to take off her clothes, but he was drunk and ham-handed. Christine's one-piece bathing suit, which she was still wearing under her street clothes, also frustrated him.

She believed he was going to rape her. She tried to yell again for help. When she did, Kavanaugh put his hand over her mouth to stop her from yelling. It became hard to breathe. She began to think she might not only be raped but also killed.

Judge was watching from another bed or a small couch nearby. He urged Kavanaugh on. But then he told his friend to stop. Christine tried to make eye contact with Judge, pleading with her eyes for him to intervene. Initially, it didn't work.

At some point, Judge jumped on the bed where Christine was pinned, but Kavanaugh continued his groping and grinding. The second time that Judge jumped on the bed, he toppled Kavanaugh and

Christine onto the floor. That moment gave Christine a small window in which to flee.

She ran across the hall to the bathroom, locked the door, and waited there. Eventually, she heard Kavanaugh and Judge leaving the bedroom, laughing. They stumbled down the narrow staircase, knocking into the walls on each side as they descended.

When she felt enough time had passed, Christine unlocked the bathroom door, went downstairs, and left the house. She suspects that she grabbed Ingham, who probably drove her home. The details of that hasty departure are no longer clear.

The return home to her parents in Potomac has stuck with her, however. Christine says her father was waiting when she got home; Paula was watching TV in a room upstairs. Christine was fearful that her appearance would reveal that something bad had happened involving boys and beer. She was too ashamed and afraid to tell her parents about it. She also didn't want to be grounded.

Christine made it past her father to her bedroom without arousing suspicion. Relief washed over her. Because she hadn't been raped, she reasoned, nothing of consequence had happened.

Yet the memory of that experience stayed with her. Only years later, after finally discussing it with a therapist, did Ford come to understand what she had gone through as an emotional trauma whose tentacles had reached many corners of her psyche, contributing to a fear of flying, relationship problems, and the near derailment of her academic performance at the end of high school and the beginning of college. She struggled through the latter two years at Holton; her grades suffered. The school's college counselor told her that some top-tier private colleges were out of reach. She chose the University of North Carolina at Chapel Hill. She partied hard there, and her academics continued to suffer. She remembers getting a D in a business statistics class. One friend, Dan Goldstein, urged her to pull herself together. Christine later recalled Goldstein telling her, "You're really smart, and you're just like totally messing up." He suggested she buckle down and major in psychology, because the required classes could be taken in any order. She followed his advice.

Christine began raising her GPA senior year. She volunteered at an Alzheimer's research lab run by the National Institutes of Health in the Research Triangle, working there two days a week to help with experiments on mice. She took a gap year to work as a receptionist at a group psychology and psychiatry practice on East-West Highway in Bethesda, learning basics about the field; during that period, she applied to graduate schools. Then, in 1989, she moved to Malibu to earn a master's degree in psychology at Pepperdine University.

California agreed with Blasey. She made new friends and developed a passion for surfing. In 1998, after earning a doctorate in philosophy and psychology at the University of Southern California, she accepted a research position at Stanford University and moved north to Mountain View, in the heart of Silicon Valley. There she met a soft-spoken mechanical engineer, Russell Ford. They were married among the redwoods.

By 2018, Christine and Russell had settled into a routine in Palo Alto with their two adolescent sons. Russell worked for a company that developed early-stage medical products using innovative technology. Christine taught at both Stanford and Palo Alto University while continuing her research at Stanford's medical school. The Fords lived in a renovated house where they occasionally rented out a spare bedroom to summer interns working at local tech companies.

They socialized with other parents in the community, attending sports events and sometimes vacationing together in Hawaii, one of Christine's favorite spots. They attended Stanford football and basketball games, and Ford, who studied scientific statistics as part of her job, developed an encyclopedic knowledge of the teams' performances.

Disarmingly casual and low-key, Christine often wore baseball caps over her long blond hair, keeping one from a Stanford Rose Bowl in her collection. She loved to teach. Outside of classroom hours, she'd meet students at a local coffee shop to discuss their coursework.

Christine's unaffected demeanor, however, belied a competitive streak. During her kids' basketball games, for instance, she'd scream encouragement from the bleachers. Her friends found it funny, given that her usual persona was that of a laid-back surfer girl. "I'd be like, 'I can't sit with you, you're stressing me out,'" Jay Backstrand, her friend and fellow sports parent, recalls joking with Ford.

During the years preceding the Kavanaugh nomination, Christine had kept tabs on his career. She had also begun grappling with her memories of the assault. In 2012, she shared the broad contours of it with Russell during a session with their couples therapist. She had told Russell before their marriage that she had experienced a sexual assault but left out the exact details.

At one point the Fords argued when Russell questioned Christine's desire to add a second front door to their house as part of a lengthy and costly home renovation. Christine explained that it stemmed from her experience of being sexually assaulted in a locked upstairs bedroom as a teenager, thus confiding in another person about this vivid recollection for the first time in thirty years. In the aftermath of that conversation, she talked through the experience much more in individual therapy. She also related it, initially without mentioning the assailant's name, to a few of her friends in Palo Alto.

Over a pizza dinner one evening in 2013, Ford revealed her

experience to her friend Adela Gildo-Mazzon, whom she had met at their children's elementary school years before. The two were discussing something personal, and Ford looked stressed and drawn. Gildo-Mazzon asked what was wrong, putting her hand on top of Ford's to comfort her.

Ford said she was having a tough day. She had been remembering a painful experience from her teenage years, an assault in which she had almost been raped "by two drunken guys," one of whom was a well-known federal judge.

The topic arose again three years later with Ford's friend and fellow parent Keith Koegler, in a Palo Alto park as they watched their sons play. It was the summer of 2016, and Brock Turner, a Stanford swimmer who had been found guilty of sexually assaulting an unconscious woman lying by a dumpster late one night, had recently been sentenced to six months in jail. (The relatively short sentence, which followed a unanimous jury verdict, was met with national outrage, much of it directed at the local judge on the case, who was later recalled.)

Standing on the periphery of the game with Koegler, Ford brought up the Turner verdict and said that she had also been assaulted as a young woman, by a man who was now a federal judge in D.C. When Ford didn't elaborate, Koegler chose not to press, believing that an assault survivor should take the lead in such discussions.

One evening the following year, Ford ran into her friend Rebecca White, who was out walking her dog in their Palo Alto neighborhood. White had recently posted on Facebook about her own sexual assault at the hands of someone she knew, and Ford said she had endured a similar experience. She added that her perpetrator was a prominent judge who might one day land on the Supreme Court.

White asked Ford what she would do if the man was nominated, and Ford said she didn't know. "That," White told her friend, "would change your life."

WHEN KAVANAUGH'S NAME first emerged on the short list to succeed Kennedy on the high court, Ford was on the beach in Santa Cruz, where her family had a small second home. As a professor with summers off, she typically spent much of June and July at the house, surfing and spending time with friends while her boys attended a state-run junior lifeguard camp. (Russell often stayed behind in Palo Alto to be near his work, but he joined them for weekends.) Now Christine was suddenly reading news on her smartphone that the man she remembered as her assailant was in the running for a lifetime judicial position, alongside other conservative judges.

Ford felt compelled to share her experience with officials in Washington. She wanted her memory of being assaulted by Kavanaugh to be considered in the decision-making process, even if the president and lawmakers ultimately concluded that her experience was too dated or irrelevant.

"I just felt like I needed to tell them what happened," Ford said later. "If this is the only bad thing he's ever done, okay, people are going to decide what they're going to decide. And I don't know if this is the only bad thing. I wasn't thinking, 'Oh, he did this to me, therefore he shouldn't be on the court.' I wasn't in that place at all. That wasn't how I was thinking about it.

"He did something to me when I was my kid's age," she continued, adding of government decision makers, "and I thought they should know, in case they care."

Ford realized that Kavanaugh's conduct might not have continued after high school, that she had "no idea what he was like as an adult," and "he could have been Mother Teresa." But she believed that the assault she remembered should be disclosed nonetheless.

In early July, when the Supreme Court short list was breathlessly covered in the press, Ford saw Kavanaugh as largely interchangeable with the other candidates—"They were all kind of similar," she recalled—assuming he would therefore be easy to replace if her experience with him was deemed disqualifying. And given that President Trump reportedly wanted to reach a decision quickly, it seemed to Ford that time was short.

Keeping the information to herself did not feel like an option. "That would be a not okay thing to do," she said, "retain that information and not share."

Ford debated her options both internally and out loud with friends on the beach. She was leery of coming forward publicly, for fear of bringing unwanted scrutiny on herself and her family, so telling her story to a media outlet seemed untenable. Going directly to a member of Congress or the Senate was another idea, though Ford wasn't sure how to discreetly reach legislators. She also considered contacting Kavanaugh directly to tell him about her recollection of the assault in 1982 and to suggest that they talk it through in private, rather than on a more public stage. "Let's not do this," she imagined saying to him. If she couldn't get through to Kavanaugh, Ford reasoned, she could try looking up Mark Judge to see if she could reach Kavanaugh through his old friend.

Despite her recollection of Judge's bystander role, in which he'd initially avoided intervening but eventually did—laughing in the aftermath of the assault—Ford still remembered having liked Judge. She remembered him during those years as funny, outgoing, and a little wild—qualities that also described her as a teenager.

Ford, who wasn't much for phone calls, began texting with a circle of four or five friends, saying that she had relevant information about a potential Supreme Court justice and needed advice.

Koegler was one of them. Two days after Kennedy's retirement announcement, Ford had revealed to him in an email the identity of her alleged assailant. Now, over text messages and during a brief visit to Santa Cruz, Koegler and his wife, Elizabeth, also a tech industry lawyer, advised Ford to get a lawyer who could help her explore private ways to share this information.

Keith Koegler was concerned about the possible impact on his friend if she went public. "You don't," he told her, "want to be in the middle of another Anita Hill thing."

ON FRIDAY, JULY 6, Ford left a message at the Palo Alto district office of her congressional representative, Anna G. Eshoo, a Democrat from California: she had information to impart regarding a candidate for the Supreme Court.

That same morning, Ford followed a friend's advice to contact the *Washington Post* tip line, and texted the following, through WhatsApp: "Potential Supreme Court nominee with assistance from his friend assaulted me in mid 1980s in Maryland. Have therapy records talking about it. Feel like I shouldn't be quiet but not willing to put family in DC and CA through a lot of stress." About an hour later she added: "Brett Kavanaugh with Mark Judge and a bystander named PJ."

The initial response was silence, which frustrated Ford. She had information she considered relevant to the nomination process, given her sense that Kavanaugh was likely to be the president's Supreme Court nominee. She had come to believe it was important to tell officials about her formative experience with him while a variety of candidates were still under consideration. She wanted both Eshoo's staff and *The Washington Post* to get back to her.

Four days after that, Ford texted the *Post* again: "Been advised to contact senators or NYT. Haven't heard back from WaPo." She then received a text back that said, "I will get you in touch with reporter," and was subsequently connected to Emma Brown, on the investigative team.

Meanwhile, the White House was gearing up to announce Kavanaugh as Trump's Supreme Court pick. Judges, litigators, and policy wonks around the country were abuzz, given Trump's efforts to build suspense around four finalists and a down-to-the-wire decision. This reality show approach prompted some on Twitter to echo *The Bachelor* in suggesting that the president would ask his nominee, "Will you accept this robe?"

On Monday, July 9, Trump named Kavanaugh. That same day, Eshoo's district chief of staff, Karen Chapman, returned Ford's call and arranged for her to meet with Eshoo. Chapman apologized profusely for not calling back earlier. She now realized the gravity of what Ford had to say.

FOUR

Lux et Veritas

Light and Truth

O n the day that Trump announced his selection of Kavanaugh, Mark Krasberg, also Yale '87, emailed his fellow classmate Kenneth Appold. "Hey—your old roommate might
become a Supreme Court justice," he said. "What do you think
of that?"

Appold, now a professor of Reformation history at Princeton Theo-
logical Seminary, did not immediately tell Krasberg what had come
to mind: his clear memory of being told by a friend that Kavanaugh
had exposed himself to classmate Deborah Ramirez at a party in the
freshman dorm Lawrance Hall.

Also around that time, Karen Yarasavage, Yale '87, texted her classmate Kerry Berchem, Yale '88, a *Wall Street Journal* op-ed endorsing
Kavanaugh for the Supreme Court.

Berchem and Yarasavage had been close friends in their Milford,

Connecticut, high school as well as schoolmates at Yale, but they had been in touch less consistently lately, due to career and family obligations. Yarasavage is married to Kavanaugh's close friend at Yale, Kevin Genda.

Happy to reconnect, Berchem met Yarasavage for drinks at the Yale Club of New York City, where they chatted about old times as well as Kavanaugh's potentially huge new role. Then, on July 16, Yarasavage followed up by texting a black-and-white photo from her and Genda's rehearsal dinner, depicting the soon-to-be bride and groom standing next to Kavanaugh, along with their mutual friends David White (known as "Whitey") and Deborah Ramirez. "We all look so fresh faced," Yarasavage wrote. The next day, Berchem posted the photo on her Facebook page, tagging Yarasavage so that both of their friend groups could view it.

Then Yarasavage mentioned finding "a box of college photos" and floated the name of a male classmate who was known for pulling down his pants.

"Makes me so nostalgic," wrote Yarasavage. "Would love to be able to turn back time for a month or so!" Yarasavage went on to say that she had sent the wedding photo to Dave White, who was in touch with *The Washington Post*.

Months later, Berchem would find herself wondering whether these exchanges with Yarasavage were simply two old friends reconnecting over old times or whether there was some subtext. Had Yarasavage—or even Kavanaugh through Yarasavage—been attempting to head off the Ramirez story, months before it became public? Had Yarasavage mentioned the male classmate known for pulling down his pants to shift attention off Kavanaugh? And had she dug up a photo of Ramirez and Kavanaugh smiling together at her rehearsal dinner to preempt potential allegations regarding their history? Is this why, as the texts suggested, Dave White had requested the wedding photo to send to *The Washington Post?*

In 1983, Kavanaugh had been admitted to Yale out of a competitive pool of more than ten thousand applicants. (Although he would later say that he had "no connections" to the school, in fact his grandfather Everett Edward Kavanaugh had been an undergraduate in the class of 1928.) At the time, under Yale's residential college system, students were divided into twelve dorms, most of which had freshman housing on Old Campus, the grassy, four-acre quadrangle. Kavanaugh lived in Lawrance Hall, the freshman building on Old Campus for Ezra Stiles residential college.

Kavanaugh wasn't placed in one of Lawrance's coveted suites. Instead he was put in D01, a room in the basement, which he shared with James Roche, a swarthy, easygoing football player from Northern California. The subterranean double room, with only one high window, was nicknamed "the Sewer," because it had flooded a year before.

Kavanaugh didn't click with Roche, who, a few months into freshman year, seized on the opportunity to have his own space by moving into an unoccupied room across the hall (jokingly referred to as a "psycho single"). But Kavanaugh's room connected to C01, a suite of five guys, two of whom became Kavanaugh's good friends: Dave White, a wide receiver on the football team, and Paul La Monica, who managed the Yale football and baseball teams.

As an undergraduate at Yale, Kavanaugh was only a few hours from his hometown by train. But Yale was a world away from Georgetown Prep. In high school, Kavanaugh had been a successful varsity athlete, the object of girls' attentions, a top academic performer, and a popular member of the in-crowd. In college, he found himself in a sea of straight-A students, unable to make the varsity basketball team and largely unlucky when it came to women. Perhaps as a result, Kavanaugh focused instead on building strong male friendships, getting good grades so that he would get into law school, and decompressing with alcohol, sometimes in large quantities.

While many of his classmates would be lured by Wall Street, Kavanaugh early on seemed to have his eye on a public sector career on the bench.

"Half of our class went to First Boston," said Ken Appold, referring to the white-shoe investment bank that is now part of the Swiss financial behemoth Credit Suisse. "He could have done that, too."

Malcolm Frank, who had a room adjacent to Kavanaugh in Stiles College during junior and senior years, said Kavanaugh could be tireless when it came to studying. "He would go down to Store 24 on Broadway and buy a two-liter bottle of Coke and at ten o'clock he would stick that bottle on his desk—'I'm just going to work until I collapse or until I'm done'—and go till three or four at night," Frank said. "It always left a very strong impression. If I got up to go to the bathroom, there he was, still at it. If you asked me a year ago, 'Who's the Brett you know?' That's the person that I knew."

Kavanaugh kept his bedroom neat, decorating it with a poster of his favorite Redskins player, John Riggins, breaking through the Miami Dolphins defense to cruise forty-three yards into the end zone during Super Bowl XVII, in 1983.

"His desk was what was notable," Frank said. "Most people's desk things are randomly strewn. His was almost like an assembly line— work was stacked up and he was going to move right through it.

"What really stood out for me was his intellectual curiosity," Frank continued. "He would get deeply immersed in his classes, particularly history. He never had an arrogance about him personally. He was pretty down-to-earth, but he lived this life of the mind. If something grabbed his interest, he'd go very deep on it."

Other classmates described Kavanaugh as decent, modest, and considerate. Tom Mercein, who played football at Yale and was in a fraternity with Kavanaugh, called him "the finest person I knew at Yale," adding that "he had a kind soul."

Kavanaugh's diligence and ambition were not apparent to everyone, though, in part because he played them down. He was viewed as a regular guy—blending in rather than standing out. He would make fun of himself, a goofy quality that earned him the jocular nickname "Brett Tool Kavanaugh."

Kavanaugh also came across as straightforward and uncomplicated. Classmates generally found him easy to be around but did not get to know him on a deep level—they shared good times but not confidences. Some friends likened the seemingly angst-free Kavanaugh to "ham on white."

Perhaps because Kavanaugh deemphasized his academic side, many of his peers failed to realize his sharp intelligence. Marc Schindler, a classmate, said he was surprised to hear Kavanaugh singled out for academic honors at graduation and remembered thinking, "Wow, who knew that Brett was that smart? He seemed like an average guy."

Traugott Lawler, an emeritus professor of English at Yale, who became the "master," or faculty head, of Stiles College when Kavanaugh was a senior, realized only later that Kavanaugh was academically strong. "I have a vague memory of people saying, 'Brett doesn't act like it, but he's a real student,'" Lawler recalled. "He certainly did not come off as a brain or an intellectual."

Kavanaugh didn't make a strong impression on young women either. Roughly six feet tall, clean-cut, with a stiff smile and a tendency to be chubby, Kavanaugh seemed socially insecure. He rarely appeared to be in a relationship and was affectionately teased for getting "no play" from girls.

"He was a virgin through college," one friend said. "He was no sort of womanizer or lothario."

At parties and the local bar, Demery's, Kavanaugh appeared to use alcohol as a social lubricant in order to feel empowered around men and emboldened toward women. "Brett would hang out with guys who were getting the girls, and Brett was not getting the girls and sort of knew he had no chance of getting the girls," one male classmate said, "so he just would get really drunk."

Athletics continued to be an important aspect of Kavanaugh's schooling. Several of the jocks on campus soon became his closest friends. These included Kevin Genda and David Todd, both varsity soccer players.

Basketball was still Kavanaugh's best sport, though he did not make the varsity team. He played anyway, joining the junior varsity team and playing pickup hoops on the fifth floor of Yale's Payne Whitney Gymnasium with an assortment of students, professors, and locals.

"We had basketball every day," Kavanaugh would later say. "Those were intense, really intense afternoons, early evenings of basketball. And then I played JV basketball that year, practice every day, lots of games, and then in the spring, basketball again for the same kind of captain-led workouts, which were every weekday, a lot of running, a lot of lifting.

"I was very focused on doing as well as I could in school," he added, "and I was very focused on trying to be the best basketball player I could be."

While many of his classmates got involved in current events—

protesting apartheid in South Africa, for example—Kavanaugh seemed to steer clear of politics, instead writing about sports for the *Yale Daily News*, where he produced about two dozen articles over three years. "I've never known him to be a culture warrior or a religious right kind of guy," said Bradford Berenson, one year Kavanaugh's senior at Yale College, who clerked for Justice Kennedy right before Kavanaugh, and served with his old classmate in the Bush White House.

Rusty Sullivan, another sportswriter at the *Yale Daily News*, later said, "If you had asked him back then, 'You have the option of becoming a Supreme Court justice or having a six-year career in the NBA,' I think he would have picked the NBA."

Along with playing and writing about sports, Kavanaugh enjoyed watching them in his downtime. He was a diehard Washington Redskins loyalist, remaining glued to the teams' games—as well as those of the Notre Dame Fighting Irish and the Baltimore Orioles—while drinking beer in dorm common rooms, shouting at the TV in frustration over a fumbled ball or a bad call. "He got mad when the Redskins lost," one classmate recalled.

In a Yale culture dominated by intellectuals and artsy types, Kavanaugh and his friends were somewhat anomalous—large, rowdy, heavy-drinking athletes who congregated at weekend parties, their volume growing louder throughout the evening.

The bathroom shared by Kavanaugh's room and the adjacent group suite often reeked of vomit. It was so bad that visitors often opted to use other bathrooms.

At parties Kavanaugh stayed close to the keg, earning a reputation for "holding up the wall" because if he moved away, he would fall down drunk.

He was also known for avoiding conversation with women or disparaging them. "He would talk to women differently than I would talk to them, and not kindly—he was really arrogant and aggressive, he did not have a healthy respect for them," said one classmate. "It was not appropriate behavior. His mother would be ashamed if she heard the things that he said to girls."

David Thompson, who was two years younger than Kavanaugh, remembered returning to his room in Morse residential college—adjacent to Stiles—late one night when he encountered Kavanaugh at the gate, trying to get in.

"I said, 'What are you doing? The key doesn't work; that's a Stiles key,'" Thompson recalled. "He said, 'This is Stiles.' I said, 'This is Morse. You live in Stiles; Stiles is over there.' He was sort of belligerent. He argued with me that he was at Stiles. I half carried him, half cajoled him over to Stiles." Kavanaugh tried his key there, which worked, and, after entering, his neighbor recalled, "slumped down inside the gate."

This bumbling side of Kavanaugh was fully in evidence the night he joined the Delta Kappa Epsilon fraternity, or DKE (prounouned "Deek"). Although fraternities were not big at Yale at the time, DKE in the 1980s was just developing an active Yale chapter, which would become infamous for drunkenness and misogyny. Lynne Brookes, who was captain of the varsity field hockey and lacrosse teams, encountered Kavanaugh in the middle of campus on Tap Night, when candidates for the college's fraternities are "tapped" for membership. Kavanaugh was wearing a leather football helmet, grabbing his crotch, hopping on one leg, and chanting, "I'm a geek, I'm a geek, I'm a power tool. When I sing this song, I look like a fool."

A 1985 photograph in the *Yale Daily News* showed an initiation rite of DKE brothers (not including Kavanaugh) marching across campus, waving a flag made out of women's underwear. The fraternity also organized the annual drinking contest known as "Tang," in which contestants downed plastic cups of warm beer as fast as possible.

A 1986 opinion piece in the college newspaper said that pledges were forced to walk around campus reading *Penthouse* magazine aloud and yelling lines like "I'm a butthole, sir" in response to frat brothers questioning them. Despite these sordid moments, DKE had a history of churning out future leaders, counting among its alumni no fewer than five American presidents, including Yale graduates George H. W. Bush and George W. Bush.

In September 1985, Kavanaugh and a group of his friends came to blows with a local New Haven man at the bar Demery's after attending a UB40 concert. Kavanaugh was questioned by the police after tossing the ice from his glass at the man. Kavanaugh's close friend Chris Dudley—who hit the man in the head with his drink—was arrested, taken to the station, and later released.

In his senior year, Kavanaugh was tapped for the all-male secret society Truth and Courage (TNC), which was popular among athletes and better known at the time by its nickname, the "Tit and Clit" club.

One evening that fall, after a night of heavy drinking, Kavanaugh and a few of his fellow TNC members were walking toward Naples Pizza when they passed a pickup truck parked on College Street that belonged to one of the society's members. The truck's owner later said he "heard some pounding noises and turned and saw somebody hitting my pickup truck with his hands," then smashing a black cargo box in the back.

"I realized it was Brett Kavanaugh," the classmate said. "He was uncontrollably, incoherently drunk. He's beating on the car in the open in the middle of the street on a busy evening.

"We never had a beef; we did not even know each other," he added. "I stopped him from damaging my vehicle and I asked him repeatedly, 'What the hell are you doing? What are you doing?' I remember his response to this day: he just looked at me blankly and turned and walked down College Street."

The classmate chose to address the issue at the society's next session, saying Kavanaugh's behavior was unacceptable. "His response again was really quite remarkable," he recalled. "Not a single word, nothing."

In the 1980s, binge drinking among teenagers had reportedly reached record levels. Alcohol was everywhere on campuses. At Yale, although the drinking age in Connecticut had been raised to twenty in 1983, students generally drank with impunity, rolling kegs into dorm stairwells and serving booze in their suite common rooms. To offset the winter doldrums, "Feb Club" ensured there was a party every night during the month of February. Pierson residential college hosted the Tuesday Night Club—a weekly keg party held in a basement area known as the "slave quarters."

Krasberg, who was in Stiles College, remembers one multi-keg party during freshman year in the C and D entryways of Lawrance, organized by Kavanaugh, Dave White, and Krasberg's C11 suitemate Paul Lisella. "I was present when they were talking about planning the party—buying the kegs, deposits, logistics," Krasberg said.

There was one keg left over, as Krasberg remembers it, so the guys had another party the following night—this time in the C11 common room. To keep the beer cold after the ice ran out, the guys kept it in a trash barrel filled with snow from the Old Campus quad.

This may have been the party that Deborah Ramirez, one of Kavanaugh's classmates, attended in Lawrance during her freshman year, where she ended up playing a drinking game in a circle of people that included Kavanaugh.

While both were raised Catholic, Ramirez and Kavanaugh came from very different worlds. His parents had second homes in the Florida Keys and on Maryland's Eastern Shore and were featured in a 1985 *Washington Post Magazine* article about redecorating their brick colonial using tiles from Portugal for a custom-made dining table. Kavanaugh was a veteran of raucous drinking parties from his high school days and was comfortable among the experienced East Coast students at Yale.

Ramirez grew up in a split-level ranch house in working-class Shelton, Connecticut, and had a sheltered upbringing. Her inexperience made her different from many of her Yale classmates, who entered college with a kind of armor born of privilege, entitlement, and sophistication. It also made Ramirez something of an easy mark.

During the drinking game, Ramirez said the guys kept picking her to drink more, and she became inebriated. At one point, someone strapped on a fake penis and pointed it at her. Then, later, Ramirez said, she had a penis thrust in her face. She remembered pushing it away, saying, "That's not a real penis." But this penis was real, she would recall; she had accidentally touched one for the first time. It was something she hadn't planned to do until she was married.

She remembered Genda and Todd laughing at her confusion that evening, and Kavanaugh pulling up his pants, looking "puffed up, like he just did something really, really great," and tilting his head back, also laughing. She remembered hearing David White yell down the hall, "Brett Kavanaugh just put his penis in Debbie's face."

"Now my reputation—this nice, innocent girl is just shattered," she later said in an interview. "And I don't even know why David and

Kevin would laugh at me like that. Those are the memories that have stayed."

To someone with more life experience, thicker skin, or a stronger sense of self at the time, the encounter might have been unremarkable—juvenile behavior by a bunch of boys. Indeed, to Kavanaugh himself, it may well have been just a little harmless, drunken fun. But to Ramirez it was devastating, affirming the very self-doubt she had hoped to conquer by facing down Yale in the first place: that she wasn't smart enough, pretty enough, rich enough, savvy enough, or tough enough to belong there.

"This whole identity had been ripped away from me," she said. "I had gone through high school, I'm the good girl, and now, in one evening, it was all ripped away. I'm no longer the good Catholic girl, I'm no longer the one who makes good choices, they make it clear I'm not smart."

Ramirez bottled away the experience, finding it too humiliating to discuss. She does not remember telling anyone about it at the time. At some point during her remaining college years, she sat across from her mother in a restaurant and confessed through tears, "Something happened at Yale." But even then, that was as far as she could go. "It was extremely painful," her mother, Mary Ann LeBlanc, said. "I thought she was raped; that's how hysterical she was. She did not want to talk about that. It was like a dead subject—*don't go there*, because it hurt so much."

Ramirez didn't want to disappoint her mother. "I had been drinking, I had touched a penis, I had been raised Catholic," Ramirez said. "How do you tell this mom, who raised this girl who didn't drink before she went to college, and now this? I didn't give her enough credit—she could have handled it."

LeBlanc asked at the time whether Ramirez wanted her to report the incident to the school, and Ramirez said no. It wasn't until Kavanaugh was nominated and Ramirez's story surfaced that her mother learned the details.

"I wish this did not happen to my daughter," LeBlanc said, trying not to cry. "She's always been a good person who went after good things."

Within a couple of days of the party, Ken Appold stood in a Lawrance Hall entryway and was told by two Stiles freshmen (whose identity he can't recall) what Kavanaugh had done to Ramirez. "It was fresh in their recollection," Appold said. "One person saw it; the second person was hearing the story from him for the second time."

"Her story is exactly the same as I was told at the same time," he added. "This isn't the kind of thing you forget." Appold said he was told an additional detail, however, that Ramirez does not remember: that after she pushed the penis away, Kavanaugh went with Genda into the bathroom, became erect, came back out, and tried it again.

"That was the story as I heard it," Appold said.

Michael Wetstone, another classmate, also later confirmed to *The New Yorker* that he remembered Appold telling him about the same incident in graduate school.

Also shortly after the Yale party, Kavanaugh's classmate Richard Oh overheard a female student emotionally describing making contact with a fake penis, saying, "It's not real," and then realizing it was real, a story he attested to in an affidavit for Ramirez's lawyers. "My memory of the story matches Debbie Ramirez's account, and I don't know her," Oh said in an interview. "There was no communication between she and I. We had these stories independently."

FIVE

Onus Probandi

The Burden of Proof

Anna Eshoo had spent two decades in Congress, focusing on issues like biotechnology, environmental protection, net neutrality, and access to health care for families and children. An elegant seventy-five-year-old woman with short hair and dark features, she was comfortable meeting with constituents.

On July 20, Ford met Eshoo at her Palo Alto office. The congresswoman had asked her staff to schedule Ford as her last appointment of the day, so that they would not be pressed for time.

Going into the meeting, Eshoo had two priorities: to establish her office as a safe and private space where Ford could speak freely and to follow Ford's lead on what, if anything, to do with her recollections. She didn't want Ford to feel forced into anything.

The two women sat down in Eshoo's rectangular conference room.

"Tell me your story," the congresswoman said.

They spoke for close to two hours, during which Ford haltingly shared the details of her encounter with Kavanaugh thirty-six years earlier, at times through tears.

Listening to her story made Eshoo cry, too. She asked what Ford wanted to accomplish. Ford said she wanted to share her information with the president or other key decision makers involved in the Supreme Court nomination. But because of her fierce desire to protect her family's privacy, Ford wanted to report the incident to those people anonymously.

Ford struck Eshoo as honest. She had a strong sense of civic duty in coming forward. But there was also a sense of naivete about what that might mean, given the ease with which tips about public officials could leak to the public and the difficulties that so often ensued.

Ford mentioned that she had followed Kavanaugh's career over the years, expecting that at some point he would be considered for the Supreme Court. She had felt compelled to speak out, she said, when he finally landed on the short list.

Eshoo sensed no partisan agenda. Ford "doesn't have a political bone in her body," she later said. "She was intelligent, sensitive. She had a real gentleness about her," she added. "But she had little to no awareness about what my world is."

Ford at that point in her life was far removed from the political culture of her native Washington. She had moved to California three decades earlier and essentially never looked back. She visited with her family once a year for family get-togethers, usually in Rehoboth Beach, Delaware. Her brothers, both lawyers, had remained in the D.C. suburbs, raising families, and her parents continued to live in the Potomac house where she was raised, her father working well into his eighties. But Ford had no firsthand sense of the political gamesmanship that existed inside the Beltway and the hardening of the partisanship that was by now coursing through the community in which she had been reared.

A registered Democrat, Ford had at various points been both a Republican and an independent. She held more liberal views than her family and was involved with local efforts to preserve Monterey Bay. She had participated in a local Women's March protesting Trump administration policies in 2017 and a march to advocate for science research funding in April 2018. But for the most part, she was inactive in national politics. Her political donations in recent years had consisted of $80.50 given to Democratic causes through the nonprofit technology platform ActBlue. Of that total, $27 was directed to a committee for the progressive Bernie Sanders during the 2016 election cycle, when Trump won the presidency.

Toward the end of their conversation, Ford told Eshoo that she was in conversations with a *Washington Post* reporter. Eshoo found that puzzling. Wasn't Ford hoping to stay anonymous? Tipping off the *Post* as a reluctant source seemed like tiptoeing into a lion's den.

The congresswoman asked what Ford wanted her to do.

"Well, what is it that you *can* do?" Ford replied.

Eshoo said she could start by contacting a trusted colleague. She meant Dianne Feinstein. Feinstein, a longtime senator from California, was both Ford's representative and the ranking Democrat on the Senate Judiciary Committee, the very panel that was evaluating Kavanaugh. Ford's information would be in more capable hands with Feinstein, Eshoo thought, given her direct role in vetting judicial appointees.

Under the Appointments Clause of the United States Constitution, the president has the power to nominate federal judges, and the Senate, not the House, has the power to "advise and consent." Advice and consent was loosely defined in the Constitution, but in modern times the Senate adopted a committee vetting process, usually culminating in multiple days of public hearings before approving or denying the confirmation with a majority vote. Still, the president maintains the constitutional right to pull his nominee at any point.

Eshoo had known Feinstein for many years, having served on the San Mateo County Board of Supervisors when Feinstein was mayor of San Francisco. She was one of the women elected along with Feinstein—as well as California senator Barbara Boxer—in 1992, the so-called Year of the Woman, just after the divisive Clarence Thomas/ Anita Hill hearings.

She reached Feinstein the following day, a Saturday. "I told her that I had something that I thought was very serious," Eshoo recalled. Without providing Ford's name, she explained her meeting with their mutual constituent and the account that Ford had shared.

Feinstein seemed to appreciate the gravity of the situation. She asked Eshoo to have the constituent write a letter to her, reiterating her story.

On July 29, during a visit with her parents back east, Ford sat down to write the letter. It was her first time committing her high school experience to paper, and reliving the memory was difficult. It was a short, lacerating read:

"Brett Kavanaugh physically and sexually assaulted me during High School in the early 1980's," Ford wrote. "He conducted these acts with the assistance of his close friend, Mark G. Judge. Both were 1-2 years older than me and students at a local private school. The assault occurred in a suburban Maryland area home at a gathering that included me and 4 others. Kavanaugh physically pushed me into a bedroom as I was headed for a bathroom up a short stairwell from the living room. They locked the door and played loud music, precluding any successful attempts to yell for help. Kavanaugh was on top of me while laughing with Judge, who periodically jumped onto Kavanaugh. They both laughed as Kavanaugh tried to disrobe me in their highly inebriated state. With Kavanaugh's hand over my mouth, I feared he may inadvertently kill me."

The letter went on to describe how she escaped, and also mentioned running into an uncomfortable-looking Mark Judge at Safeway. But she asked in three places that it remain secret, signing before her name the phrase "In Confidence." To Ford, a research scientist, anonymity was a cornerstone of professional life. Patients whose behavior or symptoms she reviewed were respected as private citizens. The names of volunteer participants in experiments were withheld from studies and analysis. So, although the context was different, Ford expected no less from the people around her now.

Ford emailed her letter on Monday, July 30, to Eshoo's aide, Chapman. Per the congresswoman's specific instructions, Chapman then immediately emailed the letter to Eshoo's D.C. chief of staff, Matthew McMurray, who hand-delivered Ford's letter to Jennifer Duck, Senator Feinstein's Democratic staff director for the Senate Judiciary Committee.

Feinstein spoke on the phone with Ford the next day. Ford sounded vulnerable and emotional, very unsure of how best to proceed. Feinstein found her credible and urged her to permit an investigation. But that, in the senator's view, entailed making the claims public. The FBI couldn't do much with an anonymous tip, she believed, and in order to spur an official probe, she would have to share its contents with her Republican colleagues who ran the Judiciary Committee.

Ford was unbending. She was not ready to lose her anonymity. "She reiterated her desire that I keep the letter confidential and not share it with anyone when we spoke," Feinstein later said.

Feinstein's staff began researching whether the Judiciary Committee could hire an outside, independent lawyer to investigate Ford's allegations. But they couldn't—at least not without explicit permission from the GOP chairs of the Rules Committee and Judiciary Committee. And doing that risked breaking their promise to Ford to keep her allegations a secret.

Among Ford's friends in Palo Alto, a consensus was building that she should hire a lawyer. At first, Ford was reluctant; she had brought her information to her legislators' attention, and her confidentiality had been assured. Given her desire to stay behind the scenes, she wondered, what benefit could a lawyer bring? She didn't like the idea of ratcheting up what was already a stressful process.

But far as they were from the corridors of Washington power, Ford's circle knew judicial nominations were highly sensitive. Her friends Keith Koegler and Elizabeth Hewitt, a married couple who were both lawyers, were strongly in favor of Ford retaining an attorney who could advise her on working with investigators or lawmakers on the Senate Judiciary Committee. Ford might eventually need a veteran's advice on how to navigate public attention, if her name was inadvertently—or purposefully—leaked.

In late June or early July, just days after Ford had first wondered out loud how to convey her memories to the White House, Koegler, Hewitt, and another friend began texting contacts in and around Palo Alto for advice. Ford's was an unusual situation, given its intimately personal nature combined with the high political stakes, and they wanted to help her proceed thoughtfully. So they canvassed fellow parents and professionals they felt they could trust to suggest ideas, without identifying Ford by name.

Word quickly got to Sheryl Sandberg, Facebook's chief operating officer, who had long been rumored to be a candidate for Democratic political office, through her sister, Michelle, a pediatrician and clinical teacher at Stanford. Sheryl also advised retaining a lawyer. She put together a list of people who she had heard specialized in such cases and passed it back to Michelle, who shared it with one of Ford's friends. Other suggestions came from family members and the office of Senator Feinstein, whom Ford had asked for referrals.

By early August, Ford was vacationing in Rehoboth Beach with Russell, their boys, and her parents. She had no intention of telling her mother and father about her experience with Kavanaugh, or the fact that she had now shared it with a U.S. senator. So when she decided it was finally time to interview some lawyers, she did so from the back of her car in a Walgreens parking lot, near the Blaseys' beach house, where she had some privacy.

Larry Robbins, a name partner in the K Street law firm Robbins, Russell, was one of the first people she talked to. Robbins, an experienced, even-keeled litigator who had argued eighteen cases before the Supreme Court, had been recommended to Ford by a relative. Discussing her experience with Robbins, a patient listener, Ford felt an immediate comfort level.

Ford explained that she had considered contacting Kavanaugh directly. "That's quite an idea," Robbins replied.

From her car in the drugstore parking lot, Ford also talked to lawyers at Katz, Marshall & Banks, a boutique Washington firm that handles whistleblower and employment matters. The Katz firm had been suggested by Feinstein's office. Its lead partner, Debra Katz, had featured prominently in a legal network founded by the National Women's Law Center, a nonprofit organization focused on gender equity, to represent women and girls facing sexual harassment and gender discrimination in the early days of the #MeToo movement in 2017. The conversation went well enough that Ford agreed to meet Katz and Lisa Banks, her longtime legal partner, a few days later.

It was cloudy and humid on the evening of August 6 in Linthicum Heights, Maryland, when the three got together at an airport Hilton. Katz, a slim, intense attorney with close-cropped dark hair who had been visiting her father in Florida, flew into the nearby Baltimore/Washington International Airport. Katz, who was known for speaking her mind, was the more assertive of the two. Banks, a brunette with softer features who drove to the hotel straight from Washington, tended to be the more conciliatory voice.

Katz and Banks had reserved a nondescript fourth-floor conference room. Over coffee, they gave Ford a brief overview of the type of law they practiced. They also talked through Ford's memories and motivations. Because of the heightened concerns about the future of the Supreme Court and the treatment of women, it was clear that the national reaction to Ford's recollection could be explosive.

The lawyers found Ford entirely believable. Her conviction that the incident had happened and that the perpetrator was Kavanaugh was unshakable. Her memory of the layout of the house and other details was intricate. That Ford had met Kavanaugh on prior occasions and knew his face, they felt, gave her memory additional power. It was much less likely for a sexual assault victim to be confused about her attacker's identity if she had met that person before.

Partway through the meeting with Ford, Katz and Banks stepped out of the room to confer. Ford had a strong case, they felt, and she would need experienced counsel. Though it had the potential to be a significant drain on their time, they wanted to help her, and were willing to do it pro bono, given how expensive the bills could eventually be.

Katz and Banks returned to the room and offered to represent Ford, who accepted. They arranged a polygraph test for the next day.

. . .

On August 7, a former FBI agent named Jeremiah Hanafin arrived at the Hilton with a Dell Inspiron notebook computer, an arm cuff for measuring heart rate, and a pneumograph for tracking chest activity. He greeted Ford and Banks, who had reconvened in a separate but similar conference room. The three talked at length about Ford's recollections of Kavanaugh. Then Hanafin asked Ford to provide a written account of those memories and left her alone with Banks.

Ford filled a legal-pad page with her account, pinpointing the same details she had given Feinstein. When Hanafin returned, she signed the statement "Christine Blasey," in a sloping cursive; the former FBI agent would use the document as the basis for asking questions. Then Banks left the room and sat in the hallway while Hanafin talked to Ford one-on-one.

Their conversation and the polygraph that was administered afterward made for a strenuous experience. Having just attended the funeral of her grandmother, who had died at age one hundred after a stint in hospice, Ford had only one night in the Washington area before flying to visit her husband Russell's family in Manchester, New Hampshire. The test took far longer than she had expected and seemed to cover her whole life story. It was painful to relive the Kavanaugh experience in such detail.

The examination rested on two key questions: (1) "Is any part of your statement false?" and (2) "Did you make up any part of your statement?" Ford answered no to both questions. Hanafin concluded that the test results did not indicate deception.

SIX

Ambitio

Ambition, or
Courting the Vote

For many people, late August 2018 was punctuated by the usual rituals that mark the end of summer: packing away beach towels, stocking up on school supplies, and accepting that the days would soon be growing shorter. But for Brett Kavanaugh, it was crunch time. On September 4, the day after Labor Day, he would go before the Senate Judiciary Committee for the first round of hearings in his confirmation for the Supreme Court.

Kavanaugh wasn't entirely new to this process, having come before the committee to be evaluated for the D.C. Circuit in 2004 and again in 2006. But the stakes for a Supreme Court seat would be considerably higher, the scrutiny even less forgiving. He knew he would have to walk the political tightrope, appearing partisan enough to satisfy the Republican base—in particular, the staunchly opinionated Trump, who could pull Kavanaugh's nomination at any time—but not so partisan that Democrats could declare him insufficiently impartial for the court.

So Kavanaugh did what he always did: his homework. The judge pored over opinions from his tenure on the District Court, focusing on the more controversial ones he was likely to be grilled about, such as the case on Obamacare and the one involving a pregnant undocumented teenager. Perhaps he would be asked in more detail about his accumulated debt of between $60,000 and $200,000, which Kavanaugh had explained was due to home improvements and having bought Washington Nationals tickets for himself and friends.

In preparing for the hearings, Kavanaugh drew on his carefully cultivated social graces as he made the customary rounds of senators' offices—brandishing his hail-fellow-well-met demeanor and a pocket copy of the Constitution.

He also rehearsed the way presidential candidates practice for debates. His coaching team included heavyweights like Don McGahn, White House counsel; Bill Burck, Kavanaugh's friend and former deputy in the Bush White House; Zina Bash, a former Trump White House aide who once clerked for Judge Kavanaugh; and Roman Martinez, also a former clerk, who worked as an assistant to the solicitor general at the U.S. Department of Justice before going into private practice.

Also in the mix was Bill Shine, who was forced out as a Fox News executive over his handling of sexual harassment scandals and subsequently became Trump's deputy chief of staff for communications before rising to White House communications director.

Even Senators Orrin Hatch and Lindsey Graham lent a hand. Both Republicans were senior members of the Judiciary Committee and proud supporters of Kavanaugh. Graham, a close ally of President Trump's, would be named chair of the committee when Grassley stepped down later that year. Hatch was one of a handful of senators who had been on the committee since the Clarence Thomas hearings.

Grassley's right-hand man Davis, working sixteen-hour days at this point preparing for the hearings, would joke to colleagues of Kavanaugh, "We're going to drag his ass across the finish line."

In a way, Kavanaugh's entire life had been a preparation for this moment—the careful avoidance of controversy as he made his way through the finest educational institutions, the cultivation of important mentors, the connections to people in power.

After graduating cum laude from Yale in 1987, Kavanaugh went straight to Yale Law School, which was neck and neck with Harvard at the time for the nation's top rank. Kavanaugh did not stand out to his peers there, who remember him sitting in the back of class, rarely raising his hand, and holding no leadership positions except as one of the notes editors on the *Law Review*, a job in which he handled student-written pieces (unlike the more prestigious articles editors, who handled professionally written pieces).

The stars who stood out from that period included John C. Yoo, who was two years behind Kavanaugh. Yoo went on to become a principal author of the Justice Department's so-called "torture memos" in the George W. Bush administration, which provided the legal justification for harsh interrogation techniques.

Nevertheless, Kavanaugh achieved a strong enough record in law school to secure plum summer associate positions—at Pillsbury Madison & Sutro; Miller Cassidy Larocca & Lewin (now part of Baker Botts); the white-shoe Washington firm Covington & Burling; and Williams & Connolly. He also managed to impress Judge Walter K. Stapleton of the U.S. Court of Appeals for the Third Circuit in Wilmington, Delaware, a Reagan appointee who hired Kavanaugh right out of Yale for a clerkship in March 1989.

"He had one of the most impressive résumés I have ever seen, and believe me, I have seen a lot of résumés," Stapleton said in his testimony for Kavanaugh's 2006 confirmation. "At the point in time I met him he had received an honors grade in every course he had taken at Yale Law School save one."

After working for Stapleton, Kavanaugh hardly needed to prove himself in another clerkship. But in 1991 he jumped at the chance to fill an opening in the chambers of Judge Alex Kozinski of the Ninth Circuit in Pasadena, California. Despite a reputation for working clerks to the bone, Kozinski was widely respected as an incisive intellect and sharp wit. More crucial to Kavanaugh, Kozinski was a known feeder to the Supreme Court.

The two forged a close relationship that continued well into the years that followed. In a 1991 *Yale Law Journal* article, Kozinski quoted Judge Patricia Wald's description of the judge-clerk relationship as "the most intense and mutually dependent one . . . outside of marriage, parenthood, or a love affair," and added that "judge and law clerk are in fact tethered by an invisible cord for the rest of their mutual careers."

Kozinski invited Kavanaugh to help screen clerks for Justice Anthony Kennedy. They coauthored a book and sat on panels together. From 2009 to 2014, both served on the Judicial Conference of the United States, a select group of judges who make policy for federal courts. In 2006, Kozinski—along with Judge Stapleton—introduced Kavanaugh at his D.C. Circuit confirmation hearing, calling him "my good friend" and praising his "sense of humanity."

Kavanaugh hired Kozinski's son, Clayton, as a clerk in his Washington chambers, even though Clayton was not among the highest-achieving students in his Yale Law School class. Other Kozinski alumni also factored into Kavanaugh's career. Burck, the lawyer who would later determine which of Kavanaugh's documents were publicly released, was a former Kozinski clerk who later represented Kozinski after the harassment accusations. Burck, too, worked in the George W. Bush White House and became a good friend of Kavanaugh's; he would attend the judge's East Room nomination ceremony and his confirmation hearings.

The closeness between Kavanaugh and Kozinski was evident in 2015, when they were both panelists at a Federalist Society event at the National Lawyers Convention. Sitting next to each other onstage at the Mayflower Hotel, in Washington, Kavanaugh said he "learned from the master," affectionately patting his former mentor on the shoulder. Kavanaugh also laughed heartily when Kozinski joked that "being a judge means never having to say you're sorry."

Learning about Kozinski's alleged misconduct "was a gut punch for me. It was a gut punch for the judiciary. And I was shocked, and disappointed, angry, swirl of emotions," Kavanaugh later testified. "No woman should be subjected to sexual harassment in the workplace, including in the judiciary, especially in the judiciary."

When asked whether, prior to the fall of 2017, he had any knowledge of Judge Kozinski inappropriately kissing, touching, or fondling anyone, Kavanaugh answered, "No."

He also said he was not one of the clerks, judges, or others on the infamous email "Easy Rider Gag List" to whom Kozinski distributed sexually explicit photos and videos, including a photograph of naked women painted to look like cows. "I do not remember receiving inappropriate emails of a sexual nature from Judge Kozinski," Kavanaugh told the Judiciary Committee.

Those denials struck many of Kozinski's former clerks as wholly implausible, given the judge's regular blue jokes and reputation for inappropriate behavior.

"Kavanaugh knew," said Brian Lehman, who quit his clerkship

after confronting Kozinski about his inappropriate conduct in 2000. (Among other things, Lehman reported that Kozinski had shown him a video of naked women skydiving, thinking it was funny to watch their breasts flapping in the wind.)

"He put up with it for a reason," Lehman added of Kavanaugh. "You put up with that for a year and after that Kozinski would use that power to promote you."

Heidi Bond, one of Kozinski's former clerks, wrote in *Slate* that Kavanaugh's assertion under oath that he did "not remember" any sexual comments made by Judge Kozinski strained credulity. "This last response leaves me wondering whether Kavanaugh and I clerked for the same man," Bond wrote. "Kozinski's sexual comments—to both men and women—were legendary."

But others viewed attacks against Kavanaugh in light of Kozinski's misdeeds as unfair. "To refuse to confirm Brett Kavanaugh simply over his association with Kozinski is McCarthyism, pure and simple," wrote Steven G. Calabresi, a Northwestern University law professor and current chairman of the Federalist Society. "It is guilt by association."

In 1991, Kozinski called the Yale Law professor George L. Priest and said he needed to replace his law clerk Alex M. Azar II, who had abruptly left after just six weeks on the job. (Azar said through a spokeswoman that he had no knowledge of nor had he witnessed any sexually inappropriate behavior by Judge Kozinski, therefore his leaving was unrelated.)

Kozinski said he was seeking a clerk with "good judgment, who's solid, who's easy to get along with," recalled Priest, who said Kavanaugh came to mind. Priest had been less impressed with Kavanaugh's performance in his torts class than he was with his performance on the basketball court during pickup games.

"He was a very decent ballplayer and honest—he did not call bad fouls," Priest said in an interview. "I wouldn't say he was a great student; he was a good student. But I got to know his character from basketball."

In addition to Kavanaugh's good sportsmanship, he wasn't a "flaming radical," like many Yale Law graduates, Priest said, so he recommended him to Kozinski.

Kavanaugh later described his phone call from Priest as "life-changing." And while Kavanaugh's Kozinski experience may have come back to haunt him during his 2018 confirmation hearings, it served him very well throughout the intervening years. "You cannot understand Kavanaugh's philosophy as a judge without understanding Kozinski's judicial philosophy," Lehman said. "Everything about Kavanaugh—how he interprets a statute, the role of regulatory agencies, the Second Amendment, the death penalty, abortion, even how many times he drafts an opinion—is influenced by that clerkship and the years he stayed in touch with him. You keep part of that voice with you throughout your career."

Kavanaugh had also, during his career, been slowly but steadily shoring up the conservative bona fides required of a Supreme Court prospect under a Republican president. While in law school he had joined the Federalist Society's Yale chapter, which had been founded in 1982 by three Yale college friends—Calabresi, Lee Liberman Otis, and David McIntosh—as a Reagan-emboldened antidote to largely liberal elite law schools.

This put Kavanaugh out of step with the majority of students and professors at Yale. In aligning with the conservative Supreme Court chief justice at the time, William Rehnquist, Kavanaugh recalled in a 2017 speech to the right-leaning American Enterprise Institute, "that often meant, in the Yale Law School environment of the time, that I stood alone."

This side of Kavanaugh was little known in Yale circles. Despite his conservative predilections, he did not talk politics with peers or publicly take partisan positions.

"In the passionate intellectual atmosphere of Yale Law School, none of us can say that Judge Kavanaugh stood out as ideological at all," said twenty-three of his classmates in an August 2018 letter of support to the Judiciary Committee. "He was not a person with an agenda. Rather, he was a thoughtful classmate and loyal friend who obviously loved the intellectual challenges of the law and the good company of his peers."

Randy Berholtz, one of those who signed the letter, said Kavanaugh struck him as a liberal Republican. "I was sort of surprised that people thought of him as a conservative Republican," said Berholtz, who added parenthetically that Kavanaugh had "nice hair."

"I just did not see him as that. He was very establishment—more Bush than Reagan or Trump," Berholtz added. "He's the type of guy who you saw and you thought, 'Here's a nice guy who seems like he's going along with the crowd.' I never saw him getting into ideological debates. He was not the smartest, most aggressive one there."

Indeed, during law school, Kavanaugh seemed to grow more circumspect. With the real world looming and intense competition for the most prestigious clerkships and corporate positions, he and his classmates realized that these three years could determine the rest of their lives.

There were a few glaring reversions to juvenile antics, like a bus trip to Boston for a Red Sox game and barhopping that left Kavanaugh and more than two dozen classmates falling out of the bus onto the front steps of Yale Law School before dawn.

On the bus, Kavanaugh's roommate Steve Hartmann tried to review notes for his labor law final the following morning "while people were doing group chugs from a keg," Kavanaugh recalled in a 2014 speech to the school's Federalist Society chapter. "Fortunately for all of us, we had a motto: 'What happens on the bus stays on the bus.' Tonight, you can modify that to 'What happens at the Fed Soc after-party stays at the Fed Soc after-party.'"

There was also the night during his 1989 summer stint at Covington & Burling in D.C. when Kavanaugh showed up with a female paralegal to a firm event at the now-defunct Brickskeller bar—famous for more than a thousand choices of beer from all over the world. One of the associates who was walking into the bar saw Kavanaugh drunkenly carrying the paralegal down the front staircase, "sort of like you would carry a bride across the threshold," he said. "He got to the bottom of the steps and fell down onto the sidewalk."

The law firm subsequently took Kavanaugh aside and told him, "'This is not appropriate,'" the associate recalled. "'You don't bring paralegals to summer associate events.'"

Even early in his career, Kavanaugh was notably driven and ambitious for a career as a judge. "He's a great example of those kinds of people who have their eye on a prize for many years," said one fellow summer associate, Darryl Brown, who also clerked with Kavanaugh on the Third Circuit, "and take every step to pursue it."

Regarding members of the opposite sex, Kavanaugh continued to seem like a neophyte—without a longtime girlfriend or much dating. Still, at least one of the women Kavanaugh went out with briefly in law school described him as "incredibly thoughtful, intelligent, hardworking," and "ethically beyond reproach."

Many of the seven students Kavanaugh lived with during the third year of law school did not share his political predilections. But the eight guys nevertheless forged a strong bond and kept in close touch after graduation, reuniting every year for long weekends of hiking, sailing, rafting, or biking. Their annual trips took them to spring training for major league teams in Florida as well as to Wrigley Field, the World Series at Yankee Stadium, and Las Vegas.

Their group was known to some in law school as the Tall Boys, because most of them—with the exception of Kavanaugh—were of noteworthy height. They included James E. "Jeb" Boasberg, who eventually became a federal judge in Washington's district court, in part because Kavanaugh—when he was vetting judges for President Bush—recommended him. The Tall Boys lived together in a dilapidated red-brick house at 61 Lake Place in New Haven, behind Payne Whitney Gym and just a few doors down from the house occupied by Kavanaugh's college fraternity, Delta Kappa Epsilon.

The housemates watched *Jeopardy!* together or ESPN *SportsCenter.* Kavanaugh was known for organizing weekend tailgates at the Yale football games, "limited dance moves," and unsophisticated eating habits that included spaghetti with ketchup and pizza without any toppings.

After law school, they spent one of their reunion weekends on a rented boat out of Annapolis, Maryland, in 2001. The details of that weekend aren't clear, but apparently Kavanaugh wasn't keen to hear them repeated outside of their close group of friends. In a September 10 email after the trip, he wrote, "Reminders to everyone to be very, very vigilant w/r/t confidentiality > on all issues and all fronts, including with spouses."

When asked about the email in his confirmation hearings, Kavanaugh said he was referring to his impending first date that evening with Ashley Estes, the West Texan presidential aide he would eventually marry, whom he had talked about "at some length" over the past weekend.

Another law school housemate, Kenneth Christmas, who is African American and has deep family roots in Mississippi, though he was raised in California, recalled a long drive he and Kavanaugh took together to Bucks County, Pennsylvania, on their way to one of their annual weekends. On the trip, Christmas shared his "bewilderment over those who deny the continuing effects of slavery and Jim Crow laws," as well as his belief "that the laws of our country must remain responsive to historical prejudice, discrimination, oppression, and mistreatment of African Americans," said Christmas in his testimony on Kavanaugh's behalf during the confirmation hearings.

"Judge Kavanaugh listened and asked questions for the whole ride," added Christmas, now an executive consultant. "There was no doubt left in my mind following that ride that Judge Kavanaugh deeply cared—and still cares—about truly understanding my black experience and point of view."

Issues of race appeared to weigh heavily on Kavanaugh's mind as a federal judge, too. When asked on his 2018 Senate Judiciary Committee questionnaire to list the ten most important cases in which he had participated, for instance, Kavanaugh named as the tenth an employment discrimination case involving a former Fannie Mae employee who was called the n-word.

"Calling someone the n-word, even once, creates a hostile work environment," Kavanaugh wrote in joining the majority's opinion ruling for the employee.

"No other word in the English language," Kavanaugh wrote in his concurrence, "so powerfully or instantly calls to mind our country's long and brutal struggle to overcome racism and discrimination against African-Americans."

As a law student, Justice Kavanaugh in the *Yale Law Journal* called for enforcement of a 1986 Supreme Court decision barring race discrimination in jury selection. In his term as a Supreme Court justice, Kavanaugh would in June 2019 write in his majority decision on a case that involved keeping black people off juries: "Equal justice under law requires a criminal trial free of racial discrimination in the jury selection process."

As a judge, Kavanaugh modeled himself after Justice Kennedy, a wizened, patrician presence, for whom he clerked between 1993 and 1994. Kennedy valued input from his clerks, bringing them into his office for discussions that would go on for hours, where he'd scribble on a whiteboard the pros and cons of a given case: "This argument favors this side, but what about this argument?" Kavanaugh recalled in a radio interview after Kennedy announced his retirement.

Kennedy, a notorious swing vote on the Supreme Court, had succeeded in alienating and endearing himself to both political parties—becoming a conservative hero for decisions such as overturning D.C.'s gun ban; a liberal hero for votes like favoring gay marriage. "He received tremendous criticism over the course of his career. And yet he was one who stuck to his principles," Kavanaugh said. "It's not easy to do, and he's done it consistently over time, recognizing that that's the role of a judge."

If Kavanaugh had made a point of seeming politically neutral early in life to maximize his options, now he doubled down on partisanship when presented with a path to power. In the late nineties, he answered Ken Starr's call to leave a position at the firm Kirkland & Ellis and join the team of young Federalist Society lawyers—known as "the elves"—who would make the case to impeach Bill Clinton.

While Kavanaugh's zealotry may have been strategic, it struck those around him as deep and genuine. Clinton's conduct got under Kavanaugh's skin, particularly the president's philandering with a former intern, and Kavanaugh made no secret of his personal feelings on the subject.

"He went nuts trying to get Clinton to be held accountable for a moral failure," one Yale College classmate said, "and he concluded it's not possible to get a president out."

At Yale College's tenth reunion in 1997, Kavanaugh made clear in conversations with friends that he was offended by the idea of Clinton taking advantage of Lewinsky when he was president and of Paula Jones, a former Arkansas state employee, when he was governor.

For example, Kavanaugh condemned Clinton as a governor "using state police to stand outside the door while he would have his wicked way with this woman," a Yale College classmate said. "He would get wound up about that. He categorized Hillary as a true believer, but he said Bill's a bad guy."

While some came to question Kavanaugh's passion on the Lewinsky matter, one of his fellow elves said there was "a little bit of an Ahab mentality that set in," adding that there was "distaste in the Starr office for the Clintons, based on a general feeling they were sleazy, whether or not what they had done was illegal."

That Ahab mentality was evident in Kavanaugh's position on the investigation of Bill Clinton: Starr should question the president aggressively and unflinchingly when it came to the details of his sexual relationship with Lewinsky.

"I am strongly opposed to giving the President any 'break' in the questioning," Kavanaugh wrote in a memo on August 15, 1998, adding, "The president has disgraced his office, the legal system and the American people by having sex with a 22-year-old intern and turning her life into a shambles."

Kavanaugh added in the memo that Clinton had fired back "with a sustained propaganda campaign that would make Nixon blush," and he urged Starr to ask explicit questions like "If Monica Lewinsky says that you inserted a cigar into her vagina while you were in the Oval Office area, would she be lying?"

At the same time, Kavanaugh did not necessarily want Clinton publicly shamed, arguing against the inclusion of sexual details in the published report—advice Starr disregarded—and later expressing dissatisfaction with the report's wide release.

"I regret that the House of Representatives did not handle the report in a way that would have kept sensitive details in the report from public disclosure," Kavanaugh said in his 2018 Senate questionnaire, "or, if not, that the report did not further segregate certain sensitive details."

Kavanaugh also later took issue with the role of an independent counsel, given his Starr experience, which Democrats would point to as a meaningful clue to how Kavanaugh would view special counsel Robert Mueller's investigation into the Russians' 2016 election interference.

"It makes no sense at all to have an independent counsel looking at the conduct of the president," Kavanaugh said in a 1998 speech at Georgetown University Law Center, adding in a law journal article that same year that the statute underlying the investigation "creates, almost by definition, a scenario whereby the President and the independent counsel are adversaries."

"The nation certainly would have been better off if President Clinton could have focused on Osama bin Laden," he later wrote, in a 2009 law journal article, "without being distracted by the Paula Jones sexual harassment case and its criminal investigation offshoots."

Kavanaugh would find himself and his colleagues rushing from the White House as an airplane hijacked by bin Laden's associates bore down on Washington three years later. The coordinated events of that day—during which planes crashed into the World Trade Center, the Pentagon, and a field in Pennsylvania—were a horrifying act of terrorism.

Even during the Starr investigation, however, Kavanaugh managed to keep politics largely separate from his personal life. Rich Roberts, his law school classmate, is married to Janice Cook Roberts, whose stepfather is Vernon Jordan. Jordan, Bill Clinton's close friend and adviser, was a central figure in the Lewinsky controversy. Yet Kavanaugh did not let these events affect their friendship.

"We did not talk about that stuff," Roberts said. "That was never an issue in terms of us being able to spend time together and hang out and enjoy each other's company."

Still, Kavanaugh increasingly became a fixture in Republican politics. In 2000, Kavanaugh—who had left the independent counsel's office to return to the law firm Kirkland & Ellis—was part of the legal team that represented the American relatives of six-year-old Elián González, who wanted to keep the child in Miami despite his father's wishes to have custody of him in Cuba. He also helped represent George W. Bush in the then-governor's successful fight for the presidency after the Florida recount in the 2000 election, legal challenges that went all the way to the Supreme Court.

In 2001, Kavanaugh quit his job at Kirkland to join the White House counsel's office, where he specialized in judicial appointments. In 2003, he became assistant to the president and staff secretary. He traveled all over the world with the president on Air Force One and worked closely with him in the West Wing.

"Love the guy," Kavanaugh said of Bush in a May 2018 commencement address at Catholic University's law school, adding that the president "lives on the sunrise side of the mountain. That's the place to live. Be the optimist. The happy warrior."

Kavanaugh also met his future wife, Ashley Estes, in the Bush White House. The president's personal secretary, Estes, like George W. and his wife, Laura, had grown up in West Texas. An Abilene native whom a family friend would later describe to the town's local newspaper as "sweet" and "the All-American girl," Estes herself had a long history with Bush, having served as his personal assistant when he was governor of Texas and worked for the Bush-Cheney presidential campaign.

President Bush and the first lady hosted a sit-down dinner for the couple in the White House's elegant Rose Garden and attended their wedding, in 2004 at Georgetown's Christ Church. At Kavanaugh's swearing in to the federal bench in 2006, Bush joked that the judge's wedding "was the first lifetime appointment" he'd arranged for Kavanaugh. Bush presided over that Rose Garden ceremony after the Senate approved Kavanaugh for a place on the U.S. District Court of Appeals on the D.C. Circuit; Justice Kennedy administered the oath and Ashley held the Bible.

Ironically, the very political affiliations that had led to that Circuit Court appointment risked derailing it. Democratic senators pounced on the issue of Kavanaugh's partisanship during the hearings, dragging out the confirmation process, which stalled between hearings in 2004 and hearings in 2006. Senator Chuck Schumer of New York accused Kavanaugh of having "a more partisan record than any single nominee who has come before us, Democrat or Republican," telling him, "You have been more active in more political causes, hot-button issues than anyone."

Schumer called Kavanaugh "the Zelig of Republican politics," drawn magnetically to some of the most controversial and high-profile issues of the prior decades, like the Whitewater investigation and the Bush administration's backing of the Iraq War.

"If there's been a partisan political fight that needed a good lawyer in the last decade, Brett Kavanaugh was probably there," said Schumer. Kavanaugh's nomination to the D.C. Circuit, he added, was "not just a drop of salt in the partisan wounds, it's the whole shaker."

During his twelve years on the D.C. Circuit, Kavanaugh established himself as a mainstream, establishment conservative on issues like the Second Amendment, campaign finance, and separation of powers, more in the mold of Justice Roberts than Justice Samuel A. Alito Jr.

While he often ruled along predictably conservative lines—curtailing environmental protection regulations, for example, and expanding executive privilege—the judge generally brought a pragmatic approach to the bench.

Temperamentally, Kavanaugh developed a reputation as decent, well prepared, and collegial. "He asks the pertinent questions, he asks them in an extremely nice manner," said A. J. Kramer, a federal public defender, in his 2018 testimony before the Judiciary Committee. "Not all judges are like that."

Nevertheless, Kavanaugh left no doubt about his political loyalties, giving more than fifty speeches to the Federalist Society and aligning himself with prominent Republicans. He also became part of the so-called "Eureka dinners" on the first Monday of every month at D.C.'s Bobby Van's Steakhouse or the Caucus Room Brasserie, where attendees included Viet Dinh, a senior legal adviser to Rupert Murdoch; John Yoo, who penned the 2002 torture memos; and Alex Azar, the onetime Kozinski clerk who later became Trump's health and human services secretary.

Sometimes Kavanaugh defied expectations—arguing, for example, that Supreme Court precedent indicated a compelling interest in access to contraception or overturning the conviction of an Osama bin Laden associate, though that conviction had been important to the Bush administration.

In 2009 Kavanaugh wrote for the court that the pro-choice Emily's List, which supports female candidates, had the right to spend unlimited amounts of money promoting issues or candidates of their choice. Even the ACLU recognized that Kavanaugh had been sympathetic to claims related to Title VII, which prohibits employment discrimination (although the ACLU also said that he ruled against more often than for civil rights complainants).

In a 2016 opinion, Kavanaugh said an attorney had been ineffective in his representation of a woman for failing to retain an expert on battered women's syndrome. "He wrote a primer essentially on the defense of battered women's syndrome for lawyers," said Kramer, who has argued in front of Kavanaugh more than twenty times in criminal cases.

Kavanaugh tried to keep politics out of his classrooms as a visiting professor at Harvard, Yale, and Georgetown—some students didn't even realize he was Republican—and away from his judicial clerks. "Having known the judge for almost ten years and having worked with him very closely, I myself do not know what his views are on the political issues of the day," Rebecca Taibleson, who clerked for him in 2010 and 2011, said in her Senate testimony, "and as a law clerk, it would have been unthinkable to even mention the political implications of a case."

Kavanaugh approached each case with "an open mind," Taibleson added, "and a foundational commitment to the belief that either side might be right."

Kavanaugh also selected his four annual law clerks from across the political spectrum and made a point of hiring women, having been alarmed at reading a 2006 *New York Times* story about the "sudden drop" in female law clerks on the Supreme Court. During Kavanaugh's dozen years on the D.C. Circuit, more than half of his clerks—twenty-five out of forty-eight—were women, and he later testified that more of his clerks went on to Supreme Court clerkships than did those of any other federal judge.

"After hiring us, Judge Kavanaugh goes to bat for us," Taibleson said in her Senate testimony. "Studies have shown that women are often at a disadvantage on those fronts, but Judge Kavanaugh is a force of nature."

She added, "I know of no federal judge who has more effectively supported women in this profession."

Kavanaugh's female law clerks also said he was sensitive to the challenges of work-family balance. Sarah Pitlyk, who clerked for the judge in 2010–11, was initially nervous about working for Kavanaugh as the mother of a toddler, an unorthodox stage of life for a high-profile clerkship. "He said, 'You're a mom coming to clerk. I haven't done this before, you haven't done this before,'" she recalled, speaking on a Heritage Foundation panel in 2018. "Let's figure out what we need to do to make the clerkship just as rewarding for you as it would be otherwise, but also to make it possible for you to be a mother while you're doing it.'"

The judge himself demonstrated a commitment to family, making time to coach the girls' basketball team associated with his church, Blessed Sacrament, part of a network of Catholic Youth Organization teams in the area. After Sunday games, he would bring his daughters to the family's usual five-thirty mass at the church, sometimes still in their uniforms, reported *The Washington Post*.

Maureen E. Mahoney, a former deputy solicitor general and an appellate lawyer at the firm Latham & Watkins, said in her testimony that for more than a decade Kavanaugh "has been instrumental in opening these doors for a new generation of women lawyers. He's been a teacher, adviser, and advocate for women in ways that unquestionably demonstrate his commitment to equality and that will ultimately reduce persistent gender disparities in the legal profession."

Some Kavanaugh critics posit that the judge focused on hiring women to preempt the very charges of sexual misconduct that surfaced during his confirmation. Others suggest that, with diverse hiring at a premium, he was merely trying to be politically correct to enhance his standing as a candidate for the Supreme Court.

During the confirmation process, *The Guardian* and *The Huffington Post* published articles alleging that the married Yale law professors Amy Chua, the author behind the bestselling book *Battle Hymn of the Tiger Mother*, and Jed Rubenfeld, who in 2018 was himself accused of inappropriate conduct toward female students, had told students that Kavanaugh liked his clerks to have a "certain look" and exude a "model-like" femininity. (Chua dismissed these allegations as "outrageous.") And one former Yale Law student said in an interview that when she was preparing to meet with Kavanaugh about a clerkship, Chua advised, "'Make sure to dress outgoing,'" without specifying what that meant.

Taibleson in an interview dismissed these assertions as "laughable."

She, along with other female former clerks, instead described Kavanaugh as a mentor who was never inappropriate but championed their professional development long after they'd left his chambers and had continued to keep in touch with them. "Often as a woman in the workplace, you know when one of your bosses or your colleagues is creepy or inappropriate—a little bit too flirty or a little bit too touchy—and Judge Kavanaugh was the opposite of that," Taibleson said. "He was so above board with us, I would never have thought twice about getting a lunch or a dinner with him."

As he neared an opportunity on the Supreme Court, Kavanaugh began writing decisions that Democrats saw as dog whistles to the Republican base. "He used his circuit court decisions to telegraph to the interest groups, 'I'm your guy, I'm your guy, look at me,'" said Senator Sheldon Whitehouse, a member of the Judiciary Committee, in an interview.

In October 2017, Kavanaugh dissented from a decision in the case *Garza v. Hargan* that allowed an undocumented seventeen-year-old in federal custody to obtain an abortion. He wrote that the ruling was "ultimately based on a constitutional principle as novel as it is wrong: a new right for unlawful immigrant minors in U.S. Government detention to obtain immediate abortion on demand."

"He was strongly partisan in his opinions," said Adam Benforado, who clerked for Judge Judith Rogers on the U.S. Court of Appeals for the District of Columbia Circuit. "He was angling himself for the Supreme Court to appeal to future Republican presidents who would be picking people who were ideologically pure. That's how his opinions read. They are strongly activist."

Benforado, who now teaches law at Drexel University, was one of the more than 2,400 law professors who later signed a letter arguing against the judicial character of Kavanaugh. "Rather than simply applying the law, he was writing expansively," Benforado said in an interview, "essentially legislating from the bench."

Since Kavanaugh had yet to weigh in on the right wing's signature issue of abortion—offering some indication of how he would vote on *Roe v. Wade*—*Garza* was widely considered a bellwether for how he might treat a future case that could overturn *Roe.* "That was seen by everybody as his audition," said Akhil Reed Amar, the Yale Law professor. "He did not have an abortion case, and if you don't have an abortion case you won't be in the club."

"If you want to be a judge, you have to pick a lane," Amar added, "and he picked his lane."

SEVEN

Vides Stygiam Paludem

You Are Gazing at the Stygian Swamp

A s the first woman mayor of San Francisco, the first female senator elected to represent California, and the first woman to sit on the Senate Judiciary Committee, Senator Dianne Feinstein was accustomed to uncharted political terrain. Having served on the Select Committee on Intelligence and overseen a nearly six-year review of the Central Intelligence Agency's detention and interrogation program, she was also accustomed to keeping secrets.

But sitting opposite Brett Kavanaugh in her office to discuss his Supreme Court nomination was exquisitely awkward for the eighty-five-year-old lawmaker. It was August 20, and Feinstein for more than three weeks had been aware of allegations that could derail Kavanaugh's confirmation. She had fulfilled her promise to Ford to keep her claims against Kavanaugh confidential. Now, during one of the customary courtesy calls court nominees make to influential senators, Feinstein had to keep silent as Kavanaugh soberly described his jurisprudential philosophy, removing a miniature United States Constitution from his pocket for emphasis.

The senator and her staff had reviewed their options. Passing Ford's letter on to the FBI in a redacted, anonymous form—which was all Feinstein felt she could do, given Ford's plea for privacy—would not have allowed the agency to conduct much of an investigation. Nor could Ford's allegations be investigated discreetly by an outside lawyer, given that the permission of the Republican chairs of the Judiciary and Rules committees was required and leaks were likely to follow.

"It would have been irresponsible and unconscionable to open her up to attacks when she did not want to come forward and had no way to defend herself," Feinstein said in a statement for this book.

Jennifer Duck, the Democratic staff director for the Judiciary Committee, felt strongly that Feinstein had no choice but to respect Ford's wishes. Duck, a tall woman with long, curly hair and watery blue eyes, had served for five years as Feinstein's chief of staff, and early in her career worked as a project assistant for the Illinois Council for the Prevention of Violence. "The first rule as a victim advocate is," said Duck, "it's up to the victim."

However, it was around this very time that Ford's name would start to trickle out. In Palo Alto, where Ford resided, the small group of friends and colleagues in whom she had originally confided seemed to have expanded to a larger circle, though neither she nor her friends could figure out exactly how. Ford, despite her low-key and scholarly life, was one or two degrees of separation from some of the most influential players in tech and finance. Palo Alto itself was politically left-leaning, home to prominent Democratic donors like the Google cofounder Sergey Brin; Laurene Powell Jobs, the philanthropist widow of Apple founder Steve Jobs; and Reid Hoffman, the venture capitalist who had cofounded LinkedIn. In Santa Clara County, where Palo Alto sat, nearly three-quarters of the votes in the presidential election of 2016 had been cast for Hillary Clinton.

Late in August, after Ford began teaching her fall classes, reporters from a variety of publications began calling her to ask about Kavanaugh. Some were persistent. One day a reporter from *BuzzFeed* knocked on her door in Palo Alto, asking questions about the alleged assault. Ford said she wasn't interested in discussing it. But days later, the same reporter appeared in Ford's Stanford classroom, where the professor mistook her for a student until the reporter confronted Ford after class at her car.

Keith Koegler is one of a number of Palo Altans—including Representative Eshoo—who suspects the leak came from somewhere in their local community. Emotions around the subject of sexual assault were strong, thanks to outrage over the recent Brock Turner sentencing. So was opposition to Kavanaugh. It wasn't hard to imagine that someone who knew that Ford was Kavanaugh's accuser wanted to pressure her into going public with her claims as a way to threaten his confirmation. Or some well-meaning person with knowledge of the details could have repeated them to the wrong party, spreading chatter that eventually reached a reporter.

"There were just a handful, four or five people, that she was talking to," Koegler said of the initial round of discussions Ford had with friends. "And those people were turning around, talking to a larger set of people, trying to figure out what to do," he said.

Even as Ford was speaking hesitantly to *The Washington Post* about the tip she'd provided over the summer, her name had made its way to the offices of not just *BuzzFeed* but also *The New Yorker*. The online news organization *The Intercept* would soon pick up news about the existence of Ford's letter. Ford's information would soon ripple out beyond her grasp.

WHEN THE FIRST DAY of Kavanaugh's Supreme Court confirmation hearings arrived, on Tuesday, September 4, 2018, the Ford allegations had yet to surface. Instead, the Democratic members of the Senate Judiciary Committee were focused on Kavanaugh's documents—specifically the thousands of pages from the judge's years in the Bush White House that they said they had been deprived of seeing.

Just moments after the hearings got under way, chaos erupted, with multiple interjections from disgruntled Democrats on the dais. Protesters in the gallery were forcibly escorted from the room by uniformed guards as they shouted objections to Kavanaugh, whose wife and daughters looked visibly uncomfortable. Grassley tried to control his temper, citing the protesters' right to free speech.

Senior Democrats were having none of it. "The committee received just last night—less than fifteen hours ago—42,000 pages of documents that we have not had an opportunity to review or read or analyze," said California Democrat Kamala Harris, interrupting Grassley's opening remarks.

"You're out of order. I'll proceed," replied Grassley.

Harris persisted: "We cannot possibly move forward, Mr. Chairman, with this hearing—" she said, before being cut off.

"I extend a very warm welcome to Judge Kavanaugh," continued Grassley, undeterred, "to his wife Ashley, their two daughters—"

Amy Klobuchar, the moderate Democrat from Minnesota who was known for her folksy demeanor, stepped in. "Mr. Chairman, I agree with my colleague Senator Harris," she said, adding, "I believe this hearing should be postponed."

Richard Blumenthal, the Connecticut Democrat, said, "Mr. Chairman, if we cannot be recognized, I move to adjourn."

The Senate Democrats said the 415,000 pages of documents they had received, plus an additional 42,000 just before the hearings started, amounted to a mere 7 percent of the writings and emails Kavanaugh had composed, read, or participated in over the course of his career. They also argued that the Republicans had done an end run around the usual process, allowing Kavanaugh's friend and attorney Bill Burck to determine which documents were released, rather than the National Archives, as usual.

The Republicans maintained that the volume of Kavanaugh's entire paper record of more than one million pages was too large to be evaluated, given his experience in the Bush White House, the federal court, and the independent counsel's office over many years.

Behind the scenes, Grassley's team watched the document fight play out with satisfied amusement, thinking the Democrats would look foolish for getting so worked up about a bunch of paperwork. They'd piddle away their political capital on a fight over emails, Republicans thought, while Kavanaugh cruised to confirmation on his squeaky-clean image and distinguished record of jurisprudence.

But the Democrats were loath to drop the matter. They were still smarting from how Judge Merrick Garland had been treated in 2016 and embittered about the confirmation of Gorsuch, who was installed partly thanks to McConnell's changing of the rules.

"We should have a thorough understanding of the nominee that's put before us so that we can vet them," said Cory Booker, the Democrat from New Jersey. "To go into this hearing without those documents is an undermining of the constitutional role to which we have all sworn an oath to uphold."

Republicans, appearing legitimately concerned about the document dispute, in turn complained that Democrats were simply trying to drag out the hearings and sink a Trump appointee. "This fight is nothing more and nothing less than an attempt by our Democratic colleagues to relitigate the 2016 presidential election," Senator Ted Cruz said. "My Democratic colleagues are not happy with the choice the American people made. But as President Obama famously said, 'elections have consequences.'"

The hearing went on for six hours, with Kavanaugh's two young daughters being ushered out by Ashley at one point to avoid the room's heat and discomfort. Toward the end of the day's proceedings, three people spoke on Kavanaugh's behalf: Condoleezza Rice, who had been secretary of state during the George W. Bush administration; Senator Rob Portman, the Republican from Ohio; and Lisa Blatt, a lawyer who had argued thirty-five cases before the Supreme Court—more than any other woman—and a self-described liberal Democrat and feminist.

"Brett is wise," Rice said, adding, "Brett listens. Especially to those with whom he disagrees. And in our charged environment, when we have become almost tribal, living in echo chambers and often finding comfort in the company of only those with whom we agree, this is an indispensable quality for the responsibilities of the Supreme Court."

Finally, Kavanaugh began his remarks. He acknowledged his character witnesses and family, as well as his gracious treatment by the president and first lady. He spoke about the impact on his judicial career of his mother, Martha, sitting behind him in a ruffled green top, her hair in blond waves, alongside his father, in a dark suit and peacock blue tie.

"My mom taught me that judges don't deal in abstract principles," Kavanaugh said, "they decide for [sic] real cases, for real people, in the real world. And she taught me that good judges must always stand in the shoes of others."

"I have given it my all in every case," he said of his work as a circuit court judge. "I am proud of that body of work, and I stand behind it." He acknowledged the seventeen judges he had served alongside as both colleagues and friends, singling out Garland—who under different circumstances might have been his fellow justice on the high court—for his "superb" leadership as chief judge on the circuit court. He quoted Alexander Hamilton: "The rules of legal interpretation are rules of common sense." It was a notion his mother had also invoked as a prosecutor.

Perhaps attempting to parry the inevitable questions about his political inclinations, given fears that he would provide the fifth vote needed to reverse *Roe v. Wade*, Kavanaugh spoke of his objectivity. "Judges do not make decisions to reach a preferred result. Judges make decisions because the law and the Constitution, as we see them, compel the results," he said. "I am a pro-law judge."

A deft political operator, Kavanaugh included something for everyone in his speech. A mention of Justice Kennedy, allowing liberals to hold out hope that Kavanaugh would be a swing voter. A sports reference about the high court's "team of nine" that highlighted Kavanaugh's collegiality. A reference to "men for others," which by now was the grounding mission of Georgetown Prep and Kavanaugh's nod to a life of public service. A gospel reference that spoke to Kavanaugh's charitable endeavors and gave comfort to the religious right. Praise for Title IX, which equalized educational opportunities for girls and was important to feminists.

The only mention of sexual harassment came on day two of the hearings, when the Democratic senator Mazie Hirono of Hawaii asked Kavanaugh the same question she'd made standard issue for all nominees during her tenure: "Since you became a legal adult, have you ever made unwanted requests for sexual favors or committed any verbal or physical harassment or assault of a sexual nature?" He answered no.

Kavanaugh had expected his confirmation to be contentious. He had lived through similar questioning when he was being evaluated for the D.C. Circuit. What he did not expect was the story about his past that reared its head a week later. In light of the battle for his reputation, the arguments over access to his documents would come to seem tame.

AT 5:24 P.M. ON Wednesday, September 12, *The Intercept* reported that Democrats on the Senate Judiciary Committee had asked to view a Kavanaugh-related letter. The letter had been authored by someone affiliated with Stanford University, the report stated, and Feinstein had refused to turn it over. The piece was scant on details, laying out only the rough gist of the Ford story with no actors other than Kavanaugh identified.

Though different accounts of the letter were circulating, "one consistent theme was that it describes an incident involving Kavanaugh and a woman while they were in high school," wrote Ryan Grim, the reporter. "Kept hidden, the letter is beginning to take on a life of its own." The piece mentioned that the woman who was at the center of the letter was being represented by the whistleblower attorney Debra Katz.

Thin as it was, the piece had a seismic effect. In a hastily convened gathering of her Democratic colleagues on the Senate Judiciary Committee that evening, Feinstein finally acknowledged the letter. The group urged her to turn it over to the FBI, which she quickly did. Meanwhile, the news media was afire over the *Intercept* story. Reporters scoured their contacts for sources at Stanford, and social media was rife with speculation. Ford's outing was assured—the only question was how soon it would happen.

On September 13, Feinstein publicly acknowledged the existence of the letter. "I have received information from an individual concerning the nomination of Brett Kavanaugh to the Supreme Court," she said in a prepared statement. "That individual strongly requested confidentiality, declined to come forward or press the matter further, and I have honored that decision. I have, however, referred the matter to federal investigative authorities."

The New York Times published additional details: "Two officials familiar with the matter say the incident involved possible sexual misconduct between Judge Kavanaugh and a woman when they were both in high school."

The White House quickly countered. "Throughout his confirmation process, Judge Kavanaugh has had sixty-five meetings with senators—including with Senator Feinstein," said spokeswoman Kerri Kupec, "sat through over thirty hours of testimony, addressed over two thousand questions in a public setting and additional questions in a confidential session. Not until the eve of his confirmation has Senator Feinstein or anyone raised the specter of new 'information' about him.

"Senator Schumer promised to 'oppose Judge Kavanaugh's nomination with everything I have,'" Kupec added, "and it appears he is delivering with this eleventh-hour attempt to delay his confirmation."

The Senate Judiciary Committee pushed forward, deciding—on the same day that Feinstein's statement was released—to vote on the nomination seven days later, September 20. The Supreme Court's new term was set to begin October 1, and committee Republicans hoped to seat Kavanaugh by then.

The Ford letter was referred to the FBI (with Ford's name redacted), which passed it on to the White House (as an addendum to Kavanaugh's already completed background check), which sent the information to the Senate Judiciary Committee.

"Upon receipt of the information on the night of September 12, we included it as part of Judge Kavanaugh's background file, as per the standard process," an FBI spokesperson said at the time. Giving the letter to the FBI had been Feinstein's first thought upon receiving it, before determining that doing so would violate Ford's confidentiality. Even so, some of Feinstein's colleagues disagreed with her methods. "Looking back on it, I think that letter should have gone to the FBI immediately," said Illinois Democrat Dick Durbin in an interview later.

The reportorial theorizing kindled by the *Intercept* story also coursed through the private sphere. On September 13, Mark Krasberg, one of Kavanaugh's Yale College classmates, saw a story on the website *ThinkProgress* headlined "Brett Kavanaugh Has a Mysterious #MeToo Problem." Citing the *Intercept*'s report on the letter to Feinstein, the story said, "Supreme Court nominee Brett Kavanaugh may have committed a very serious crime—possibly even a sex crime. Or maybe he didn't."

After seeing that article, Krasberg, now a research assistant professor of neurosurgery at the University of New Mexico, emailed his fellow alumnus Kenneth Appold, saying, "What do you think of this?" In response, Appold told him about hearing from a friend during their freshman year that Kavanaugh had exposed himself to Deborah Ramirez at a Yale dorm party.

Meanwhile, at least four Democratic senators had heard about the

Ramirez allegation through various channels and were trying to find out more, including Senator Mazie Hirono. The Ramirez story wasn't the only one in the wind. So was another potentially important example of Kavanaugh's behavior in college that had never surfaced publicly.

The offices of at least two senators on the Judiciary Committee learned that one of Kavanaugh's classmates, Max Stier, had seen a drunk Kavanaugh with his pants down at another freshman-year party where his friends brought Ramirez's drunk friend Tracy Harmon over and put Kavanaugh's penis in her hand. The story made its way to the FBI but was never investigated. At least one other Yale student remembered hearing that Harmon had transferred out of Stiles residential college at Yale because of Kavanaugh, though exactly why was unclear.

Stier is a respected thought leader on federal government management issues in Washington, as the founding president and chief executive of the Partnership for Public Service. He was featured in Michael Lewis's book *The Fifth Risk*. Stier relayed his recollections to senators during the confirmation process and later made clear his willingness to share them with the FBI, but he refused to speak about them publicly. Harmon, whose surname is now Harmon Joyce, has also refused to discuss the incident, though several of her friends said she does not recall it.

On September 14, the Ford allegations surfaced—without Ford's name—in an online *New Yorker* story, written by Ronan Farrow and Jane Mayer, two investigative reporters who had directly relevant experience. Mayer had coauthored a book on the Clarence Thomas hearings. Farrow had recently garnered accolades for being among the first reporters to break the Harvey Weinstein sexual harassment allegations in print. "The complaint came from a woman who accused

Kavanaugh of sexual misconduct when they were both in high school, more than thirty years ago," the article said, adding that Senate Democrats had referred the complaint to the FBI for investigation.

That same day, Team Kavanaugh quickly mobilized to debunk the early, incomplete stories. Judiciary Committee staffers directed reporters to the judge's six previous FBI background investigations since 1993 as proof that Kavanaugh was clean. As details of the allegations unfolded, the committee's Majority Nominations Unit paired with the committee's Oversight and Investigations Unit for an inquiry that continued over the following month and ultimately involved about forty attorneys, law clerks, and others. Mike Davis, the Senate nominations chief, didn't know exactly what he was facing with the alleged Stanford accuser. But he wanted to be as prepared as possible. He was determined to not let some anonymous, potentially specious accusations sink his candidate without a fight.

Kavanaugh's personal supporters tried to beat back the substance of the claims that he had mistreated a woman in high school. Working quickly through a network of Kavanaugh's female friends, Meghan McCaleb, a graduate of the Catholic girls' school Georgetown Visitation who had married Scott McCaleb, a Kavanaugh schoolmate from Georgetown Prep, overnight got sixty-five women to sign a letter defending the nominee's character.

"Through the more than 35 years we have known him, Brett has stood out for his friendship, character, and integrity," the women stated. "In particular, he has always treated women with decency and respect. That was true when he was in high school, and it has remained true to this day."

Among the signatories were Renate Dolphin, the Stone Ridge alumna who had been taunted by Kavanaugh and his friends in high school but hadn't known it; Maura Kane (formerly Molloy), who had married Kavanaugh's close friend Tom Kane, from Georgetown Prep, and was Meghan McCaleb's sister; and Suzanne Matan, who was mentioned in Kavanaugh's 1982 calendar and would sit stoically behind him in the first row of the public area during his contentious final confirmation hearing.

The letter was sent to Grassley on September 14 and then out to the press. Kavanaugh also issued his own statement, distributed by the White House. "I categorically and unequivocally deny this allegation," he said. "I did not do this back in high school or at any time." It was a bold move, considering that he had not yet heard any of Ford's claims.

"It puzzled me that he was setting himself up for an easy refutation by people who have different memories," said Appold. "He could have simply said he had no recollection of harming those women, but if he did anything that offended them he was sorry."

In fact, it was unclear from Ford's own account whether Kavanaugh was cognizant of his own actions—or their damaging impact on her—at the time. She told Feinstein and others that Kavanaugh was very drunk when the incident occurred, which suggested his memory might have been impaired. She also said that during the assault, both Kavanaugh and Judge had been laughing, with Judge jumping on the bed, the second time toppling both her and Kavanaugh to the floor. Perhaps Kavanaugh had no recollection of the event because he was too drunk to remember it. Or perhaps he had blanked on it because it had registered with him at the time as harmless—and therefore forgettable—horsing around.

"When he came out before even knowing who the accuser was and before even knowing the substance of the allegations and left himself no wiggle room at all—and when he found out more he doubled down," said one former classmate, "I said to my wife, the only way I would ever have made such a statement is if I was 100 percent sure."

After reading Kavanaugh's denial, Krasberg was moved to alert the media, given that he knew about the Ramirez story from his friend Appold. "I remember saying to myself, 'Hey, not so fast there, bud, that's not what I know about you,'" Krasberg said, referring to Kavanaugh. "Then I phoned Jane Mayer."

Krasberg also spoke to his former roommate Richard Oh, now an emergency room doctor in California, who had yet another memory that dovetailed with Appold's. Oh recalled overhearing a female classmate emotionally recounting a recent party at which a fake penis turned out to be real. Krasberg urged Oh to relay his memory to Mayer at *The New Yorker*, which he did.

What was ultimately compelling to Krasberg was that his two classmates each had their own memories of hearing the story, and Ramirez's full account of the incident, when it emerged, appeared to confirm them both.

EIGHT

Iudicans Iudicem

Judging the Judge

On September 16, the world learned the identity of Kavanaugh's high school accuser in *The Washington Post*.

Ford had come to realize that her name was going to emerge one way or another, and that it was better to recount the experience in her own words. Senator Kamala Harris, the assurgent California lawmaker who was soon to announce a presidential bid, had learned of the existence of Ford's letter—if not its author—and was pressuring Feinstein to brief Senate Judiciary Committee Democrats on it. So Ford turned back to Emma Brown, the *Post* reporter who had first responded to her anonymous early July tip.

"Emma was not pushy and was respectful," said Koegler, who lived through Ford's deliberations. "So that was who got the story."

Early in the week of September 10, Brown traveled to California to interview Ford. But Ford, who asked Brown to hold off on publication until she was sure she was ready to be unmasked, remained deeply uneasy about the prospect of thrusting herself and her family into an often unforgiving spotlight.

"Literally right up to the publication deadline, she was not sure," Koegler said.

Then came the *Intercept* story on Wednesday—which contained the broad strokes of the Ford recollections without her name—and the briefing of committee Democrats that Harris had argued for. Knowing that her story was now a news event that was unlikely to recede anytime soon, Ford gave the green light to Brown. Her story was published online on a Sunday afternoon and on the front page of the *Post's* paper edition the following morning.

The impact was immediate. Reporters swarmed around the Ford house in Palo Alto, prompting neighbors to warn Christine off staying at home. Russell, driving one of their sons back from a soccer tournament in Lake Tahoe, was overwhelmed with incoming calls and messages. The couple's friend Elizabeth Hewitt had taken the Fords' other son to a local swim club along with her own children while her husband, Keith Koegler, monitored the television coverage at home. While he was doing that, Christine researched hotel options and responded to her own flood of messages. Many were supportive. Some on social media or sent to her professional email address, however, were quite menacing.

Around the nation, people far removed from Palo Alto and Washington were reeling at the news. The backdrop of an intense national #MeToo movement, the public sensitivity to a president who had boasted of grabbing women "by the pussy," the possibility of a Supreme Court candidate who might prove the decisive vote in overturning *Roe v. Wade*, and Ford's demonstrable proximity to Kavanaugh's high school circle all combined to throw Kavanaugh's candidacy into serious jeopardy.

Ford immediately drew comparisons to Anita Hill in 1991; her story involved mistreatment by a male Supreme Court nominee that was sexual in nature. Like Hill, Ford had never intended to share her experience. But, once drawn into the public fight, Ford—like Hill—would prove unwavering in her account.

Suddenly, a confirmation process whose biggest flashpoint so far had been a tiff over concealed documents was mired in full-blown scandal. The Judicial Crisis Network, a conservative dark-money group, would end up spending about $22 million in campaign-like videos to support Kavanaugh ("For conservatives, he's a grand slam"). The National Rifle Association also spent large sums ("Your right to self-defense depends on this vote"). Demand Justice, a liberal group, focused on pressuring Republican senators to oppose Kavanaugh.

Republicans tried to take control of events, arguing that the release of the Ford letter was a last-ditch effort by Democrats to scuttle Kavanaugh's nomination. Particularly galling to them was the fact that Feinstein had met with Kavanaugh about his nomination and yet said nothing, which became a popular talking point among conservatives.

"When Senator Feinstein sat with Judge Kavanaugh for a long period of time—a long, long meeting—she had this letter. Why didn't she bring it up?" Trump said at a September 18 news conference. "Why didn't the Democrats bring it up then? Because they obstruct and because they resist. That's the name of their campaign against me."

Even some Democrats were frustrated with Feinstein, whom they felt had mishandled the situation by not sharing the letter with investigators or her colleagues. California state senator Kevin de León, who was vying for Feinstein's seat the following month, accused her of wanting to "assist" and not "resist" the president and his policy agenda. But Feinstein had not felt she had any option. Months later, in email responses to questions for this book, she still sounded vexed by the position she had found herself in and the mountain of criticism that resulted.

"I stand by my decision to not forward her letter to the FBI until after the media had made the story public," Senator Feinstein wrote. "Dr. Ford repeatedly requested confidentiality and I honored those requests."

Some Republicans seemed more open to Ford's story. Arizona senator Jeff Flake, who heard about the *Post*'s piece while traveling in Utah, immediately called for a hearing so that Ford could testify.

"I felt strongly that she needed to be heard," Flake said in an interview later. "And after fits and starts, a lot of my colleagues agreed." Some senators wanted to have the hearing the following day. That, however, proved unrealistic.

The immediate question was whether Ford would come forward in person and testify publicly about her recollections. On September 17, Ford's lawyer Debra Katz told CNN that her client was willing to do so. Kavanaugh himself was arguing for an immediate hearing. Committee Republicans scheduled one for Monday, September 24. Staffers also arranged for a sworn telephone interview with Kavanaugh on September 17. On that call, he unequivocally denied all allegations made by Ford.

The Holton-Arms community began weighing in on behalf of their former student. Susanna Jones, its head of school, lauded Ford's coming forward: "As a school that empowers women to use their voices, we are proud of this alumna for using hers." Still, Jones was in an awkward position, given that the Holton community ran the political gamut. Justice Gorsuch's daughter was one of her students. And Kimberly Jackson, a 2008 graduate, had been selected provisionally by Kavanaugh to clerk on the Supreme Court if he was confirmed.

Twenty-three members of Ford's 1984 class sent a letter to the committee attesting to their classmate's "honesty, integrity, and intelligence." More than six hundred Holton alumnae signed a letter saying that Ford's "experience is all too consistent with stories we heard and lived while attending Holton. Many of us are survivors ourselves."

For Ford, however, the warm words of confidence were being drowned out by violent threats to her safety and well-being. On Tuesday, September 18, Katz and her law partner Lisa Banks wrote to Grassley that, since their client's name had gone public, "her worst fears have materialized."

Ford had been targeted for "vicious harassment" and even death threats, they noted, and her family had been forced to relocate. Katz and Banks also said Ford had been impersonated online and that her email had been hacked. The attorneys took issue with the committee's hastily scheduled public hearing and the idea that she should "testify at the same table as Judge Kavanaugh . . . to relive this traumatic and harrowing incident. The hearing was scheduled for six short days from today and would include interrogation by Senators who appear to have made up their minds that she is 'mistaken' and 'mixed up.' . . . No sexual assault survivor should be subjected to such an ordeal." An FBI investigation was the logical first step before scheduling such a hearing, the lawyers argued.

That same day, Mark Judge and Patrick Smyth, two of the three other boys Ford recalled being present at the party where she was assaulted, said they had no memory of the gathering and had never seen Kavanaugh engage in any such misconduct.

"I do not recall the party described in Dr. Ford's letter," Judge said in a September 18 letter to Senate leaders, issued by his lawyer, Barbara "Biz" Van Gelder, of the firm Cozen O'Connor.

Smyth said the same day through his own lawyer, Eric Bruce, of the firm Kobre & Kim, "I have no knowledge of the party in question;

nor do I have any knowledge of the allegedly improper conduct she has leveled against Brett Kavanaugh."

The firestorm Ford now faced was harsher and meaner than she'd anticipated. In addition to the email hacking and security threats, she was deluged with hate mail and attacked viciously on social-media channels like Facebook and Twitter. Her home address was publicized, paving the way for unwanted visits, vandalism, or worse. Her family and friends on both coasts were besieged by journalists. She realized that she'd not only have to live elsewhere for a while but also take time off from teaching.

Genuinely frightened, Ford met with local FBI agents to report the many security issues. She also arranged for a costly protective detail that began on September 19, just seventy-two hours after the *Washington Post* story had been published. Ron Conway, a local angel investor who had helped launch Airbnb and had heard of Ford's troubles through a mutual friend, helped her identify a security team to hire. Along with some travel security costs and local housing expenses, that team was ultimately paid for by a GoFundMe account arranged by Ford's friends and colleagues. But at the time, it wasn't at all clear whether the Ford family would have enough money to cover their expenses.

The GoFundMe campaign eventually blew far past its goal of $150,000, raising a total of more than $647,000 in a little over two months. (In late November, Ford would shut down the site with a note of thanks, saying any unused funds would be directed to "organizations that support trauma survivors.")

The Palo Alto community also showed its support in other, more public ways. Local activists chartered a plane to fly above the city with a sign that read THANK YOU, CHRISTINE. WE HAVE YOUR BACK. A Sunday-night vigil at the corner of Embarcadero Road and El Camino

Real attracted more than a thousand well-wishers, some of them young women. Holding candles and signs that read GO CHRISTINE! and BELIEVE WOMEN, they cheered at passing drivers who supportively honked their horns and spoke out about the dangers of staying silent about sexual assault. "My daughter has to know that if something were to happen to her, she's just a couple of years younger than Christine was then," one of the participants, Mora Oommenn, told the San Jose *Mercury-News*, "so she needs to know that we're behind her, that there are adults who will listen to her and her experience will be taken seriously."

Meanwhile, Team Kavanaugh was bracing for battle. On Wednesday, September 19, Mike Davis, Grassley's lieutenant, trumpeted on Twitter: "Unfazed and Determined. We will confirm Judge Kavanaugh."

That tweet did not go over well among Kavanaugh's critics. After Twitter commentators accused him of bias, Davis backtracked the next morning, posting a tweet that said, "To clear up any confusion, I was referring to Democrats' partisan political attacks and their refusal to take part in the committee's thorough and fair investigation. I deleted the tweet to avoid any further misinterpretation by left wing media as so often happens on Twitter."

In reality, Davis's tweets were an intentional ploy meant to serve as a bat signal to the right—rallying it to wake up to what was at stake—and they worked. Watching him come under fire for defending a bread-and-butter GOP judicial nominee only endeared Davis— and, by extension, Kavanaugh—further to their party. "I heard you caused a ruckus," Grassley, whose distaste for political mudslinging was continually evident to Davis, would later say. But the senator's trust in his aide continued unabated. Grassley always backed his staff, and, having started his career in the senator's mailroom, Davis knew it.

The political fight was already well under way behind the scenes.

Davis and his colleagues on the Senate Judiciary Committee staff repeatedly contacted Katz and Banks, looking to solidify plans for their intended Monday hearing. But Katz and Banks continually pushed back, saying their client needed more time to prepare for such an appearance, given her distant location and the threats she was fielding as a result of her allegations against Kavanaugh.

"They were saying, 'She'll testify Monday,'" recalled Banks. "And we were saying, 'Well, that's ridiculous.'"

Then Edward Whelan, a friend of Kavanaugh's and onetime clerk to Justice Antonin Scalia who was the president of the Ethics and Public Policy Center, a prominent conservative research organization, stepped forward. Whelan published a series of tweets suggesting that Ford's allegations amounted to a case of mistaken identity and that in fact it was Chris Garrett—known as "Squi" to Kavanaugh and his friends—who may have groped and silenced her in his Chevy Chase childhood home.

"Dr. Ford may well have been the victim of a severe sexual assault by someone 36 years ago," Mr. Whelan wrote. "Her allegations are so vague as to such basic matters as when and where that it is impossible for Judge Kavanaugh to *prove* his innocence."

Whelan pointed out that Garrett and Blasey had briefly dated before the alleged incident. Garrett's home then was within walking distance of the Columbia Country Club, which put it in the right vicinity as the location for the events she had alleged. Whelan's posts included photographs of Garrett, suggesting his appearance was similar to Kavanaugh's.

The Whelan tweets quickly made Davis's into a sideshow. Here, a powerful Washington lawyer had dragged a private citizen into the fray, seemingly without even a private warning. Political players were appalled; some cried conspiracy. Steve Schmidt, a longtime Republican strategist who had been critical of the Trump administration, called it "inconceivable" that the Whelan posts had been issued without the approval of White House and GOP officials. Reports soon surfaced that Whelan had met privately with Senator Orrin Hatch and that Hatch's spokesperson, Matt Whitlock, had retweeted another Whelan tweet promoting a mistaken-identity theory, telling people to "keep an eye on Ed's tweets the next few days." (After Whelan's thread came out, Whitlock deleted the tweet and denied having known what Whelan was planning.)

Ford was disturbed by the posts. She thought there was no chance the assault had occurred at Garrett's house. Garrett, after all, had been her steady for a time preceding the alleged incident with Kavanaugh; she knew him, and she knew his house in Chevy Chase. Even after breaking up, Ford and Garrett had been friendly enough that when he landed in Sibley Memorial Hospital with a medical problem—she couldn't remember what it was, though pictures from that time show Garrett with one arm in a sling and a band around his upper body—she had taken the bus there from school one afternoon to visit him. (Classmates from Georgetown Prep also faintly remembered Garrett's injury and hospital stay.)

On Thursday evening, *The Washington Post* reported that the "mistaken identity" argument was a central plank of the planned Kavanaugh defense against the Ford allegations. Whether the plan was to suggest it was someone else or to point the finger at a specific person—as Whelan did—is unclear.

Whelan, who had served as a counsel to the Senate Judiciary Committee and worked with Kavanaugh in the Bush White House, later apologized and deleted the posts, calling his behavior "an appalling and inexcusable mistake of judgment." He subsequently took a leave of absence from work, but returned a month later. Garrett, a social studies teacher at a private school in Atlanta, remained publicly silent. Even friends from Prep would have trouble connecting with him.

On Friday, September 21, Trump weighed in again. "I have no doubt that, if the attack on Dr. Ford was as bad as she says, charges would have been immediately filed with local Law Enforcement Authorities by either her or her loving parents," the president said on Twitter. He also said Kavanaugh was "a fine man" who was "under assault by radical left wing politicians."

This was crucial messaging for Kavanaugh, who knew how essential the president's backing was.

THAT FRIDAY MORNING, the Washington lawyer Michael Bromwich was in Chicago on a client matter when he heard from Ricki Seidman. Seidman, a bespectacled blond-haired strategist who worked at the public relations firm TSD Communications, had been involved with a slew of Supreme Court nomination battles, starting with Anita Hill's. She had also helped run the "War Room" during Bill Clinton's 1992 campaign for president, setting election strategies for the notoriously undisciplined Arkansas governor.

In addition, Seidman had worked as the director of scheduling and advance in the Clinton White House; as deputy associate attorney general in the late 1990s, working on issues of school safety, civil rights, and other domestic policy matters; and as Joe Biden's communications director during the 2008 presidential campaign, when he was Barack Obama's running mate. She had also advised companies like Google, Bechtel, and Facebook.

Seidman had been introduced to Ford by Katz and met Ford over coffee in August in California. Like Katz and Ford's other attorneys, Seidman was donating her time to help the professor, motivated by a sense of duty. With her call to Bromwich, she was asking another professional to do the same, this time because Ford needed a lawyer with more experience in handling congressional hearings.

Bromwich was also a D.C. insider and an ally of the Clinton and Obama administrations. A trim former prosecutor with a salt-and-pepper beard and a professorial mien, Bromwich had been the Justice Department's inspector general during the Clinton administration and participated in many congressional hearings. He had also worked under Rudolph Giuliani in the U.S. Attorney's Office in Manhattan, represented the government in the Iran-Contra matter, and supervised an effort to overhaul the nation's Minerals Management Service after the Deepwater Horizon oil spill of 2010. Bromwich had spent many years in private practice and was currently acting as a corporate monitor to Walmart and Apple.

He was up for advising Ford, too. "I live for interesting stuff," he said in an interview later.

Bromwich and Seidman arranged for an introductory phone call to be held later on September 21, which Bromwich dialed into from Chicago's Midway International Airport, where he was about to catch a flight back to Washington. Katz and Banks laid out the situation for him: Davis and his colleagues were insisting that Ford testify on Monday, which would give her little or no time to prepare. And Grassley was signaling that the offer was final.

"It was very intense," remembered Bromwich. "They were getting a lot of pressure."

The Ford team spoke to Davis again on Saturday, this time with Bromwich—who had been working out at a local Crunch Fitness when the call was arranged—dialing in from the gym's spinning room. Both sides, which had been dueling in the media, felt irritated with the growing impasse.

Ford, her lawyers told Davis, was willing to testify publicly. But there were certain conditions that would have to be met in order to ensure her comfort level, which was already low. Among them: scheduling the hearing later than Monday, which had become a nonstarter for their client, and making sure that, if a date and open hearing could be agreed upon, Ford would be permitted to sit before the committee alongside her counsel, rather than at a table by herself, as was more customary.

Davis kept signaling that he was ready to walk away, as if Ford and her lawyers were simply too unreasonable to negotiate with. "I think their intelligence was, she wasn't coming," Katz later speculated of the Davis team in an interview. Because of that, much of the dialogue with the committee staff, she said, was "clarifying, saying, 'She's coming.' We just wanted this to be fair."

Up until the middle of that weekend, however, the Republicans threatened that it was Monday or nothing. Also, mindful of the optics, Grassley's office wanted to hire an outside female prosecutor to interview Ford at the hearing instead of having the all-male panel of Republican senators do it themselves. And they wanted the prosecutor to have fifty uninterrupted minutes for questions, a condition that Feinstein's staff would not allow. Instead, the ranking member wanted each side to have the same amount of time and to take turns. They were also furious that Davis wouldn't give up the name of the prosecutor the Republicans planned to hire. The reality was, his team had been dialing madly around the country to find someone who was willing to do the job and only finalized their selection on Saturday.

Despite the rhetorical headbutting, Davis tried at times to reassure them that they would make Ford feel comfortable. "Senator Grassley is committed to providing a safe and respectful environment," Davis said repeatedly, invoking his boss's penchant for being the nice guy. (Indeed, Grassley found the mean-spirited partisanship infusing the process distasteful, and displayed a deference to Feinstein, his most senior counterpart on the committee, insisting that his staff refer to her as "the ranking member.")

But Davis himself, a man known for cutting asides and gallows humor even among his friends, came off as aggressive. "Is this your final offer?" he would say when the Ford team talked through its conditions. The whole thing had the feel, at times, of a rancorous financial negotiation.

Still, by Saturday afternoon, they had the contours of a deal for Ford to testify the following Thursday. So shortly after two p.m., the attorneys wrote Davis an email, telling him that Ford was coming: "Dr. Ford accepts the committee's request to provide her firsthand knowledge of Brett Kavanaugh's sexual misconduct next week."

KATHLEEN CHARLTON HAD ROOMED with Robin Pogrebin at Yale and graduated in 1987. By Monday, September 17, Charlton had learned that news outlets were pursuing the Ramirez story. The following Thursday, September 20, she called her friend and classmate David Todd, who told her that *The New Yorker*'s Ronan Farrow had contacted him.

"Todd also shared the surprising news that Brett had called him," Charlton said in a statement she ultimately submitted to the FBI. "He said that Brett was giving him a heads-up that press would likely make contact and wanted to make sure Dave would share 'no bad.' It seemed Dave understood this to mean he was not to speak ill of Brett's history."

Todd also told Charlton that he had responded to Farrow's questions about the assault details by saying, "I definitely don't remember that."

Pogrebin, who was covering the Kavanaugh confirmation for *The New York Times*, learned about the conversation from another classmate. The next day, September 21, she called Todd to ask him about it. Charlton immediately received an angry text from Todd: "Don't F****** TELL PEOPLE BRETT GOT IN TOUCH WITH ME!!! I TOLD YOU AT THE TIME THAT WAS IN CONFIDENCE!!!"

Charlton would later say publicly, "From the content and all-capital-letters of the text, Dave seemed to feel that there was a great deal at stake for Brett if Brett's fears of exposure ever became public."

ON SEPTEMBER 22, nearly a week after the Ford story surfaced, Leland Keyser, through her lawyer, gave a statement to the media and the Senate Judiciary Committee, saying she did not know Kavanaugh and had "no recollection of ever being at a party or gathering where he was present, with, or without, Dr. Ford." The following day, Keyser told a *Washington Post* reporter in a brief interview at her home that while she didn't recall the situation, she believed Ford's allegations.

To Keyser, a petite blond woman with a blunt but friendly bearing, the Ford account was an unwelcome development. Keyser's adult life had not been easy. After graduation, she had parlayed her athletic talent into a career in golf, playing professionally herself and then founding the women's golf program as a Division I sport at Georgetown University. In 2005, she had led her team to a second-place finish at the Big East Women's Golf Championship as its coach.

But since then, she had been derailed by a multitude of ailments, undergoing numerous back surgeries, a knee replacement, and other treatments, leaving her unable to work. A Mayo Clinic chronic-pain program helped, but she still had many bad days. She had lost a boyfriend after a diving accident—at the Columbia Country Club pool, of all places—in her early twenties and been divorced twice. Her Holton friends had often worried about her health and ability to cope.

Now reporters were camped out at Keyser's Silver Spring home, watching what felt like her every move. She couldn't sleep and was upset about her lack of privacy. To escape the attention, she checked into a hotel in Bethesda. But when even that didn't calm her nerves, Keyser flew to Michigan to stay with a friend. She was eventually captured on film by *Daily Mail* reporters in a baseball cap and shorts, looking stressed and disheveled.

KAVANAUGH SPENT HOURS holed up in the Eisenhower Executive Office Building, preparing for his testimony with White House counsel Don McGahn; the former Fox News executive Bill Shine; Raj Shah, a White House spokesman; and Sarah Sanders, Trump's chief spokeswoman. The president's counselor and frequent public defender Kellyanne Conway was also involved.

During these practice sessions, or "moots," Kavanaugh was questioned so intensely and continually on the Ford allegations that he grew angry. He marveled that, after twelve years on the federal bench, he was having to defend his sexual history rather than his deep legal record or even his thousands of pages of emails and other documents from his many public roles. A September 25 preparatory phone call with Grassley's staff was just one in a series of indignities.

"Okay. So we're on the same page," a staffer said on the call, "I'm going to define 'sexual or romantic behavior' as kissing, touching, or penetrating her genitals, anus, or breasts; touching or penetrating your—her touching or penetrating your genitals or anus; seeing her genitals, anus, or breasts; or her seeing your genitals or anus."

It was not the sort of job interview Kavanaugh ever imagined for himself.

To HELP HIS MENTOR deal with the onslaught, Travis Lenkner, a Chicago-based litigator who had clerked for Kavanaugh during his second year on the D.C. bench, flew to Washington to head up the judge's support team. Lenkner weighed in on media appearances and organized the various efforts by friends and associates to back the judge, including letters of support from former classmates and interviews with Kavanaugh surrogates.

On September 25, Lenkner himself, a polished speaker with sandy blond hair, a polka-dot tie, and a poker face, appeared on *PBS News-Hour* to discuss Kavanaugh. Addressing the notion that Kavanaugh had assaulted Ford, Lenkner said Kavanaugh, like anyone, had moments from his youth that he'd look back on and "cringe" over. But those things, he added, are "far from what has been alleged here."

"To say that someone drank beer in high school or in college," Lenkner said, "is a far cry from saying that a sexual assault ever came close to occurring."

In assisting Kavanaugh, Lenkner was aided by a handful of other former clerks, as was the practice with most Supreme Court nominees. Many came from Kavanaugh's initial years on the bench, a time when a judge is learning the job and relationships with his or her clerks are often at their most intense. Now Kavanaugh's inner circle of clerks included Zina Bash, who had gone on to work for Senators Ted Cruz and John Cornyn before becoming a Trump administration aide; Porter Wilkinson, who was now the chief of staff to the board of regents at the Smithsonian Institution; and Roman Martinez, a partner in the firm Latham & Watkins's appellate practice who had been an assistant in the Solicitor General's Office, representing the federal government in litigation.

These former clerks shared an abiding loyalty to their former boss that was not unusual. But Kavanaugh's particular attention to his past employees and quick recall of the details of their lives had cemented that rapport. While they worked for him, Kavanaugh engaged his clerks in rigorous debate before oral arguments, invited them to lunches to discuss their careers and families, and, with Ashley, hosted them at his Chevy Chase home for holiday dinners. Jennifer Mascott, who testified on Kavanaugh's behalf during the first round of Senate hearings, noted that he had remained involved in developing her career at every stage in the eleven years since she'd left his chambers.

Now she and her former colleagues had a chance to repay Kavanaugh's generosity. They went into high gear to defend their mentor. Davis, who was trying to maintain a distance from Kavanaugh himself, went to them when he wanted to share a message or relay an informal question. Davis made clear to the clerks that this was not a legal fight they were in. It was a political one.

NINE

Innocens

The Innocent

ometime between September 8 and 12, Ramirez's mother, Mary Ann LeBlanc, was watching television during a visit to her daughter in Boulder, Colorado, when a report on Kavanaugh's nomination came on the screen. Hearing his name, Ramirez peered over the railing from the upstairs level of her house and said out loud, "He drank a lot."

It wasn't until Monday, September 17, when Ramirez was sitting at her desk at work, that she discovered her personal relevance to Kavanaugh's confirmation. She picked up a message on her office voicemail from *New Yorker* reporter Ronan Farrow, a name she did not know, given her limited media consumption. She also received a message on her cell phone from Beth Reinhard, a reporter at *The Washington Post*. When Ramirez stepped out and returned Farrow's call, he told her he was looking into allegations of sexual misconduct against Kavanaugh at Yale.

"I actually said, 'I don't have any stories about Brett Kavanaugh and sexual misconduct,'" Ramirez recalled. Farrow told her he was trying to verify a story "about a night when someone exposed himself to you."

Ramirez said, "Oh, that—that I remember clearly. I can't talk about that right now; I'm at work."

Ramirez had grown resigned to that experience the way she had many other painful encounters at Yale. People made fun of how she spoke, namely the way she dropped consonants from words like "mitten" and the name "Martin." In Spanish class, classmates ribbed her for not being better with the language, since her last name is Ramirez. Some questioned whether she was re-wearing the same pair of jeans and called out her knockoff black-and-red Air Jordan sneakers.

"It was not about how I thought of me," Ramirez said. "It was how they looked at me."

Sometimes the insults were delivered as humorous asides that nevertheless proved hurtful, including comments like "My mom told me I could find one of you in my backyard." Or when she'd go over to someone's house: "Hide the knives." Or questioning her admission to Yale on the merits: "How did you get in here? Is it because you're Puerto Rican?"

"I never got it, but I knew it was about me being Puerto Rican," Ramirez said. "I just knew it had to be a joke about me. It was all supposed to be funny and people trying to separate me from my Puerto Rican-ness, like, 'I don't think of you as Puerto Rican.' What does that mean—because if you did, you would think less of me?"

Ramirez wasn't new to prejudice. She'd had to argue her way into the honors class at her high school. Her mother worried that, at Yale, her daughter would feel inferior. But Ramirez was determined to press forward. "I was used to being underestimated," she said. "I was used to people thinking, 'How did she do that?'"

"My mom would have preferred me to go to a smaller college—looking back at it, she was right," she said. At a place like Yale, "they invite you to the game, but they never show you the rules or where the equipment is."

To some extent, Ramirez was experiencing the harsh reality that all Yale students face: "You think you're badass in high school, then you go to Yale and you have to work your ass off just to be average," said Andy Thurstone, a classmate. He added of Ramirez, "I think she was a little overwhelmed with that."

Ramirez's father, who is Puerto Rican, rose through the Southern New England Telephone Company, having started as a cable splicer. Her mother, who is French, was a medical technician. One of three children—her sister, Denise, is eighteen months younger, and her brother, Mark, seven and a half years younger—Ramirez took pride in her parents' work ethic and enjoyed her childhood's simple pleasures: swimming in their aboveground pool, taking camping trips, riding behind her father on his snowmobile.

She was a diligent, obedient student, becoming valedictorian at her Catholic elementary school, St. Lawrence, and excelling at her Catholic high school, St. Joseph. "She dedicated everything to school—she did not get in trouble, I don't even think she dated," recalled LeBlanc. "She just was determined to succeed, and she was going to go out and get it. And she did." Ramirez worked summers serving ice cream at Carvel, driving there in the used car she'd bought with $500 of her babysitting earnings. Unable to afford full freight at Yale (nearly $13,000 at the time for tuition, room, and board; $72,100 in 2019), her parents had to take out loans. To chip in, Ramirez, who studied sociology and psychology, also obtained student loans and had work-study jobs on campus, including serving food in the dining halls and cleaning dorm rooms before class reunions.

She was a cheerleader her freshman year, sometimes positioned at the pinnacle of the pyramid, but learned quickly that although cheerleading was cool in high school, it didn't carry the same cachet in college.

For Ramirez, Yale was full of painful ironies like that. People would call her Debbie Cheerleader or Debbie Dining Hall or start to say "Debbie does . . ." as a play on the 1978 porn movie *Debbie Does Dallas*. But Ramirez, who had limited sexual experience and knowledge, didn't understand the reference.

"She was very innocent coming into college," Liz Swisher, who roomed with Ramirez for three years at Yale and is now a Seattle physician, later recalled. "I felt an obligation early in freshman year to protect her."

Over and over again, friends use the same words to describe Ramirez: guileless, sweet, shy, naive. They called her "the Debster."

"While many of her friends at Yale were boisterous and borderline obnoxious, Debster was always slightly in the background, seemingly our shadow of good conscience," said Ramirez's close friend Tracy Harmon Joyce in a written statement. "Debster has integrity and character, and is honest to a fault."

While Ramirez may have come into Yale with the determination to prove herself, her experiences there—most powerfully the Kavanaugh encounter—made her question whether she belonged. "I've never said anything good about Yale," she said.

Still, she made some close friends, including Harmon, Swisher, Lynne Brookes, and Karen Yarasavage, a member of the Yale basketball team. Yarasavage, who did not respond to interview requests for this book, made Ramirez a bridesmaid in her wedding and the god-mother of her youngest daughter.

At that Baltimore wedding, in 1997—when Ramirez was photographed in a group that included Kavanaugh—Kerry Berchem, a Yale schoolmate, noted that Ramirez stayed by her side, steering clear of her usual group. "I thought it was weird that she hung out with me so much," Berchem, now a lawyer in private practice in New York, said later. "These are your friends; you hung out with them all the time in college. Why are you not hanging out with them now?"

After college, however, Ramirez began to cut ties with Yale altogether. Having sold accident and disability insurance and then worked as a medical sales rep, Ramirez in 2002 started volunteering with the Safehouse Progressive Alliance for Nonviolence, or SPAN, a nonprofit organization that assists victims of domestic violence—including women who have been sexually assaulted. In 2004, she became a staff member there, working as a victim's advocate coordinator and eventually joining the organization's board, on which she continues to serve. While working there, Ramirez began to understand her identity as a person of color with light-skinned privilege.

It was this feeling of alienation that made Ramirez begin to distance herself from her past, leaving her Yale friends confused about why she had grown distant. "If I felt like a person in my life wasn't going to embrace my journey or would somehow question it," Ramirez said, "I just let them go."

ON THE EVENING of September 17, once she had returned from the office, Ramirez called Farrow back and began a conversation that continued over that week. Talking to Farrow was cathartic, enabling Ramirez to finally be able to reckon with her Yale experience.

In debating whether to cooperate with the *New Yorker* story, Ramirez ultimately realized she had two choices: come forward and join Ford or stay silent. "Which one can I live with?" Ramirez said she asked herself. "I knew I couldn't live with my own self-judgment and blame of knowing I did nothing at all."

But while her initial motivation was to stand with another survivor, she ultimately realized she was also standing up for herself. "It wasn't altruistic by the time it was done," she said. "I was doing it for me, too."

On September 18, Ramirez called to prepare her mother for what might be coming out in the media. LeBlanc recalled Ramirez telling her that "something happened at Yale" all those years ago. Since coming forward now was not initially Ramirez's idea, LeBlanc was later "upset that anybody thought she started this story."

Rumors of the Ramirez account, circulating in Washington, made their way to Colorado senator Michael F. Bennet. Bennet, in turn, suggested that the attorney Stan Garnett—who had served for nearly ten years as the district attorney for Boulder County—reach out to Ramirez, which he did.

Ramirez knew Garnett from her work at SPAN, one of the two major domestic violence safe houses in Boulder County with which Garnett worked closely as district attorney. On September 18, she hired Garnett to represent her. An imposing man—one part politician, one part cowboy—Garnett had been the Democratic nominee for Colorado attorney general in 2010. He had recently rejoined the law firm of Brownstein Hyatt Farber Schreck.

"I told Debbie, 'Your obligation is only one thing: to tell the truth,'" Garnett said. "Your obligation is not to figure out whether it impacts Brett Kavanaugh's ability to be on the Supreme Court. I will help make sure that you are protected as you go through the process."

Protecting Ramirez meant connecting her with a communications strategist and helping evaluate her security needs, given the death threats experienced by Ford. Garnett had a security consultant come to Ramirez's house, who warned Ramirez that members of the media might pay neighbors to let them peer into her windows and that drones might be launched around the perimeter of her property. Garnett also contacted the Boulder police chief and the Boulder sheriff, both of whom he knew well. He encouraged Ramirez to shut down her internet presence and to make sure her phone number was unpublished.

On September 21, Garnett invited John Clune onto Ramirez's legal team. Clune, who looks more like a laid-back ski instructor than a hard-driving criminal lawyer, started his career as a prosecutor—serving as chief deputy district attorney for Eagle County. He had come to specialize in representing survivors of sexual abuse and was known for his sensitive work with victims. In 2007, he started the Boulder law firm Victim Justice Initiative, developing a national practice representing targets of sexual assault and other violent crimes. In 2009 he cofounded the Rocky Mountain Victim Law Center, and in 2013 he joined Hutchinson, Black and Cook, a Boulder-based firm, where he now focuses on representing students and families on campus rape and Title IX matters.

Ramirez contacted Swisher, Harmon Joyce, and her sister, Denise, asking if she'd ever told them about her experience with Kavanaugh. She also reached out to James Roche, Kavanaugh's freshman-year roommate and a close friend of Ramirez. Roche, now the CEO of a San Francisco software company, had only a vague recollection of hearing about the Ramirez incident, but he also told *The New Yorker*, "I cannot imagine her making this up," adding that he remembered Kavanaugh as "frequently, incoherently drunk."

"Is it believable that she was alone with a wolfy group of guys who thought it was funny to sexually torment a girl like Debbie?" Roche added. "Yeah, definitely. Is it believable that Kavanaugh was one of them? Yes."

Ramirez's efforts to backstop her memories with friends would later be used against her; Republicans suggested that she was trying to construct a story rather than confirm one. But her lawyers quickly understood that this type of deliberative behavior was typical of Ramirez: while she was ultimately confident of her memories, she wanted to double-check them.

Ramirez decided it was important to let Farrow use her name, that her allegations would have less credibility and force if they were anonymous. "With all my work with survivors, I knew, 'I have to use my name,'" she said. "My story is not the same if I don't use my name." She would not, however, allow Farrow to use the names of her friends; she wanted to protect them, in particular Yarasavage and her three daughters.

"That was one of my biggest struggles," she said, adding of Yarasavage, "I loved her. I still love her. She asked me to be the godmother of her daughter, and now their father was in the room and this is going to impact them."

That loyalty wasn't reciprocated by Yarasavage—or a number of others. Ironically, in finally coming to terms with her feelings of alienation from her alma mater, Ramirez set herself even further apart, at least from a certain crowd. Dave Todd, Dave White, Karen Yarasavage—along with fellow classmates Dan Murphy, Dino Ewing, and Louisa Garry—gave *The New Yorker* a statement in response to Ramirez's allegations, describing themselves as "the people closest to Brett Kavanaugh during his first year at Yale."

"He was a roommate to some of us, and we spent a great deal of time with him, including in the dorm where this incident allegedly took place," the statement said. "Some of us were also friends with Debbie Ramirez during and after her time at Yale. We can say with confidence that if the incident Debbie alleges ever occurred, we would have seen or heard about it—and we did not.

"The behavior she describes would be completely out of character for Brett," they continued. "In addition, some of us knew Debbie long after Yale, and she never described this incident until Brett's Supreme Court nomination was pending. Editors from *The New Yorker* contacted some of us because we are the people who would know the truth, and we told them that we never saw or heard about this."

Right before the *New Yorker* article posted, Farrow called Ramirez to tell her about that statement. To her, it was like a sock to the stomach. "At that time, I looked at it as: they signed a statement against me," she said. "I felt so betrayed and hurt, it was like being in the room again. They signed a statement to lock it in the room."

Garry and Ewing later asked that their names be removed, saying they "did not wish to dispute Ramirez's claims." Garry, now a high school teacher and coach, had testified before the Senate Judiciary Committee on Kavanaugh's behalf on September 7, describing how she had met Kavanaugh on the first day of college, run marathons with him over the years, and brought her students to his courthouse for a field trip.

As the *New Yorker* piece was being finalized, Ramirez had trouble sleeping. She would nod off from exhaustion but then wake up with her mind racing. So when the magazine's photographer for the story, Benjamin Rasmussen, told her the dawn light at 6:30 a.m. would be best for a portrait, Ramirez had no problem agreeing to that early hour. Before taking the picture, in a park near her house, Ramirez thought carefully about what to wear. "I wanted to present all of me," she said.

She ended up choosing a shirt that read PUERTO RICO; an Indian shawl from her husband Vikram Shah's family, "so Vikram was wrapped around me"; and jeans, because they reflected her understated lifestyle. Shah held the light screen, and as Ramirez looked at him with tears in her eyes, she thought, "I'm sorry I put you through this."

John Clune was supposed to fly out to Montana for a child sexual abuse case on the morning of Sunday, September 23, but he got up extra early to stop at Ramirez's home on his way to the airport. The disjointed quality of Ramirez's story was consistent with those of many victims Clune had dealt with in his career: they have a sharp memory of certain details, a fuzzy recollection of others.

"If somebody is going to make something up, they don't make something up with all these holes in the story," Clune said. "Your memory is not bad if you're not restricted by the truth."

Clune recognized that the incident Ramirez described was not akin to rape; but it still registered with him as aggressive, humiliating, and wrong. "This was deliberate hazing that was done to try to make fun of her and get a laugh at her expense, and to do that in a sexual way that's creating a hostile environment," he said. "That's the kind of thing that sets the table for sexual violence."

"She was targeted," he added. "She's the quiet, shy person who was there, and it was funny for them to get her drunk and it was funny for Brett to do this. Somebody gets a laugh at the expense of someone who is probably the most vulnerable of the group."

The *New Yorker* story posted that evening. "After six days of carefully assessing her memories and consulting with her attorney, Ramirez said that she felt confident enough of her recollections to say that she remembers Kavanaugh had exposed himself at a drunken dormitory party, thrust his penis in her face, and caused her to touch it without her consent as she pushed him away," the story said. "Ramirez is now calling for the F.B.I. to investigate Kavanaugh's role in the incident."

The article included an anonymous quote from Yarasavage, stating, "This is a woman I was best friends with. We shared intimate details of our lives. And I was never told this story by her, or by anyone else. It never came up. I didn't see it; I never heard of it happening."

The story included a statement from Kavanaugh denying the allegations: "This alleged event from 35 years ago did not happen. The people who knew me then know that this did not happen, and have said so. This is a smear, plain and simple. I look forward to testifying on Thursday about the truth, and defending my good name—and the reputation for character and integrity I have spent a lifetime building—against these last-minute allegations."

The White House also provided *The New Yorker* with a statement. "This 35-year-old, uncorroborated claim is the latest in a coordinated smear campaign by the Democrats designed to tear down a good man," said White House spokeswoman Kerri Kupec. "This claim is denied by all who were said to be present and is wholly inconsistent with what many women and men who knew Judge Kavanaugh at the time in college say. The White House stands firmly behind Judge Kavanaugh."

ON SEPTEMBER 23, Ramirez placed a NO TRESPASSING sign on her garage, alongside another sign on her garbage can that said I HAVE NO COMMENT and that referred reporters to Garnett, with his phone numbers. *The Washington Times* then published an article with a photo of that sign and a headline suggesting that Ramirez was refusing to talk to the Senate Judiciary Committee.

Directing people to Garnett spared Ramirez some of the ugliness that was coming her way. But instead Garnett started getting death threats, so the sign on her garbage can was replaced with another one: PLEASE DEMAND AN FBI INVESTIGATION FOR DR. CHRISTINE FORD AND DEBBIE RAMIREZ'S CLAIMS.

"For a few days there, it was just incredible—I had people sending bizarre and foul and pornographic emails—there was a drone clearly over my house," Garnett said. "There were reporters over at my house.

"By the time the story broke, most of the craziness was directed at me and John," he added, "because we were the people who could be found publicly."

The Republicans had to seize control of events that were spiraling out of control. Though the Ramirez story was not as damning as Ford's—and potentially muddied Ford's clarion account—the allegations nevertheless fed a troubling narrative and threatened to derail, or at least delay, Kavanaugh's confirmation. At 7:43 p.m. on September 23, just hours after the *New Yorker* story posted online, Mike Davis decided to be proactive, emailing Garnett to ask when Ramirez would be available for an interview with Senate Judiciary Committee investigators. He added that Grassley's staff had only learned of these allegations from the *New Yorker* article.

"Democratic staff should have made Republican staff aware of these allegations to fully probe them rather than drop an eleventh-hour allegation at the tail-end of the confirmation process," Davis wrote. "But we are determined to take Ms. Ramirez's statement and investigate further as necessary as quickly as possible."

Garnett responded that he would get back to Davis, which Clune did the following afternoon, emailing that Ramirez "would welcome an investigation by the FBI into this information and would cooperate with such. On appropriate terms, she would also agree to be interviewed in person."

After seeing the *New Yorker* story, Bill Pittard, a lawyer at the D.C. firm KaiserDillon, which specializes in white-collar defense, did something he'd never done before: emailed a lawyer he hadn't met to offer his assistance. Pittard, who had previously served as the acting general counsel and deputy general counsel for the U.S. House of Representatives, specializes in helping officials of the legislative branch or clients preparing for congressional hearings.

"I emailed Stan on Monday morning to say, 'Looks like an interesting matter,'" Pittard recalled. "'If you need any help with the congressional piece—which seems likely to come now that this allegation is out there—feel free to let me know.'"

Pittard was brought on board the following day, September 25 (all of Ramirez's attorneys worked pro bono, with the hope that perhaps outside contributions might compensate them down the road). He then communicated to the Judiciary Committee that Ramirez hoped to see an FBI investigation into her allegations and would agree to testify. "I thought there was no way the world would move forward without hearing from Debbie," Pittard said.

The New York Times had also been tracking the Ramirez story over the past several days and ultimately made the difficult decision to hold off on publishing her allegations in the absence of corroboration. "Neither *The New Yorker* nor *The New York Times*, which attempted to verify Ms. Ramirez's story last week, were able to find witnesses acknowledging the episode," the *Times* wrote on September 25, adding that it had not obtained an interview with Ramirez.

The *Times*'s decision not to go with the Ramirez story—the paper instead followed up with a profile of her and Kavanaugh at Yale—quickly became ammunition for those who questioned Ramirez's veracity or sought to discredit her account.

On September 25, in a phone interview with Senate Judiciary Committee staffers about the Ramirez allegations, Kavanaugh—in addition to reiterating his denial of the events—cited the *Times*'s decision not to publish. "*The New York Times* says as recently as last week, she was calling around to other classmates saying she wasn't sure I had done this. And you know, I think—I think we're—this is an outrage for this kind of thin, uncorroborated, thirty-five-year-old accusation to be leveled in this fashion at this time.

"After all these years, with all this time, and all these descriptions with no corroboration and with her best friend saying she never heard about it, you know, I'm—I'm really just, you know, stunned," Kavanaugh added. "And outraged. It's the twilight zone."

Though the *Times* and *The Washington Post* both decided against publishing stories, various media outlets picked up on it nonetheless, giving the allegations weight as confirming a pattern in Kavanaugh's behavior.

That weight threatened to grow even heavier two days later when, on September 25, a Washington-area woman named Julie Swetnick came forward with her own alarming accusations. Swetnick, who had graduated from a Montgomery County public high school three years before Kavanaugh left Georgetown Prep, posted a statement on Twitter through her lawyer, Michael Avenatti. She said that she had observed Kavanaugh as a high school student at parties where women were plied with alcohol or drugs and "gang raped" by "trains" of boys—including Kavanaugh and Judge—who lined up outside of bedrooms. She said that she had been raped by multiple boys as well, at a party where Kavanaugh and Judge had both been present, and she believed she had been drugged with quaaludes or another substance.

These deeply troubling charges were ambiguous in critical respects. Swetnick stated plainly in an affidavit that she had been raped and likely drugged by boys at a 1982 party. But she didn't link Kavanaugh and Judge to the rape, other than to say they had attended the party where it occurred. She said Kavanaugh and Judge had "spiked" punch at the parties and "targeted" girls "so they could be taken advantage of" and even "gang raped." She said she had seen both boys "lined up outside rooms" awaiting their "turn" with a girl inside. But she lacked specifics on dates, locations, and the girls who were involved.

Kavanaugh denied the charges. He told committee investigators that Swetnick's claims amounted to "an outrageous accusation" whose details he found "ridiculous." Judge also denied the claims. Many Georgetown Prep alumni, even those who thought the Ford account rang true, were also dubious. They said they had rarely, if ever, socialized with girls from Swetnick's high school, Gaithersburg, making it improbable that she had attended "well over ten" house parties in the early 1980s alongside Kavanaugh and Judge. Moreover, the idea that those boys—or any of their classmates—would have gang-raped girls on a regular basis was out of step with the sort of sexual behaviors they remembered.

"We could all be obnoxious when we got drunk, and those guys are no exception," said Joe Conaghan, a classmate from Georgetown Prep, speaking of Kavanaugh and Judge. "Obnoxious, yes. Drunk, yes. But rapists? No way."

Grassley's vetting squad—the Davis team—did not get much information out of Avenatti, who refused to make Swetnick available for questioning.

At the same time, Davis considered the pile-on of allegations a gift—the more extreme, numerous, and unsubstantiated the accusation, the more absurd they were bound to seem to any thoughtful person. Had the Democrats focused only on Ford, his reasoning went, her account could have succeeded in derailing Kavanaugh.

Ford's credibility and the damning nature of her allegations were convincing even to some Republicans. Where Swetnick's scenario lacked probability, Ford's involved a likely group of friends in a conceivable location and time period. But the Democrats pounced on *all* of the charges being leveled against Kavanaugh, which now seemed to be barreling out of nowhere, blurring into what Republicans could easily assert was a political vendetta.

Avenatti was a huge help in that regard—"manna from heaven," as Davis would say to colleagues. A brash Los Angeles lawyer who had represented the adult-film star Stormy Daniels in her claims against Trump—with whom she claimed to have had an affair that Trump then paid her to keep quiet—Avenatti was an especially polarizing figure. A slender hobbyist race-car driver with closely cropped hair and a confrontational glare, he had become a fixture on television news during the Daniels suit, which had been filed in March 2018. His combative talk toward the president had incensed the right.

But even though many pro-Kavanaugh Republicans felt Ramirez's uncorroborated memory would likely help their claims of overreach, they were not eager to have Ramirez testify. There was serious concern that Ramirez's story could add credence to Ford's, and would further slow Kavanaugh's confirmation. So instead, Grassley's team engaged in a protracted back-and-forth with Ramirez's lawyers over next steps.

The committee required some evidence of Ramirez's allegations before speaking to her, including a sworn statement from her or a phone call with investigators. "You can't get a congressional investigation opened by making an allegation without any evidence," one GOP aide said in an interview. But Ramirez's lawyers said they needed to speak with the committee before making their client available.

On Tuesday, September 25, Heather Sawyer, Davis's Democratic counterpart on the Judiciary Committee, sent Davis an exasperated email. "The Committee does not usually refuse to talk with counsel (or whistleblowers), and also does not usually place preconditions on getting on the phone to discuss next steps, so I'm not sure why that is happening here," she said, adding, "I've never encountered an instance where the Committee has refused even to speak with an individual or counsel. I am perplexed as to why this is happening here, except that it seems designed to ensure that the Majority can falsely claim that Ms. Ramirez and her lawyers refused to cooperate."

Davis fired back: "I have not refused to speak with anyone. I am simply requesting—for the 7th time now over the last 48 hours—that Ms. Ramirez's attorneys provide the Senate Judiciary Committee with any evidence that they have before we move to the next steps."

Grassley rejected a September 23 request from Feinstein for a postponement of nomination proceedings to permit investigation of Kavanaugh's conduct with respect to Ramirez. Grassley said he was "unclear why Ms. Ramirez's claims should have any bearing on Dr. Ford's testimony."

Like Garnett, Clune was mainly focused on getting Ramirez's recollections into the hands of the decision makers. "The sense was, our job wasn't to convince anybody what happened," he said. "Our job was to get the information that Debbie had to whoever was going to be doing the background investigation on Kavanaugh."

Once her story was out, Ramirez hunkered down at home, grateful for the food, cards, and visits from friends. She particularly appreciated the support from her husband, Shah, a technology consultant. They had met in 2004 through a mutual friend, and Shah was immediately struck by Ramirez's combination of tenderness and tenacity. "She was gentle," he said, "but she was very strong and determined."

Reading the article was its own new reality. Ramirez had not thought of what happened to her as sexual misconduct until she saw it described that way in *The New Yorker.* "It took 35 years later to read it in print to see it in those words," she said.

The supportive letters, emails, and texts from perfect strangers that poured in after the article's publication were overwhelming and affirming. She read every one and sometimes turned to them during the confirmation hearings for sustenance. "I would save it for a moment when I needed to read it," she said. During an interview, Ramirez pulled out a thick binder containing some of the letters that she'd saved in plastic sheaths, as well as a decorative box filled with other letters, still in their envelopes.

She read from a few of them, messages like "We're with you, we believe you, you are changing the world," and "Your courage and strength has inspired me. The bravery has been contagious."

College students wrote about how Ramirez had helped them find the words to speak for the first time about their own experiences of sexual violence. Medical students wrote about how they were now going to listen differently to victims. Parents wrote about having conversations with their kids about how bad behavior can follow them through life. One father told Ramirez he was talking to his two sons about how their generation has the opportunity and obligation to be better. SPAN received donations in her honor.

Strangers also came up to Ramirez in public, thanking her—often through tears—sometimes asking if they could give her a hug.

At the same time, the very Yale community from which Ramirez had come to feel detached circled around her. More than three thousand Yale women signed an open letter commending Ramirez's "courage in coming forward" and urging delay of the vote on Kavanaugh until "all witnesses have testified under oath."

"We demand that her allegations be thoroughly investigated and that she be treated with fairness, and given an opportunity to tell her story," the letter said.

Rebecca Steinitz, a Yale College 1986 graduate, along with Kate Manning, from the class of 1979, and Christina Baker Kline, from the class of 1986, drafted the letter—which also supported Ford—on Sunday, September 23, upon learning of Ramirez's allegations in *The New Yorker.* The alumnae were careful not to say "we believe them," but instead to convey that the charges should be taken seriously.

"White men of privilege have gotten away with an enormous amount in the centuries of our country's history, and as a white woman with nearly as much privilege, I feel like it is my duty to speak up," Steinitz said in an interview. "It's my ethical obligation. I come from the seat of power and I have to speak to its abuses."

More than fifteen hundred Yale men issued a similar letter two days later, on September 25.

"The harrowing accounts we've recently heard—of harassment, misconduct and assault—are sadly consistent with the campus culture at the time," the letter said. "We can't change what happened then, but we can speak out today: no one should be subjected to the abhorrent treatment Deborah and Dr. Blasey have described. Nobody who would do such things should be confirmed as a Justice of the U.S. Supreme Court."

TEN

Lege Dura Vivunt Mulieres

Women Live Under a Harsh Law

K eith Koegler had never met some of the people who gathered at his Cape Cod–style house, not far from Facebook founder Mark Zuckerberg's, before sunrise on Tuesday, September 25. Given the early hour, nobody was much in the mood for long introductions. But they all had one thing in common—Ford—and had assembled for a trip to Washington, D.C., to support their friend when she testified before the Senate Judiciary Committee.

There was Kirsten Leimroth, whose children had attended the same kindergartens and junior lifeguard camps as Ford's and who had become a crucial confidante on the beaches of Santa Cruz that previous summer. There was Chris Conroy, a photographer friend whose wife, Tanya, was one of Ford's closest confidantes. There was Jay Backstrand, a private wealth manager and fellow sports dad, who had offered to do whatever he could to support Ford in the wake of her

Kavanaugh disclosures. And there were two colleagues from Stanford who had been supportive throughout Ford's attempts to speak up and share her memories.

As they assembled under an overcast sky, the friends tried to keep the conversation light, chatting about their jobs and their children's activities. Before long, a couple of cars pulled up to whisk them north to a private airport hangar in Oakland. Ford, who had left Russell at home to take care of their children, had been driven separately in a secure vehicle and met them there.

She had handpicked the group for their emotional stoicism and clear-eyed counsel—taking into account their availability amid child-care responsibilities and demanding careers. She called them her "support team."

Koegler, the baseball dad, was central to the network. In the months since Ford had first shared her recollection that Kavanaugh was the teenager who assaulted her back in the 1980s, Koegler had become not just a personal ballast, but her researcher in chief.

A tech industry lawyer, Koegler was a voracious reader and a technical thinker. In his second-floor home office, he'd spent many hours that summer poring over news coverage of the nomination process, biographical information about Kavanaugh, and writings and videos produced by Mark Judge. In combing through YouTube, articles, and social networks, Koegler had learned more about the house parties at Don Urgo's and the lexicon of 1980s Georgetown Prep than he had ever thought he would care to know.

On September 24, Koegler had also signed an affidavit attesting to Ford's 2016 description of her assault as well as her identification of Kavanaugh as her assailant, two years later.

"In all of my dealings with Christine I have known her to be a serious and honorable person," he stated, just above his ballpoint signature. Ford's husband, Russell, along with her close friends Adela Gildo-Mazzon and Rebecca White, also attested to having been informed—years or months ahead of Kavanaugh's nomination—of Ford's memories of being sexually assaulted by a now prominent judge.

Koegler and his wife, Elizabeth Hewitt, whom he had met at Vanderbilt Law School, in Nashville, Tennessee, had spent many hours with Christine and Russell that summer before any hearings, studying the options for disclosing Christine's recollections to the chief decision makers in Washington without risking Ford's privacy or personal safety. They often sat on a slouchy sofa on the Koegler family's back porch while their kids hung out inside or played video games in the garage. Ford was not generally prone to taking direction from others, but in this case she sought ideas and feedback, much as she would in analyzing a set of data in her Stanford research studies.

At some point in August, Koegler strongly expressed his concern about her coming forward.

"I just worry it's going to rip you apart," he said.

As Christine's friends gathered at Koegler's house on the morning of Tuesday, the 25th, they had no idea what to expect of the next few days. It was still unclear whether she would testify publicly, given that Ford herself was somewhat imprecise about the purpose of the trip. She told friends she was simply traveling to Washington to meet with her lawyers and members of the Judiciary Committee in person.

Those well acquainted with Ford's personality—always private, typically measured—thought it was possible that she hadn't processed having already made the commitment to testify in public. In discussions with her that morning and in recent days, they'd had the impression that the talks about her appearance were still fluid, despite the widespread expectation of a televised public hearing. Ford seemed committed to share her recollections somehow in D.C., but how, exactly, that would unfold remained unclear to her friends. No matter what, they knew it would be hard for Ford, who didn't relish revisiting a traumatic story in front of millions, let alone flying across the country in order to do it. Because of that, her friends focused on trying to keep Ford feeling calm and thinking positive.

"She didn't need someone who would be high emotional drama," recalled Leimroth, a tall accountant and mother of four. "I've been told I'm Germanic, for better or worse, so I'm not up-and-down," she added of her personality. "And I was able to go."

Ford and her supporters were flying on a private plane that had been secured through colleagues of hers as a way to simplify the travel and avoid public attention. The plane belonged to two Silicon Valley billionaires: Mark Pincus, who had founded the gaming company Zynga; and Reid Hoffman, cofounder of the professional-networking site LinkedIn. In the run-up to Ford's testimony, Ford's contacts had canvassed a small group of wealthy local residents to see if they would be willing to provide transportation. Pincus and Hoffman, who co-owned a plane and recognized the personal risks that Ford was taking, quickly agreed to cover the flight.

The two men were good friends and generous donors to Democratic causes. In addition to supporting scores of congressional candidates over the prior decade, Pincus and Hoffman had contributed to the presidential campaigns of Hillary Clinton and Barack Obama. During the Obama administration, they'd had repeated contact with Obama and his team, sometimes advising on social media strategy.

Hoffman said later that he and Pincus were motivated by the simple desire to help Ford: "We believed then, as we do now, that it is important to take seriously accusations of violence against women." They wanted Ford to have a chance to air her information.

But they also knew well how radioactive the situation had become, given that their own pilots had been anxious to interact with Ford and her friends for fear of being identified and harassed by Ford's detractors later. To assuage the pilot's concerns, the billionaires hired a flight attendant to work the trip.

BUCKLING HER SEAT BELT, Ford was palpably nervous, given her long-standing fear of planes and other confined spaces. "I'm not going in front of the Judiciary Committee," she repeatedly told her friends. "I'm just meeting with people individually."

Jay Backstrand, the private wealth manager, attempted some humor. "Can I have a Bloody Mary?" he asked the flight attendant. But there was no alcohol available on board, only breakfast.

The plane landed at Dulles International Airport around 2:30 in the afternoon, earlier than expected. That meant Ford, already leery of being spotted (concealing her face in a baseball cap and sunglasses), had to linger in the private-plane hangar until the group's ride arrived. Eventually she and her friends were picked up by a security team in black SUVs.

They were driven to the Watergate Hotel, where they compared notes about whose room had a view of the site of the infamous 1972 break-in. In a small conference room off the hotel's main lobby, guarded by a hulking pair of security guards who had been hired to protect her while traveling, Ford met with her lawyers. In addition to Katz and Banks, that legal team now included Bromwich, who had joined just days before to aid with the congressional testimony, and Larry Robbins, the Washington litigator who had been one of the first to connect with Ford.

The group tried to put Ford at ease with small talk. Since she seemed emotionally drained, they kept the meeting short.

Given the ongoing discussions with Mike Davis and others on the majority staff, the lawyers understood Ford's uncertainty about whether she would meet with senators individually in a closed setting or testify to the full committee in public. "There was always the question of open or closed hearing," Banks said later, adding of Ford that "the committee had given her the option, so that had been a conversation throughout, about what was the better way to do that for her."

For Banks and her colleagues, who had been immersed in advising Ford during the week before the Watergate meeting, the public glare had also been intense. They, too, had received death threats in the wake of the *Washington Post* story, some of them misogynistic, detailed, and disturbing. Some of those directed at Katz were also anti-Semitic, she said; some had sexually violent language. "It was scary," she said. Like Ford, the lawyers quickly retained bodyguards who monitored them day and night.

In Chevy Chase, Maryland, Kavanaugh spent the days before the hearings impatient to rebut the story. It had been two weeks since the first whiff of charges against him surfaced, threatening not only his nomination but his reputation, and he was eager to speak out. Issuing prepared statements felt inadequate; he'd put out two—one on September 14, "categorically" denying the allegations, and another on September 20, calling for "a hearing as soon as possible, so that I can clear my name." But he had not yet had an opportunity to publicly defend himself.

Instead, Kavanaugh had been forced to sit tight—deferring to the decisions of those shepherding his nomination, unable to do anything except watch as the allegations mushroomed and the news frenzy intensified. In just the past few days, the incendiary charges from

Ramirez and Swetnick had been added to the mix. The Ford hearing was delayed, providing more time for Kavanaugh's political opponents to dig into his past and feed embarrassing tidbits to the media about his youthful antics. Demonstrators wearing pins that read I BELIEVE CHRISTINE FORD were being hauled away from the Capitol in handcuffs for protesting his nomination.

Not long before, Kavanaugh had been on the verge of achieving his ultimate goal. Now he found himself fielding coarse questions about genital penetration and fending off accusations of gang rape. It was a surreal and agonizing moment.

Though Trump had recently stood in the East Room and introduced Kavanaugh in glowing terms, now reports swirled about whether the president's support might be wavering. It looked very possible that the White House could decide Kavanaugh wasn't worth the Herculean push and withdraw its nomination, particularly given the time pressure of confirming a new justice before the new Supreme Court term in October and the midterm elections in November. Trump was unpredictable, after all—as likely to redouble his support of the embattled nominee as to abandon him—so Kavanaugh's confirmation seemed suddenly, dramatically uncertain.

But Trump, it turned out, wasn't going to ditch his nominee without a fight. If the president's team had heretofore delegated the housework to Grassley's crew, now it kicked into high gear to prepare for a likely second round of hearings. Starting on September 18, Don Mc-Gahn, White House counsel, along with Shine, Sanders, and one of her senior press aides, summoned Kavanaugh to the White House for three straight days of interrogation about his sexual past.

That Thursday, September 20, a group of Democratic senators sent a letter to the White House arguing that its refusal to request an FBI investigation "abandons the precedent that President George

H. W. Bush set when he asked the FBI to investigate after Anita Hill raised allegations against Judge Clarence Thomas in 1991." And an NBC/*Wall Street Journal* poll conducted between September 16 and 19 found that 38 percent of registered voters, a majority of the group, now opposed Kavanaugh's nomination. (Thirty-four percent were in favor.)

Around this time, Kavanaugh's wife, Ashley, received death threats that had to be investigated by the U.S. Marshals Service: "May you, your husband and your kids burn in hell," said one. "My condolences to you for being married to a rapist. Although you probably deserve it," said another. It was a stunning dose of the same toxic rhetoric that had been heaped on Ford and her family, emblematic of the national outrage over her accusations, though from a very different direction. Kavanaugh moved his family out of the house temporarily, though he stayed behind.

Deeply frustrated by a sense of impotence, Kavanaugh did what he could behind the scenes. He worked with Beth Wilkinson—the lawyer whom Mike Davis had told he was "pumped" about Kavanaugh's nomination—and Alexandra Walsh, experienced Washington trial attorneys. He consulted with Lenkner and his other close former clerks on communications and tactics. He and his wife tried to explain to their girls—in as much detail as each daughter could handle at her age—the maelstrom suddenly enveloping them. Kavanaugh had been just four years older than Margaret when the incident with Ford was alleged to have occurred—an age at which any associated legal records would likely have been sealed away to avoid damaging his reputation as an adult. He would later testify that talking to their daughters about Ford's allegations may have been the worst experience of his and Ashley's lives.

Finally, on September 24, the day before Ford and her friends flew east, Kavanaugh got the chance to say his piece. He and Ashley sat down with the Fox News anchor Martha MacCallum for an expansive conversation about the Ford, Ramirez, and Swetnick allegations. Grassley's team thought the Kavanaughs should do the interview at home, so they would look relaxed in their own surroundings. But the couple was concerned about the disruption a network camera crew would cause—not only to their girls but also to their neighborhood, which was already dealing with a sizable media presence. So the interview was conducted in a suite at the Madison Hotel, in downtown Washington, just a ten-minute walk from the White House.

Sitting stiffly on banquet chairs, with a conventional vase of pink and white roses in the background that looked like it had come from 1-800-Flowers, Kavanaugh repeatedly denied Ford's account, saying he couldn't recall ever meeting her, let alone having sexual contact with her, consensual or otherwise.

"I've never sexually assaulted anyone," he said time and again. He looked steadily at the interviewer, his voice focused and calm. He often repeated himself, as if sticking closely to rehearsed talking points.

Asked whether she had confronted her husband on the claims, his wife appeared to be fighting back tears. "No," Ashley said, shaking her head, her smile rueful, her hands clasped in her lap. "I mean, I know Brett. I've known him for seventeen years. And this is not, at all, character—" she said, pausing to change course.

"It's really hard to believe," she continued. "He's decent, he's kind, he's good. I know his heart. This is not consistent with Brett."

MacCallum asked about the Ramirez allegations, which had only just been published in *The New Yorker.*

"I never did any such thing," said Kavanaugh evenly. "If such a thing had happened, it would have been the talk of campus." He cited reports, published in *The New York Times* and elsewhere, that Ramirez had been calling around to see if classmates shared her memories—evidence, he suggested, of their flimsiness. "I'm just asking for a fair process," he said, over and over, using the phrase no fewer than eleven times.

Faced with one sordid accusation after another—did he flash his penis at Ramirez and laugh about it? Had he ever participated in a gang rape?—Kavanaugh remained composed throughout, his only tell being knitted brows and a modestly raised voice when asked about Swetnick's claims that he and Mark Judge had spiked punch bowls at high school parties to facilitate "trains" of boys queueing up to have their way with girls. "That's totally false and outrageous," he said. "Never done any such thing."

The interview was astounding by any measure. Not only had Kavanaugh been faced with allegations of misconduct toward women, which dwarfed those of Clarence Thomas so many years before, but he was volunteering details of his own sexual experience that were unheard of for someone in his position.

"I did not have sexual intercourse, or anything close to sexual intercourse, in high school, or for many years thereafter," he said at one point, in an effort to debunk depictions of him as a sexual predator.

MacCallum had to make sure she'd heard right: a federal judge en route to the U.S. Supreme Court had just admitted on national television that he remained a virgin through college.

Ms. MacCallum: So you're saying that through all these years
 that are in question, you were a virgin?
Judge Kavanaugh: That's correct.

Ms. MacCallum: Never had sexual intercourse with anyone in
high school?

Judge Kavanaugh: Correct.

Ms. MacCallum: And through what years in college, since
we're probing into your personal life here?

Judge Kavanaugh: Many years after. I'll leave it at that.

MacCallum also seemed to try to startle the judge, to get him off
his preconceived script, by asking him to speculate on why these assertions were being made. But Kavanaugh did not break his composure, saying only in measured tones, "I'm not going to let false
accusations drive me out of this process."

Toward the end of the interview, when MacCallum questioned
whether Kavanaugh thought he still had the president behind him,
the judge said Trump had called that afternoon to pledge his continued support, adding, "I know he's going to stand by me."

But after watching Kavanaugh on Fox, the president wasn't so sure.
According to the Trump playbook—hit back harder—Kavanaugh had
failed miserably with his tepid, awkward performance. The president
began entertaining a scenario in which the White House moved on to
plan B: pick another nominee with less baggage. "We had numerous
conversations about it through the course of time," McConnell later
told *The New York Times*, adding of Trump, "But he hung in there."
(During the toughest points of the confirmation fight, McConnell
would also assure Trump, "I'm stronger than mule piss.")

The Fox performance was vintage Kavanaugh, whom colleagues
and former clerks had described as focused and even-tempered over
the years, even in stressful situations. But Republican Senate staffers,
who thought the TV setting of drawn blinds and dim lighting looked
like a hostage situation, were also incredulous at Kavanaugh's cool

demeanor, arguing that this crucial juncture called for considerably more righteous indignation. "'I want a fair process'?" said one aide, mimicking Kavanaugh. "Why don't you say you're not a gang rapist? That would be more helpful."

Kavanaugh's closest advisers shared the feedback with him more gently. He should have been on offense, not defense. If given the opportunity, he would have to do better next time.

IN THE PRACTICE SESSIONS on the fourth floor of the Eisenhower Executive Office Building—known as "murder boards" or "moots"—Kavanaugh had been gearing up to be interrogated about the Ford and Ramirez allegations. Now he also had to ready himself for questions about his high school yearbook.

On September 24, shortly after the Fox interview, *The New York Times* reported that Kavanaugh and his close high school friends, including Mark Judge, had bragged at Georgetown Prep about their sexual interactions with Renate Schroeder—a student at the nearby girls' school Stone Ridge who was a year younger—and memorialized their assertions with a club dubbed "Renate Alumnius" in their yearbook.

The boasts about fooling around or having sex with Schroeder, which were made around the fields and hallways of Prep—and in a ditty about her that was published in an inexplicit form on Kavanaugh's friend Michael Walsh's yearbook page—were frequent and offensive during the early 1980s. All in all, Kavanaugh and thirteen other boys had Renate references on their personal yearbook pages. A group photo of the future judge and some of his closest friends in their football gear was captioned "Renate Alumni," which, in that context, suggested they had all been physically involved with her.

Through his attorney Alex Walsh, Kavanaugh denied having boasted about such sexual conquests. But Renate herself, now a Connecticut wife and mother with the married name Dolphin, called out the "insinuation" as "horrible, hurtful, and simply untrue." Although she had been friends with Kavanaugh and other members of his circle at the time, she had not known of the sexual references implied by the yearbook or the song that belittled her. She and her friends from that era said she had never had sex with any of the Prep boys.

Compared with the physical assault described by Ford, the Renate story was far less serious. But once again, details became data points. The Renate chapter wasn't just an unsavory but sadly typical teenage vulgarism; it seemed to confirm the misogynistic mindset that many Kavanaugh critics suspected he held, at least during the early 1980s, when the Ford and Ramirez events allegedly occurred.

FIRST THING WEDNESDAY MORNING, September 26, Katz, Bromwich, and their team were back at the Watergate with Ford, this time armed with a draft of prepared comments for her to consider reading at the hearing. It was about twenty pages, double-spaced, describing her mentality in coming forward and then, in some detail, the 1982 encounter she remembered with Kavanaugh and its aftermath. Ford read through it and immediately went to work with a red pen, spending about an hour and a half marking up every page. Yet even four days after the Senate Judiciary Committee announcement that she'd appear in a public hearing on Thursday, as television networks arranged for their live feeds and the public waited in nervous anticipation of what they would soon hear, she had not yet committed herself to open testimony.

Throughout the day, her team was in and out of the hotel conference room. Katz worked from her Dupont Circle office, making tweaks to the opening statement from there. Banks and Bromwich talked Ford through the likely order of the coming proceedings: she'd give her prepared remarks, then submit to question-and-answer sessions, each of which would take five minutes. The questioners would alternate between Republicans and Democrats. The Republicans had delegated as their interlocutor Rachel Mitchell, a sex crimes prosecutor from Arizona, who had flown in for the hearing.

Ford was focused. She resisted the idea of a practice session. She told her lawyers that she didn't want her answers to be scripted in any way. She wanted the wording in the opening remarks to be precise, to capture only what she remembered clearly. She would be up front about whatever she could not recall.

Around five o'clock that afternoon, Seidman entered the conference room where Ford was conferring with Bromwich and Robbins. "I need to talk to you about the hearing," she said.

She wanted Ford to concede to public testimony. "I know you intended for it to be private, and you don't want a circus," Seidman explained, "but if it's entirely private, then senators who will be making decisions won't hear your testimony." Only the members of the Senate Judiciary Committee members would hear Ford's input firsthand, Seidman added. The other seventy-nine senators who would cast pivotal votes on Kavanaugh would be informed mostly by secondhand accounts as they made their decisions.

Seidman noted that Ford's team had obtained as many provisions as possible to make Ford feel comfortable. They had secured a smaller hearing room, ensured that she could sit with her lawyers abreast, and had limited the number of cameras that would shoot the proceedings. Seidman had drawn a diagram of what the room looked like. She offered to show it to Ford.

"I don't want to see it," Ford replied. "It'll make me nervous." Nevertheless, she agreed.

CONSERVATIVES WERE APPROACHING the next day's hearings with no small amount of chagrin. Many bitterly asserted that a fair hearing— Kavanaugh's mantra in his Fox interview—appeared to no longer be possible in the United States. A person's entire career and reputation could be sullied in a matter of days, even if the accusation was thirty-six years old, the principals were young, and there was no apparent proof.

Others felt that every story unearthed—Ford, Ramirez, Renate— only confirmed the callousness of the candidate at his core. The seventeen-year-old Kavanaugh *did*, they believed, implicate the fifty-three-year-old Kavanaugh and very likely meant there were other incidents involving him out there.

The Republicans on the committee staff were frustrated. Since the Ford allegations had been made public, Davis—like Katz and Banks— had been managing a slew of other distasteful accounts about Kavanaugh, investigating each of them on Grassley's behalf. None seemed to have any substance, and the Swetnick accusations, which were bogged down in arguments with her lawyer, Avenatti, over revealing additional evidence, appeared to majority staffs and senators to be as baseless as they were outlandish. But with each allegation, thin or credible, the portrait of Kavanaugh and his high school buddy Judge as accomplices in sexual misconduct was becoming fixed in the public consciousness.

There was a story reported by a Tiverton, Rhode Island, man named Jeffrey Catalan of men named Brett and Mark sexually assaulting a woman on a Rhode Island boat in 1985, when Kavanaugh would have been a sophomore or junior in college. Catalan, after saying initially that he thought he recognized Kavanaugh from old pictures in the media, later said he couldn't be sure.

There was an anonymous tip sent to Senator Kamala Harris's San Diego office from a woman who claimed to have been raped in the back of a car by both Kavanaugh and a friend on an unknown date and location. That woman, whom Senate investigators referred to as Jane Doe, was never clearly identified, though a woman named Judy Munro-Leighton later claimed credit for the story—and then said she had made it up as a ploy to get attention.

Working regularly until 3 or 4 a.m. and deploying a staff of two dozen, Davis did his best to quash the stories like a game of whack-a-mole, upbraiding those who would air ad hominem attacks, sharing only the most important details with his boss, Grassley. Davis spent much of his forty-first birthday, which fell on the same Sunday that the committee announced Ford's September 27 testimony, sitting in his Hart building office in a blazer and khakis—weekend wear for the Grassley team—preparing for Thursday's hearings. Sitting in his spare space, which was decorated with little more than a picture from his clerkship with Gorsuch, he had a view of the atrium and the offices of Democratic senators beyond. Their windows were plastered with signs saying BELIEVE ALL SURVIVORS.

Davis himself was incredulous about Ford's story. He regarded Katz and her colleagues—who, after all, had been connected with Ford by Feinstein's office—as liberal hacks with a political agenda. Their calls for an FBI investigation, he believed, were nothing more than stall tactics, a way to obfuscate an uncorroborated story from ages ago that should not be permitted to take down an accomplished, upstanding nominee.

Kavanaugh spent Wednesday afternoon working on his prepared

statements for the next day. He labored solitarily for hours, stretching well into the night.

THURSDAY, SEPTEMBER 27, dawned cloudy but warm in Washington. At the Watergate Hotel, the Palo Alto contingent rose early and dressed for what was sure to be a draining day. Seven miles north, in Chevy Chase, Kavanaugh was putting the finishing touches on his prepared remarks, which he had shared with just one other person, his former law clerk Porter Wilkinson. Wilkinson was a young lawyer who had gone on to clerk for Chief Justice John G. Roberts Jr. before joining the Smithsonian Institution.

Shortly before 10 a.m., Ford, dressed in a midnight-blue dress and jacket, her blond hair styled into soft waves, entered the hearing room, accompanied by a large bodyguard wearing a suit with a blue silk pocket square. At the witness table, Katz, wearing a black pinstriped suit over a white shell top and glasses tipped down the bridge of her nose, sat to Ford's right; Bromwich, in a dark suit and bright blue tie, was to her left. They handed Ford materials and whispered last-minute instructions.

Behind them were Banks and Joseph Abboud, an associate who had worked closely with Katz and Banks; Ford's friends Jay Backstrand and Keith Koegler; her Holton schoolmates Cheryl Amitay and Mimi Micklitsch Mulligan; and Sandra Gichner, one of Ford's closest high school friends and now a Holton trustee. All wore Senate-issued brown witness badges.

Supporters from Ford's Holton days, as well as some of the school's current students—dressed in their pleated navy-blue-and-white plaid uniforms—also took seats, along with Leimroth and the other friends from home. Alyssa Milano, the *Charmed* actor and #MeToo activist, was in attendance, noticeable in a loose, dark top, high bun, and grave expression.

Ford's parents and two brothers, who had not learned of her experience until the summer of 2018, were absent—a detail Republicans would pounce on as evidence that her family would not vouch for her credibility. Those closer to the situation later said the reality was more complicated: while Ford's family supported her, they were also Republicans who were deeply entrenched in the Bethesda world of the Kavanaughs. This was a difficult public ordeal for them.

As the hearing got under way, the Democrats and Republicans vacillated between wanting to show courtesy to the principal witnesses and wanting to score political points.

Grassley began by thanking both Ford and Kavanaugh for appearing, and he apologized for their rough treatment by the public in the prior weeks. He also criticized Feinstein and her colleagues for harboring Ford's "secret" letter until the last minute, a letter that contained damaging allegations of which there had never been a "whiff" in preceding FBI background checks.

The senator bemoaned the leaking of Ford's name to the press, chastised his Democratic counterparts for what he described as a lack of cooperation with his own staff's investigations of the claims against Kavanaugh, and complained that Kavanaugh's other accusers—namely, Ramirez and Swetnick—had not produced evidence despite repeated requests. "This will be in stark contrast to the grandstanding and chaos that we saw from the other side during the previous four days in this hearing process," he said. Then he turned the floor over to Feinstein.

The ranking member welcomed Ford, praised her résumé, and spoke at length about the Anita Hill hearings of twenty-seven years earlier, pointing out how little had changed, given the skepticism faced by Hill—and, now, Ford. She clearly wanted to remind the American audience of the Senate's ignominious chapter in 1991, when many felt that a dignified professional woman had been unjustly humiliated and discounted. Feinstein invoked the accusations of Ramirez and Swetnick, as well as the attestations of some of Kavanaugh's college friends who by now had called his denials of bad behavior dishonest.

"The entire country is watching how we handle these allegations. I hope the majority changes their tactics, opens their mind, and seriously reflects on why we are here," Feinstein concluded. "We are here for one reason: to determine whether Judge Kavanaugh should be elevated to one of the most powerful positions in our country."

Grassley replied that he was sorry Feinstein had mentioned the "unsubstantiated allegations of other people," clearly wanting to remind viewers that stories gain credence merely by their repetition. Then he swore Ford in.

Cameras whirred as the cramped hearing room grew hushed. As soon as Ford began speaking, the posturing and partisanship that had characterized the proceedings thus far fell away. There was only a seemingly average woman who had pushed through her paralyzing fear to come to tell her story. And the whole world was watching.

"I am here today not because I want to be," began Ford in a quivering voice. "I am terrified. I am here because I believe it is my civic duty to tell you what happened to me while Brett Kavanaugh and I were in high school."

Ford's testimony played out like a master class in authenticity and simplicity. She made no sweeping statements and proffered no larger agenda. Instead, Ford stuck to the only topic on which she had authority: what she remembered and how it had affected her.

She explained how she came to meet Kavanaugh, whom she

described as "the boy who sexually assaulted me." She described what had happened at the gathering after a day of swimming and diving at the Columbia Country Club in 1982. She admitted what she did not recall.

"I truly wish I could be more helpful with more detailed answers to all of the questions that have and will be asked about how I got to the party and where it took place and so forth. I don't have all the answers, and I don't remember as much as I would like to.

"But the details that—about that night that bring me here today," she added, "are the ones I will never forget. They have been seared into my memory, and have haunted me episodically as an adult."

The account was raw and wrenching. At many points, Ford spoke hoarsely and appeared to be choking back tears, not bothering to move aside the loose lock of hair that sometimes fell over her face. The senators listened, some impassively, some with their eyes downcast. Grassley nodded almost imperceptibly.

Ford spoke about how she had grappled with her memories, telling very few friends, and leaving out specific details, until recent years. She talked about feeling an obligation to share with the committee what she regarded as relevant information while fearing for her privacy. "Sexual assault victims should be able to decide for themselves when and whether their private experience is made public," she said.

She recounted the painful process of deciding whether it was fruitless to come forward, especially once Kavanaugh's confirmation seemed all but certain. She offered a window into her own ambivalence that had surfaced as recently as two days earlier, on the plane to Washington.

"As the hearing date got closer, I struggled with a terrible choice: Do I share the facts with the Senate and put myself and my family in the public spotlight?" she said. "Or do I preserve our privacy and allow the Senate to make its decision without knowing the full truth of his past behaviors?"

She related how the decision was soon made for her when reporters swarmed her home and workplace, leaving numerous messages for her friends and bosses. She recalled giving her story to *The Washington Post* and the horrifying backlash that followed.

"My family and I have been the target of constant harassment and death threats, and I have been called the most vile and hateful names imaginable," she said. "These messages, while far fewer than the expressions of support, have been terrifying and have rocked me to my core."

She said that since September 16, she and her family had moved from one location to another, sometimes together and sometimes not. Her work email had been hacked, she said, and false messages had been distributed from her account. She had been depicted by some as a political operative, a characterization she disputed. "It is not my responsibility to determine whether Mr. Kavanaugh deserves to sit on the Supreme Court," she said. "My responsibility is to tell you the truth."

The floor was then turned over to the questioner hired by Republicans, Rachel Mitchell. The format was atypical—senators usually ask their own questions—but the Republicans had deemed it important to have a seemingly impartial female interlocutor rather than give the appearance of a bunch of white powerful men bearing down on Ford.

A meticulous and plainspoken lawyer with a short, blunt haircut and rimless glasses, Mitchell seemed ideally suited for the job—a benign, by-the-book presence devoid of prosecutorial zeal. She had not been easy to find. Republican committee staffers spent long hours contacting dozens of female lawyers about doing the questioning at the hearing. Quite a few turned them down, presumably wanting to avoid the highly charged, politicized process.

Mitchell had overseen the special victims unit of the Maricopa County attorney's office in Arizona, spent a dozen years in the sex crimes subdivision, and handled some major local cases. She was there to stand in for the male senators—to ask their tough questions, softened with a veneer of compassion and expertise. Mitchell had interviewed many sexual assault victims and mentored other young prosecutors on best practices.

It was the type of sensibility Republicans sorely needed twenty-seven years after the Hill hearings, at a time when women's professional and political advances, along with the advent of #MeToo, had led to many Americans demanding better treatment of accusers. But the fact that Mitchell was representing a panel consisting entirely of white male Republicans on the committee—some of them well into their eighties—remained unavoidable. A number of the people who attended the hearing would later say that Mitchell's presence—that of a lone woman sitting at a small desk far below the dais, asking questions on behalf of the senior male senators above her until she was cut off—was one of the most disconcerting elements of an already unsettling day.

Mitchell, dressed in a powder blue shirt and dark blue jacket, greeted Ford warmly. She urged her to let her know if she found anything confusing or unclear. But just as they began to delve into the letter Ford had written to Feinstein, Grassley cut them off.

"Ms. Mitchell, I don't know whether this is fair for me to interrupt, but I want to keep people within five minutes. Is that a—is that a major problem for you in the middle of a question?" he asked, adding that for equity's sake, he needed to move on to the next Democratic questioner.

Mitchell quickly assented.

As the hearing went on, Mitchell would pick up with her careful deconstruction of Ford's recollections of Kavanaugh, looking for inconsistencies in her account, or for additional specifics. She probed on the alleged geographical area of the assault and about whether there were any other factors in Ford's life that could have contributed to the anxiety and PTSD-like symptoms she had largely ascribed to her alleged assault by Kavanaugh. Then a Democratic senator would have a turn, thanking Ford for her testimony and asking further questions about how the alleged incident impacted her life.

Some of the Democratic rounds seemed like showboating, however well intentioned. Senators Kamala Harris and Cory Booker, both of whom would announce presidential campaigns in the months to come, made particularly long, principled speeches before directly questioning Ford. Professorial, polite, and composed, Ford repeatedly apologized for herself in a small voice, saying "I wish I could be more helpful" when she could not recall a particular detail, and timidly requesting caffeine. "I'm used to being collegial," she said at one point.

She came across as both knowledgeable—using scientific jargon like "sequelae" in reference to the aftereffects of her trauma—and, at times, strikingly naive. "I don't understand," she whispered audibly to Bromwich at one point, in response to Mitchell's targeted line of questioning about whether she had spoken to members of Congress after her August 7 polygraph.

Ford was forced to walk that fine line commonly navigated by women: appearing firm and confident without coming across as strident, unlikable, or unstable. Ford prevailed. Her equanimity would later be contrasted with Kavanaugh's overwrought delivery, which, ironically, was forgiven by many as understandable passion in the heat of self-defense.

In one of the more memorable moments of the hearing, Ford described to Vermont senator Patrick Leahy, a Democrat, what was unforgettable about her Kavanaugh memory. "Indelible in the hippo-campus is the laughter," she said tearfully, referring to the sound of Kavanaugh and Judge's hilarity during and after her alleged assault, "the uproarious laughter between the two, and their having fun at my expense."

Despite her occasionally halting delivery, Ford was firm on one point: the man on top of her had been Brett Kavanaugh. "Dr. Ford," asked Senator Dick Durbin, the Democrat from Illinois, "with what degree of certainty do you believe Brett Kavanaugh assaulted you?"

She answered without hesitating: "One hundred percent."

ELEVEN

Inde Ira et Lacrimae

Then Anger and Tears

Between the snapping cameras, the cramped and crowded room, the high dudgeon, and the whiplash of moving from one senator's stern five-minute question session to another's obsequious tone, the September 27 hearing was a surreal experience for the many glued to the proceedings. In an age of reality television, the hearing held its own, offering drama, pathos, and suspense.

Whispered arguments broke out at moments between senators and staffers—such as when Grassley openly chided a sweaty-looking Davis, and Feinstein appeared not to hear a critical snippet of information from Jennifer Duck. Mitchell's methodical queries were regularly interrupted and eventually jettisoned altogether. But almost everyone agreed—regardless of political affiliation—that Ford and her steady, anguished tone were riveting.

Banks—who had noticed her colleague's heightened emotions and said to Katz on the way into the hearing room, "Don't cry"—and Katz were particularly proud of Ford, knowing how hard it had been for their client to get to this moment. Koegler gently patted Ford's shoulder after she testified. Ford's high school friends later wrote one another text messages praising her poised composure.

Far beyond Capitol Hill, those watching the live feed on video were rapt. The Twittersphere was afire. During Ford's testimony, the National Sexual Assault Hotline said calls jumped 147 percent. Some Senate staffers tried to draw on the calming techniques they'd learned from Tara Brach, a mindfulness teacher, who as the hearings began in early September led a webinar meditation session in the Hart Senate Office Building, even as loud protests were happening in the lobby. Ashley Judd, Ellen DeGeneres, Emmy Rossum, and other prominent celebrities who had been active in the #MeToo movement lamented Ford's experience, identified with her trauma, or expressed outrage over her treatment. Many hailed her as a pathbreaker for women, speaking out about sexual assault to a broader audience—and with greater stakes—than anyone they could remember.

"Out of the blue, a hero steps up and I'm in awe," wrote the actress Sally Field. "I know the pain of these kinds of memories, Dr. Ford. Memories that are indelibly imprinted on your brain no matter how many years go by."

Charlie Baker, the Republican governor of Massachusetts, argued that there should be an FBI investigation in light of Ford's "sickening" disclosures, and that there should be no vote that week on Kavanaugh.

Men and women around the country, in living rooms, on airplanes, and in offices, reckoned with their own memories of rape or assault, or those of loved ones.

Even President Trump would speak approvingly of Ford's performance. "I thought her testimony was very compelling, and she looks like a very fine woman to me," he said to reporters the next day.

"She was a very credible witness, and she was very good in many respects."

Fox News host Chris Wallace pronounced Ford's testimony a "disaster" for the Republicans. Other conservatives agreed. "Ford seems kind. This doesn't strike me as partisan," the outspoken right-wing commentator Mike Cernovich wrote on Twitter. "This will be a tough vote."

Many Democrats agreed. "Heartbreaking, credible, and compelling," tweeted Massachusetts senator Elizabeth Warren of Ford's testimony. "I believe her, and I hope my Republican colleagues do, too."

Throughout that day, the senators on the panel received a flood of messages from friends, family, and acquaintances with memories of sexual assault, feedback that members of Congress saw as a call to action. Rhode Island Democrat Sheldon Whitehouse, Delaware Democrat Chris Coons, and Arizona Republican Jeff Flake all received messages from people who identified with Ford. It would shape their response to the testimony in the days to come.

Coons said his phone "blew up" in a way it never had before, with texts and emails from people he'd known for decades and others he'd never met before. They started offering their own stories, one after the other, "saying, 'Me, too: I have had my life changed by sexual assault,'" Coons explained later. "'It was my father,' 'It was my brother,' 'It was my priest,' 'It was my schoolteacher.'"

The Republican establishment quickly countered. Graham told the press scrum that Ford was "a nice lady" but noted that she "has come forward to tell a hard story that is uncorroborated." Louisiana senator Bill Cassidy agreed, previewing a line of defense that many Republicans would use in the coming days: However compelling Ford's account, there was no evidence to support her claims, and, therefore, they could not be accepted as truth in the face of Kavanaugh's vigorous denials (the prosecutor Rachel Mitchell would say in her final report: "A 'he said, she said' case is incredibly difficult to prove. But this case is even weaker than that").

It was an argument that even Ford's staunchest defenders could not counter. Despite her confiding in friends, her spouse, and a therapist years before Kavanaugh's ascension, Ford had not shared her experience of assault at any time remotely close to the incident itself. No diary, letter, police report, or other written account existed. Ford's parents hadn't known; her friends, including her good friend who had allegedly been present during the evening in question, had no idea. The site of the event—while theoretically traceable, given the details of its layout and its connection to a young Mark Judge—was unknown.

The closest Ford could come to pinpointing record-based evidence of the story she had shared was to suggest searching employment records associated with a summer job Judge had worked in 1982 at the Potomac Village Safeway, where Ford said she had run into him weeks after the incident and found him shame-faced. But those records, if they existed, wouldn't prove Kavanaugh assaulted her.

The doubts raised by the lack of evidence were powerful. "Just because she's had a credible story does not mean it's correct," Louellen Welsch, a sixty-two-year-old resident of Colorado Springs, told *The New York Times.* "I need to have a lot more questioning."

FORD HAD BEEN in the witness chair for more than three hours when Grassley brought the gavel down, calling for a forty-five-minute recess. Kavanaugh would take the stand next.

Ushered out by her bodyguards and lawyers, Ford was led into a waiting car beside the Hart building. Riding back to the hotel, she called her husband, Russell, who commended her clear, composed delivery. Koegler, who had accompanied Christine in the car, agreed. Christine was subdued during the ride, as if the whole experience hadn't yet sunk in.

Back at the Watergate, Ford and her supporters occupied two suites, one of which had a television tuned to the hearing. Ford didn't want to watch Kavanaugh, so she stayed in the other suite, where there were snacks, wine, and friends who came to wish her well.

Some of Ford's lawyers were there, along with her friends from Palo Alto. Members of her Holton class—including Samantha Guerry, Gichner, and McLean—also came by, along with a supportive male friend from Landon, where her brothers had gone to high school. Ford's parents, who were now in their eighties, also made an appearance. It had not been easy for the professor to share her memories with them after so many years. Her father, Ralph, had initially counseled against coming forward, presuming little could be achieved after so many years. But over time, he and Ford's mother, Paula, had come to accept and support their daughter's decision. Her brothers were not in attendance.

During the whirlwind that followed Ford's September 16 *Post* interview, the Blaseys had remained largely out of sight, turning away media inquiries. A short telephone interview with a *Post* reporter on September 25 was the extent of Ralph's public comments. "I think all of the Blasey family would support her," he said. "I think her record stands for itself. Her schooling, her jobs, and so on." He also said, "I think any father would have love for his daughter."

Christine's parents not only bore the sorrow of hearing their only daughter's allegation of assault at fifteen. They had the added awkwardness of continuing to live in the home where they raised their daughter, in the same area where the incident was said to have occurred, among many of the very same families.

In an odd coincidence, Kavanaugh's mother, Martha, as a judge had been involved in a 1996 foreclosure case over the Blaseys' house in Potomac; after the couple settled with their mortgage lender, Martha dismissed the case, enabling the Blaseys to keep their home. At another point, Ralph Blasey had been president of the Burning Tree Golf Club, an all-male establishment in Potomac, where Ed Kavanaugh was also an active member.

Because of these ties to Kavanaugh's world, Ford had avoided sharing her story with her parents as long as she possibly could. But now she could no longer protect them.

During the break after Ford's testimony, senators retired for their usual Thursday lunches in the Capitol—Republicans in the Mansfield Room and Democrats in the LBJ Room—where Senator Schumer and his colleagues agreed that Ford's account was so powerful that it should speak for itself. When it came to questioning Kavanaugh, they didn't have to go back over her testimony and could cover different ground.

Kavanaugh did not watch Ford's testimony but instead spent the first part of the hearing going over his remarks at home. Just before noon, as the judge was escorted out the side entrance of his house into one of two waiting black SUVs, a female reporter shouted, "Judge Kavanaugh, what is your reaction to Christine Ford's testimony so far? How will you make your case to the American people and the Senate Judiciary Committee?"

The gregarious, glad-handing etiquette that Kavanaugh usually modeled had been replaced by a very different, self-protective type of protocol; the judge was now in crisis mode. So he swiftly entered the car without responding to any media questions. Riding away down the street, Kavanaugh could barely be seen through a tinted window.

Once on Capitol Hill, Kavanaugh continued going over his statement at a long conference table in the Finance Committee's anteroom. His speech—which was both a defense of his record and an angry invocation of the degradations he and his family had already weathered—was, at least on paper, leagues more aggressive than his remarks during the Fox interview earlier in the week. But McGahn, who cleared the room shortly before Kavanaugh was due to testify to have a private audience with the nominee and Ashley, had some further advice.

"You need to reboot the room," the White House counsel said, according to Carl Hulse's book, *Confirmation Bias: Inside Washington's War Over the Supreme Court*, urging him to remember his life's work in getting to this point and to speak from the heart.

A few minutes later, when Davis went to fetch Kavanaugh to bring him to the committee room, the judge looked as though he had worked up a powerful head of steam. Still, Davis thought a final word on the need for an aggressive performance might help, telling Kavanaugh, "You better come out swinging."

Kavanaugh entered the hearing room stiffly, clearly agitated, and spent a moment organizing his place—moving his nameplate to one side, adjusting the microphone, squaring off his prepared remarks. He sniffed and looked up at the committee, his lips pursed and the bridge of his nose creased.

"Judge Kavanaugh, we welcome you," said Grassley. "Are you ready?"

Behind the judge sat a row of family and friends, many of them women: Ashley, looking dispirited and resigned; his mother, Martha; Suzanne Matan, a friend from high school; and Zina Bash, a former Kavanaugh clerk and one of his closest advisers. McGahn and Kavanaugh's father, Ed, were also close by. A few rows behind them, Ford's lawyers, Katz, Bromwich, and Abboud, were visible, sitting not far from Alyssa Milano.

After being sworn in by Grassley, Kavanaugh began. Immediately it was evident that this was a Kavanaugh the country had not seen before. Indeed, even some of his closest friends and colleagues were surprised by the bitter virulence that came out of the judge, whom they typically thought of as mild-mannered and even-tempered.

"Less than two weeks ago, Dr. Ford publicly accused me of committing wrongdoing at an event more than thirty-six years ago, when we were both in high school," Kavanaugh began. "I denied the allegation immediately, categorically and unequivocally. All four people allegedly at the event, including Dr. Ford's longtime friend Ms. Keyser, have said they recall no such event. Her longtime friend Ms. Keyser said under penalty of felony that she does not know me, and does not believe she ever saw me at a party, ever."

He lingered on Keyser's lack of recollection, speaking slowly and loudly. It was the first tenet of an elaborately conceived statement that served as the closing argument in his personal trial. He would return to it again and again.

"Here is the quote from Ms. Keyser's attorney's letter," Kavanaugh continued. "Quote, 'Simply put, Ms. Keyser does not know Mr. Kavanaugh, and she has no recollection of ever being at a party or gathering where he was present, with or without Dr. Ford,' end quote. Think about that fact.

"The day after the allegation appeared, I told this committee that I wanted a hearing as soon as possible to clear my name. I demanded a hearing for the very next day. Unfortunately, it took the committee ten days to get to this hearing. In those ten long days, as was predictable, and as I predicted, my family and my name have been totally and permanently destroyed by vicious and false additional accusations. The ten-day delay has been harmful to me and my family, to the Supreme Court, and to the country.

"When this allegation first arose, I welcomed any kind of investigation—Senate, FBI, or otherwise. The committee now has conducted a thorough investigation, and I've cooperated fully. I know that any kind of investigation—Senate, FBI, Montgomery County Police, whatever—will clear me. Listen to the people I know. Listen to the people who've known me my whole life. Listen to the people I've grown up with and worked with and played with and coached with and dated and taught and gone to games with and had beers with. And listen to the witnesses who allegedly were at this event thirty-six years ago. Listen to Ms. Keyser. She does not know me. I was not at the party described by Dr. Ford."

As she sat just behind her husband's right shoulder, Ashley's chin began to tremble, as if to hold back tears. Matan, the high school friend who—along with dozens of other women from that era—had signed a letter attesting to Kavanaugh's character and defended his conduct to reporters, sat tall and grave on the other side. To Kavanaugh, his family, and his supporters, this moment was the nadir of a toxic cultural moment in which good people were being ruined by unproven accusations, aided by an unhinged media and a coarse brand of political discourse that had not been seen in generations. It was a tragic, devastating experience that shook their belief in fundamental notions of fairness and due process.

"This confirmation process has become a national disgrace," continued Kavanaugh, his voice rising. "The Constitution gives the Senate an important role in the confirmation process, but you have replaced advice and consent with search and destroy.

"Since my nomination in July, there's been a frenzy on the left to come up with something—*anything*," he said, emphasizing the word, "to block my confirmation. Shortly after I was nominated, the Democratic Senate leader said he would, quote, 'oppose me with everything he's got.' A Democratic senator on this committee publicly referred to me as evil—evil; think about that word—and said that those who supported me were, quote, 'complicit in evil.' Another Democratic senator on this committee said, quote, 'Judge Kavanaugh is your worst nightmare.' A former head of the Democratic National Committee said, quote, 'Judge Kavanaugh will threaten the lives of millions of Americans for decades to come.'

"I understand the passions of the moment, but I would say to those senators, your words have meaning. Millions of Americans listen carefully to you. Given comments like those, is it any surprise that people have been willing to do anything, to make any physical threat against my family, to send any violent email to my wife, to make any kind of allegation against me and against my friends—to blow me up and take me down?

"You sowed the wind for decades to come. I fear that the whole country will reap the whirlwind."

His point that caustic political rhetoric was causing real harm was canny. In a speech about Kavanaugh's nomination, Senator Cory Booker had said that those not fighting for the personal freedoms that might be dismantled if Kavanaugh joined the Supreme Court were "complicit" in "evil." Booker even quoted Psalm 23, saying that, as a country, "we are walking through the valley of the shadow of death." It was a highly charged speech.

But Kavanaugh was disingenuous in targeting only his Democratic critics for cheapening the nation's political dialogue. His very own patron, President Donald Trump, had been among the most egregious perpetrators of acidic and denigrating talk. Trump used his speeches and Twitter posts to mock and degrade almost anyone who opposed him, calling one former female aide a "crazed, crying low-life" and a "dog," and a CNN anchor "the dumbest man on television." He had belittled the North Korean leader Kim Jong-un, who had threatened to send nuclear bombs to the United States homeland, as "rocket man" at a United Nations delegation. He had complained at a White House meeting about aspiring immigrants from "shithole countries" and insulted the IQs of his political opponents. This irony can't have been lost on Kavanaugh.

Still, he attacked the Democrats for their rhetoric and their tactics. Speaking of Feinstein, who listened with her arms folded, Kavanaugh argued that the Ford accusations had been tucked away, then "unleashed and publicly deployed, over Dr. Ford's wishes" in order to ruin his prospects. He called the multiple allegations against him, most of which had surfaced only in the prior eleven days, a "calculated and orchestrated political hit, fueled with apparent pent-up anger about President Trump and the 2016 election, fear that has been unfairly stoked about my judicial record, revenge on behalf of the Clintons, and millions of dollars in money from outside left-wing opposition groups."

For many, the Clinton reference was a low for Kavanaugh—a moment when he lost his intellectual grip and descended into score-settling partisanship far afield of the legitimate concerns over sexual assault. He was not wrong, however, about the political scar tissue that had inspired so much of the liberal anger. The treatment of Garland, the installment of Gorsuch, and a feeling that Republicans were undermining Americans' support of abortion rights, gender equality, and other issues by ramming conservative nominees onto the court all informed the Democrats' vehement opposition.

Kavanaugh then reached the central plank of his argument: a flat denial. "I've never sexually assaulted anyone," he said. "Not in high school, not in college, not ever.

"This onslaught of last-minute allegations does not ring true," he continued, echoing his mother's saying as a prosecutor about what rings true and false. "I'm not questioning that Dr. Ford may have been sexually assaulted by some person in some place at some time. But I have never done this. To her or to anyone. That's not who I am. It is not who I was. I am innocent of this charge."

He talked about his family and the impact of the allegations on them, nearly breaking down as Ashley dropped her head behind him. "I intend no ill will to Dr. Ford and her family. The other night, Ashley and my daughter Liza said their prayers. And little Liza—all of ten years old—said to Ashley, 'We should pray for the woman.' It's a lot of wisdom from a ten-year-old."

He then took a moment to compose himself, with Ashley nodding slowly, as if to silently urge him on. He spoke of his career and all the vetting he had undergone in a quarter century of public and private life, never once being accused of sexual misconduct. He said he may have met Ford at some point but did not recall it—a critical concession that helped legitimize Ford's assertion that she had known Kavanaugh and his group of friends. As if realizing that, Kavanaugh returned again to Keyser, who had said she did not know him.

Kavanaugh mentioned "two male friends who were allegedly there," and the fact that they had said, under penalty of felony, that they did not recall the incident Ford described. He said that those two men had "refuted" Ford's claims, a false and misleading turn for the habitually meticulous judge, given that, in fact, they had said they did not remember them. Kavanaugh mentioned his high school calendars, including the one he had kept during the summer in question—

considering it "both a calendar and a diary"—a habit he'd picked up from his father, who had kept detailed calendars since 1978. Kavanaugh choked up at the memory—emotion that would prove rich fodder for Matt Damon's widely watched parody of the judge on *Saturday Night Live.*

He also nearly broke down in talking about Renate Schroeder, whom he and his friends had referenced in their 1983 high school yearbook. The "Renate Alumnius," he said, had been innocuous, "clumsily intended to show affection, and that she was one of us," and "not," he added, "related to sex." It was a dodge, given that nobody had believed even then that real sex had occurred. He blamed the media "circus" for interpreting the reference otherwise, saying he was "so sorry" to Renate for the reference, as "she was, and is, a great person." The harm to Dolphin clearly affected Kavanaugh, who had indeed been her friend in high school and in sporadic touch with her since. But given the well-evidenced fact that Kavanaugh had bragged about her as a sexual conquest in high school, unless he had forgotten that fact entirely, it was his own past behavior that was paining him, too.

He then repeated that he had been a virgin until years after high school.

He spoke of his record with women—his friendships with women during and after high school, his promotion of and respect for women in the workplace. He noted that he had contingently hired four clerks to aid him on the Supreme Court if he were to be confirmed—all women.

"If confirmed, I'll be the first justice in the history of the Supreme Court to have a group of all-women law clerks," he said.

He talked more about the impact of the Ford allegations on his family. "When I accepted the president's nomination, Ashley and I knew this process would be challenging," he said. "We never expected that it would devolve into this. Explaining this to our daughters has been about the worst experience of our lives."

Then the questioning began.

Mitchell had presented Kavanaugh with a written definition of the term "sexual behavior," and she now asked him to review it. Reading the document, Kavanaugh looked irritated. He furrowed his brow, pursed his lips, sniffed, and drank water. Mitchell asked him about Mark Judge.

"Funny guy, great writer," said Kavanaugh, describing Judge as part of his circle of high school friends. "Popular. Developed a serious addiction problem that lasted decades. Near death a couple times from his addiction." Kavanaugh added, "I haven't talked to him in a couple of years." He would continue distancing himself from Judge as the hearing continued, calling him a friend of "ours" rather than "mine."

Kavanaugh then described Patrick Smyth, a friend he'd seen occasionally since high school, who had played defensive tackle on the football team and often driven him to school during their freshman and sophomore years.

Feinstein was given the floor. Her first question was why Kavanaugh hadn't supported an additional FBI investigation into the recent claims of sexual misconduct, given his confidence that the accusations were false.

Kavanaugh appeared conflicted—pulled in one direction, perhaps, by his strategic instinct to please and in another, no doubt, by having the ultimate professional trophy so close he could taste it. In a way, Feinstein's question was naive: of course Kavanaugh didn't want an FBI delay; he wanted to be sworn in.

"Senator, I'll do whatever the committee wants," said Kavanaugh, his voice rising. "I wanted a hearing the day after the allegation came up. I wanted to be here that day. Instead, ten days passed where all this nonsense is coming out—you know, that I'm in gangs, I'm on boats in Rhode Island, I'm in Colorado, you know, I'm sighted all over the place. And these things are printed and run breathlessly by cable news."

He was referring to claims of his alleged assault of a woman in Rhode Island that were later retracted by the man who raised it, and, presumably, to an anonymous account by a Colorado constituent who said he had once shoved a girlfriend up against a wall in Washington while drunk. The account was never clarified or corroborated.

Kavanaugh was increasingly red-faced, animated, and glowing with perspiration. "You know, I wanted a hearing the next day," he said. "I—my family's been destroyed by this, Senator, destroyed."

Feinstein talked about the "terrible and hard part" of the Senate confirmation process—that the panel couldn't come to a conclusion about any allegations, which in her view made an FBI inquiry even more necessary. Kavanaugh interrupted to explain that the FBI doesn't reach conclusions in background investigations. Feinstein returned to the idea that the FBI would help gather the facts. Again, Kavanaugh interrupted.

"You're interviewing me," he said, gaining steam. "You're doing it, Senator."

Mitchell then asked Kavanaugh about his drinking in high school.

"Yes, we drank beer," he replied. "My friends and I, the boys and girls. Yes, we drank beer. I liked beer. Still like beer. We drank beer. The drinking age, as I noted, was eighteen, so the seniors were legal. Senior year in high school, people were legal to drink, and we—yeah, we drank beer, and I said sometimes—sometimes probably had too many beers, and sometimes other people had too many beers. We drank beer, we liked beer."

It was misleading in one respect, and understated in another. Seniors were legal when Kavanaugh was a junior; by the time he was a senior, the drinking age had been raised to twenty-one. But throughout those years, Kavanaugh had overindulged regularly, as had many of his classmates. Mitchell asked if he had ever drunk excessively.

"Sure," he said.

She asked if he had ever passed out from drinking.

"I—'passed out' would be—no, but I've gone to sleep, but I've never blacked out," he replied. "That's the—that's the—the allegation, and that—that—that's wrong."

It was something that former drinking buddies found unlikely. But they also weren't certain it was false. Kavanaugh himself may have blacked out and not realized it.

"Did you ever wake up with your clothes in a different condition, or fewer clothes on than you remembered when you went to sleep or passed out?" Mitchell asked.

Kavanaugh smiled nervously and shook his head, as if to show that the question was preposterous or perhaps because he felt put on the spot. He held up a hand slightly as if to point out how absurd this was. "No, y— no," he answered, laughing softly.

She touched on the key aspects of Ford's story: that he had been present with her at a teenage gathering in 1982, that he had been in a room with her and Judge, that he had ground his genitals over her, that he had covered her mouth with his hand, that he had tried to remove her clothes. In each case, Kavanaugh said those things had never happened.

After a fifteen-minute break, Leahy had his five minutes with Kavanaugh. The questioning quickly devolved into an argument, the judge brimming with fury. Leahy's questions about Judge's book *Wasted*, Kavanaugh said, were not an attempt to decode a semi-autobiographical account of drinking at Georgetown Prep, but an effort "to make fun of some guy who has an addiction."

A question about the yearbook references led to an even more hostile exchange, in which Leahy muttered under his breath about filibustering and Kavanaugh repeatedly interjected with boasts about his academic prowess in high school. Indeed, Kavanaugh's tendency to resort to his record as a student seemed like its own kind of filibustering. "I'm going to talk about my high school record," he told the senator, "if you're going to sit here and mock me."

Multiple Democratic senators asked Kavanaugh to support an FBI investigation into Ford's claims, and he consistently answered that he'd do whatever the committee wanted to do, without affirming that he'd specifically back another FBI probe. Durbin asked him to turn to McGahn, in the front row, and request an FBI investigation, at which point Grassley furiously interrupted and asserted that the panel was running the investigation, not McGahn or Kavanaugh. Durbin continued to press him, flustering Kavanaugh.

"I—I welcome whatever the committee wants to do, because I'm telling the truth," Kavanaugh said.

"I want to know what you want to do," replied Durbin.

"I—I'm telling the truth," said Kavanaugh.

"I want to know what *you* want to do, Judge."

"I'm innocent. I'm innocent of this charge."

"Then you're prepared for an FBI investigation—"

"They don't reach conclusions. You reach the conclusions, Senator."

"No, but they do investigate questions."

"I'm—I'm innocent."

After Durbin finished, instead of returning to Mitchell, who had expected to use the Republican committee members' allotted time to question Kavanaugh, Grassley yielded the floor to Graham.

The South Carolina senator, who had been restless in his seat, charged forth like a bull released from its pen. He railed against Feinstein for harboring Ford's claims for weeks and meeting with Kavanaugh without disclosing them, all while her staff recommended a lawyer to the professor. "This is the most unethical sham since I've been in politics," he yelled.

"Boy, y'all want power. God, I hope you never get it," he went on, addressing the Democrats as he shook his fist. "I hope the American people can see through this sham. That you knew about it and you held it. You had no intention of protecting Dr. Ford. None."

Graham's outburst represented the release Kavanaugh had not allowed himself. The senator's id had been unleashed just when Kavanaugh had struggled to show restraint. Angry over political scores, under cultural cover from the #MeToo movement, and enabled by a salivating media, the Democrats had trashed this esteemed judge, Graham, Kavanaugh, and their allies thought, and ruined his reputation—possibly forever. It was unforgivable.

Graham turned to Kavanaugh. "Do you consider this a job interview?"

Kavanaugh responded by noting the advice-and-consent process that Congress uses to vet judicial nominees under the Constitution.

"This is not a job interview," boomed Graham. "This is hell."

He said that he intended to vote for Kavanaugh and hoped that "everybody who's fair-minded will."

Kavanaugh sat for a moment, chin tipped back, looking almost vacant as the floor passed to Whitehouse, the Rhode Island Democrat.

The hearing immediately grew contentious again. Whitehouse got back in the weeds, asking about the yearbook pages, specifically the meaning of "Beach Week Ralph Club." Kavanaugh explained that he had a weak stomach and was known for throwing up after eating spicy food or drinking beer.

Whitehouse, a former prosecutor who had been Rhode Island's U.S. attorney before running for Senate, stared at Kavanaugh over the rims of his reading glasses, appearing unmoved by the explanation.

"So the vomiting that you reference in the Ralph Club reference," he asked drily, "related to the consumption of alcohol?"

Once again, Kavanaugh resorted to his résumé with a defensive retort that led many to later accuse him of impudence and entitlement. "Senator, I was at the top of my class academically, busted my butt in school," he said. "Captain of the varsity basketball team. Got in Yale College. When I got into Yale College, got into Yale Law School. Worked my tail off."

Whitehouse persisted. "Did the world 'Ralph' you used in your yearbook—"

"I already—I already answered," said Kavanaugh. He was becoming more confrontational, as he had with Feinstein earlier.

As Whitehouse attempted to read his other questions about Kavanaugh's yearbook page, the judge jumped in. "I like beer. I like beer," he said. "I don't know if you do."

Whitehouse attempted another question.

"Do you like beer, Senator?" Kavanaugh pressed, before Whitehouse could finish.

Whitehouse was unmoved. He asked about "boofing," which is sometimes slang for anal sex, but which Kavanaugh described as a reference to flatulence. He asked about Renate; Kavanaugh repeated his earlier response on that matter. Whitehouse asked about "Devil's Triangle," sometimes slang for a sexual scenario involving two men and one woman.

"Drinking game," said Kavanaugh.

"How's it played?" asked Whitehouse.

"Three glasses in a triangle."

"And?"

"You ever play quarters?" asked Kavanaugh.

"No."

"Okay. It's a quarters game."

A few moments later, Texas Republican senator John Cornyn stepped in, reminding Kavanaugh that if he was lying, he'd be guilty of a crime. Kavanaugh evenly said he understood that. Cornyn then sympathized with Kavanaugh, much as Graham had. The claims against the judge, Cornyn said, were "outrageous, and you're right to be angry."

But Kavanaugh's calmer demeanor was short-lived, as Democratic senator Amy Klobuchar of Minnesota took over.

"Most people have done some drinking in high school and college, and many people even struggle with alcoholism and binge drinking," she said. "My own dad struggled with alcoholism most of his life, and he got in trouble for it, and there were consequences. He is still in AA at age ninety, and he's sober, and in his words, he was pursued by grace, and that's how he got through this."

She said that some had characterized Kavanaugh as a "belligerent" drinker and brought up the issue of memory loss as a result of drinking. Kavanaugh interrupted and began talking about his freshman-year roommates at Yale, including two who didn't get along, causing one to move the other's furniture out into a courtyard.

Klobuchar returned to her point. "Was there ever a time when you drank so much that you couldn't remember what happened, or part of what happened, the night before?" she asked.

He said no. She tried again: "So you're saying there's never been a case where you drank so much that you didn't remember what happened the night before, or part of what happened?"

"It's—you're asking about, you know, blackout," Kavanaugh replied. "I don't know. Have you?" He leaned back in his chair and grinned nervously, as if aware that he was going too far but unable to help himself.

Klobuchar patiently responded: "Could you answer the question, Judge? I just—so you—that's not happened. Is that your answer?"

"Yeah, and I'm curious if you have," said Kavanaugh.

Klobuchar was clearly taken aback, but she answered quickly: "I have no drinking problem, Judge."

"Yeah," he said, "nor do I."

The exchange with Klobuchar, even in light of the Clinton reference and the Graham outburst, would be regarded by many as a new low point in the Kavanaugh hearings. As damaging as the Ford allegations were, as excruciating as it had been to watch her, and as exercised as Kavanaugh had been up to then, nothing had appeared quite so impertinent as him turning the tables on a senior female senator who had just opened up about her own family history with alcohol.

Klobuchar, after all, was effectively interviewing Kavanaugh for a job as his superior in that context. She was using compassionate, deferential language and requesting honest answers. Yet Kavanaugh pounced on her, perhaps hoping to give her a sense of the personal anguish and humiliation he was experiencing.

"You don't go to where they are when they're acting that way," Klobuchar later said in an interview, likening her unruffled response to needing to "take away the keys" from an inebriated driver. As a prosecutor, she said, she was trained to let the witness continue talking rather than interrupt or assist. Still, "I just thought he would apologize to me," she added, "because it was so bad."

After an unexpected break in the hearing, Kavanaugh did, in fact, apologize, looking tearful as he did so. "Sorry I did that," he said. "This is a tough process. I'm sorry about that."

The proceedings stretched on for another ninety minutes, with Democrats continuing to push for an additional FBI probe and Republicans lamenting the hardship Kavanaugh had endured as a result of the allegations leveled against him. Mitchell had been rendered obsolete after Graham's performance, which had effectively reclaimed the floor for his party members; every other Republican senator to follow grilled Kavanaugh directly. Mitchell sat quietly at her small desk while the majority members used the time that had originally been allotted to her.

Kavanaugh was more controlled by this point. He seemed almost exhausted by the day's events. Or he may have been encouraged by the sense that the Republicans were stepping up on his behalf, shifting the hearing's dynamics in his favor. Kavanaugh didn't need to argue his case as strongly anymore; his Republican supporters were doing it for him. Where the judge had started the day looking like a villain, now he was looking like a victim.

By the time Senator Ben Sasse, the Nebraska Republican, took the floor, Kavanaugh evinced a sense of dark humor toward the whole ordeal.

"Judge, we did thirty-eight hours in public with you. Did we have any private hearings with you?" asked Sasse.

"Yes," said Kavanaugh.

"Was that a fun time for you?" Sasse answered. "When people— senators could ask questions that are awkward or uncomfortable about potential alcoholism, potential gambling addiction, credit card debt, if your buddies floated you money to buy baseball tickets—did you enjoy that time we spent in here late one night?"

Kavanaugh flashed a wry smile. "I'm always happy to cooperate with the committee," he said.

A few minutes later, Democrats raised another issue that would haunt Kavanaugh in the days to follow: his temperament. Kavanaugh's enraged tirades and aggressive retorts had raised doubts in some quarters about his fitness for the Supreme Court, a place where objectivity and a cool head are required.

Ironically, Kavanaugh had brazenly violated his very own principles about "proper demeanor," which he had articulated just two years before in a speech about "The Judge as Umpire" to Catholic University of America's Columbus School of Law. "It is important," Kavanaugh said at the time, "to keep our emotions in check, and be calm amidst the storm. To put it in the vernacular: To be a good umpire and a good judge, don't be a jerk.

"A good judge and good umpire must demonstrate civility," Kavanaugh added. "Judges must show that we are trying to make the decisions impartially and dispassionately based on the law and not based on our emotions." He also said in the speech, "It is very important at the outset for a judge who wants to be an umpire to avoid any semblance of that partisanship, of that political background."

Democrats realized this issue had traction and exploited it. "Is temperament also an important trait for us to consider?" asked Mazie Hirono, the senator from Hawaii, in the hearing's third and final hour.

Kavanaugh seemed taken aback, as if he hadn't realized how he was coming off that day. "For twelve years, everyone who has appeared before me on the D.C. Circuit has praised my judicial temperament," he said, adding that he had a "well qualified" rating from the American Bar Association.

"So you agree that temperament is also an important factor for—"

"Yes. And the federal public defender, who testified to the committee, talked about how I had—was always open-minded and how I ruled in favor of unpopular defendants, how I was fair-minded. I think, universally, lawyers who've appeared before the D.C.—"

"So the answer is yes," replied Hirono, saying she had only five minutes and needed to move on.

Booker, who spoke a few minutes later, perhaps came the closest to a traditional cross-examination. Eyes wide and searching, his left hand raised for emphasis, Booker zeroed in on a few topics, repeating the questions over and over again if Kavanaugh tried to answer indirectly. Booker bore into Kavanaugh about whether he drank on weeknights, whether he considered Ford to be a political operative, and whether he regretted her coming forward. Kavanaugh maintained his composure, answering quietly but steadily that he thought all allegations should be taken seriously and that he and his family bore no ill will toward Ford and her family.

Toward the end of the hearing, Republican senator Ted Cruz suggested that Feinstein or her staff had leaked Ford's letter, a notion that had been floated repeatedly that afternoon. Feinstein, who had been stone-faced for much of the proceedings, asked for the floor.

"Mr. Chairman, let me be clear," she said. "I did not hide Dr. Ford's allegations. I did not leak her story. She asked me to hold it confidential, and I kept it confidential as she asked."

In reality, how the story had leaked never became clear. The fact that Ford's account—even the anonymous version of it—had leaked to the number-two executive at Facebook within days of Kavanaugh's addition to the short list meant that talk had been swirling around Silicon Valley for months before Ford went public. Staffers in Congresswoman Eshoo's office and Senator Feinstein's had both known Ford's story. Ford's close friends were aware of it, and, in seeking assistance for her, they had spread it to outer circles in their network.

Knowing the accuser's current profession and a modicum of her background, it wouldn't have been hard for an informed observer to put two and two together and alert the media. And anyone who did know the details could have leaked them to serve any number of agendas.

Cornyn asked for the floor, then turned to Feinstein. "Can you tell us that your staff did not leak it?" he asked.

"Oh, I don't believe my staff would leak it. I have not asked that question directly, but I do not believe they would," she answered.

Cornyn asked how, if that were the case, the Ford letter had reached the press.

Feinstein repeated that her staff had not leaked it.

Jeff Flake, the Arizona Republican, was one of the last to speak directly to Kavanaugh. In his speech, he tried to lower the temperature.

"This is not a good process, but it's all we've got," Flake said. "And I would just urge my colleagues to recognize that, in the end, we are twenty-one very imperfect senators trying to do our best to provide advice and consent. And in the end, there is likely to be as much doubt as certainty going out of this room today."

The Louisiana Republican John Kennedy had the last word. He asked Kavanaugh if he believed in God; Kavanaugh said he did. Then, one by one, he asked Kavanaugh to say whether the allegations of Ford, Ramirez, and Swetnick were true. Kavanaugh said they were not.

Kennedy pressed him: "No doubt in your mind?"

"Zero," said Kavanaugh. Then, mirroring Ford's final words that day, he added: "I'm 100 percent certain."

"Not even a scintilla?" said Kennedy.

"Not a scintilla; 100 percent certain, Senator."

"You swear to God?"

"I swear to God."

TWELVE

Falsus in Uno,
Falsus in Omnibus?

False in One Thing,
False in All Things?

At six feet eight inches and 215 pounds, Charles Ludington, known to his friends as Chad, was an obvious star on the Yale varsity basketball team. During college summers, he'd return home to North Carolina to work at basketball camps at NC State and UNC–Chapel Hill. After graduating, in 1987, he went on to play professional basketball in France for a year.

For the first half of college, Ludington's social life revolved mostly around basketball players—his fellow varsity teammates as well as a posse that included Brett Kavanaugh.

Thirty-five years later, in mid-September, Ludington, now an associate professor of history at North Carolina State University, was contacted by several reporters who wanted to ask about Kavanaugh's college behavior. Ludington declined to be interviewed, saying that he could not speak to the judge's professional capacities. After all, his career expertise was in eighteenth-century Britain and Ireland and the history of the wine industry.

But when he listened to his former classmate insist during his Fox interview that there was never a time when he drank so much that he couldn't remember what had happened the night before, Ludington began to feel "really uneasy," he later said.

"I felt that he was very clearly misleading people about his experiences in college," Ludington explained. "This is not someone who has grown up into an adult who says, 'Yes, I did a lot of stupid things and said things I regret about women and gays in college, but I'm a man now and I'm embarrassed by those things.' That's the demeanor I expected from someone who was trying out for the Supreme Court."

Ludington began to compose an essay in his head, but he didn't do much about it. Then he watched Kavanaugh testify after Ford.

Kavanaugh's portrayal of his drinking in college did not square with what Ludington remembered: a college classmate who would drink so much that he was completely "shit-faced" by the end of an evening. The Kavanaugh whom Ludington had known would slur his words and be belligerent. To see Kavanaugh spinning his college drinking in such a misleading way made Ludington decide to speak out. "I simply wanted to say, 'This is what I do know: the idea that Brett was never blacked out is preposterous," he later recalled. "Because you don't get as drunk as he got and remember everything."

Despite the occasional concessions—"Sometimes I had too many beers," for example, and the apology to Renate Dolphin—many of Kavanaugh's classmates from both Yale and Georgetown Prep felt he had shown a lack of candor. Like Ludington, they had observed Kavanaugh drunk and seemingly out of control at times. They had been that drunk themselves and believed they would admit it under the same circumstances. Anything less, these people felt, would be fundamentally dishonest—an unforgivable trait for a Supreme Court candidate.

On September 30, the Sunday after the contentious hearings, Ludington put out a statement. "I do not believe that the heavy drinking or even loutish behavior of an 18- or even 21-year-old should condemn a person for the rest of his life. I would be a hypocrite to think so," Ludington wrote. "However, I have direct and repeated knowledge about his drinking and his disposition while drunk. And I do believe that Brett's actions as a 53-year-old federal judge matter."

He continued: "I can unequivocally say that in denying the possibility that he ever blacked out from drinking, and in downplaying the degree and frequency of his drinking, Brett has not told the truth."

It was important to Ludington—and other Yale classmates of Kavanaugh's—to emphasize that he was not objecting to the drinking; he was objecting to the dissembling.

Yalies had initially been content to remain on the sidelines regarding Kavanaugh's nomination—though many of them disagreed with his politics. But after hearing Kavanaugh, in his Fox interview and his Senate testimony, cast himself as a veritable choir boy—who had focused on academics, church, and only "sometimes" had "too many beers"—many of them felt compelled to call foul.

"Brett stood up there and lied about who he was," said classmate Lynne Brookes on ABC News. "If he's gonna lie about the little things, what about the big things?"

Similarly, Kavanaugh's freshman-year roommate James Roche was offended by the notion that a Supreme Court nominee had failed to tell the truth. Since he and the judge had once slept just ten feet apart in a small college double room, Roche maintained that he had firsthand knowledge of Kavanaugh's level of drunkenness and its aftereffects during his freshman year.

"It wasn't drunk to the point of having trouble getting up every month or two, it was frequently," Roche told Anderson Cooper on CNN. "I saw him both what I would consider blackout drunk and also dealing with the repercussions of that in the morning."

Some of Kavanaugh's high school contemporaries also said he had lied under oath. Paul Rendón, Sean Hagan, and other classmates from Georgetown Prep attested that the salacious talk about a young Renate had been much more than a simple "show of affection," as Kavanaugh had put it in the hearing. "Being a stupid teenage boy does not include cruelty," Hagan wrote on Facebook. "So angry, so disgusted, so sad."

Kavanaugh tried to suggest that some of these classmates had an ax to grind, namely Roche. Asked in his September 25 telephone interview with the Judiciary Committee why Roche had painted him as a sloppy drunk, Kavanaugh said, "I'm not going to speculate beyond what I have said. It's the twilight zone."

This was where the hearings came to feel like *Rashomon*. Was Kavanaugh a misogynist lush who lied under oath about how much he drank? Or was he simply a brainy frat boy? In the intensely tribal politics of 2018, there was no such thing as somewhere in between; Kavanaugh became a human Rorschach test. Depending on their ideological perspective, people projected onto Kavanaugh what they needed him to be—a tragic casualty of #MeToo run amok, or the consummate symbol of white male privilege, triumphing yet again.

In a furious effort to counter the blackout narrative—that Kavanaugh had often been so drunk that he very possibly did not remember his conduct—the Republican spin machine mobilized. On October 1 the White House put out statements from two of Kavanaugh's college classmates, Dan Murphy and Chris Dudley, both of whom said they never saw Kavanaugh in a blackout state.

"I not only socialized with Brett, but I was there with him at the end of the night when we came home, and there in the morning when we got up," said Murphy, one of Kavanaugh's suitemates, in his statement. "I never saw Brett black out or not be able to remember the prior evening's events, nor did I ever see Brett act aggressive, hostile, or in a sexually aggressive manner to women.

"Brett was and is a good-natured, kind, and friendly person, to men and women," Murphy continued. "The behavior I've heard other people want to attribute to him, but from people who did not live with Brett and therefore not in the same position to observe, is simply wrong, and such behavior is incompatible with what I know to be true."

Dudley, a star basketball player in college who went on to a sixteen-year career in the NBA and was the Republican nominee for governor of Oregon in 2010, referred to Kavanaugh as "one of my best friends at Yale," describing him as a student who put academics first. "His desire to work very hard and make school his number one priority helped me stay focused," Dudley said. "But like nearly every other college student, we took breaks from school and went out for drinks and to see friends. I will say it again: we drank in college. I was with Brett frequently in college, whether it be in the gym, in class or socializing. I never ever saw Brett black out. Not one time. And in all the years I have known him, I have never seen him to be disrespectful or inappropriate with women."

Tom Kane, Kavanaugh's close friend from high school, said on CNN: "To the day I die, I'll believe that he did not do this."

THERE WERE ALSO DUELING VERDICTS on Kavanaugh's temperament. Some saw an arrogant white male throwing a tantrum about being denied a position he believed was his birthright. Kavanaugh's aggressive demeanor, his disrespect toward Democratic senators—especially Amy Klobuchar—and his brazen partisanship in accusing the Democrats of avenging the Clintons, they argued, made him clearly unfit for the court. Others said his demeanor was understandable as the boiling frustration of the wrongly accused.

"His performance at that second set of hearings was disqualifying, not to mention his lies," said Kathleen Clark, a law school professor at Washington University in St. Louis who went to law school with Kavanaugh and had had him come speak to her class on several occasions.

Kavanaugh's critics were not all from the political left. Charlie Sykes, a conservative commentator, said on a podcast that Kavanaugh's performance "was breathtaking as an abandonment of any pretense of having a judicial temperament.

"It's possible, I think, to have been angry, emotional, and passionate without crossing the lines that he crossed," Sykes added, "assuming that there are any lines anymore."

Benjamin Wittes, the editor in chief of the blog *Lawfare* and a senior fellow at the Brookings Institution, concurred in *The Atlantic*: "If I were a senator, I would not vote to confirm Brett Kavanaugh." Wittes added that he wrote those words "with no pleasure, but with deep sadness," since he had a long relationship with the judge.

"He delivered on Thursday, by way of defense, a howl of rage," Wittes wrote. "His opening statement was an unprecedentedly partisan outburst of emotion from a would-be justice. I do not begrudge him the emotion, even the anger. He has been through a kind of hell that would leave any person gasping for air. But I cannot condone the partisanship—which was raw, undisguised, naked, and conspiratorial—

from someone who asks for public faith as a dispassionate and impartial judicial actor. His performance was wholly inconsistent with the conduct we should expect from a member of the judiciary."

North Dakota senator Heidi Heitkamp had been close to announcing her support of Kavanaugh. Then she watched him testify. Like many, she was put off by Kavanaugh's belligerence toward Senator Klobuchar. "That was very much a concern about his judicial temperament, but also concern about his veracity," Heitkamp later said.

More than 2,400 law professors—including about a dozen from Yale—signed a letter saying, "The concern for judicial temperament dates back to our founding," and calling Kavanaugh unfit.

"Judge Brett Kavanaugh displayed a lack of judicial temperament that would be disqualifying for any court," the letter said. "We are united, as professors of law and scholars of judicial institutions, in believing that he did not display the impartiality and judicial temperament requisite to sit on the highest court of our land."

One of the most stinging critiques came from the elderly justice John Paul Stevens, who had previously supported Kavanaugh's nomination. At ninety-eight, Stevens was one of only four living retired Supreme Court justices. Kavanaugh, said Stevens, "has demonstrated a potential bias involving enough potential litigants before the court that he would not be able to perform his full responsibilities."

The political nature of Kavanaugh's testimony also prompted some former allies to reverse their stances on his fitness for the court. Two Yale Law School classmates, Mark Osler and Michael Proctor, who had signed an August letter of support now issued a retraction.

"The reason for our withdrawal is not the truth or falsity of Dr. Ford's allegations, which are still being investigated, but rather was the nature of Judge Kavanaugh's testimony," they wrote. "In our view that testimony was partisan, and not judicious, and inconsistent with what we expect from a Justice of the Supreme Court, particularly when dealing with a co-equal branch of government."

Though he did not share Kavanaugh's political bent, Osler had originally been moved to support him, based on the nominee's qualifications. "I reached out to friends who practiced in front of him on the D.C. Circuit, who said he was smart, he was fair, and he picked good clerks," Osler said in an interview.

But during the hearings, Osler, a former federal prosecutor who is now a professor at the University of St. Thomas School of Law, in Minneapolis, was "taken aback" by Kavanaugh's performance. "It was really painful, because this was someone who was a friend, who I really respected," Osler added. "Then when I saw what I saw during the hearing, it was a gut clench."

Even Kavanaugh loyalists said his testimony was a serious mistake, though perhaps not one of his own making. Many suspected he was performing for "an audience of one," meaning President Trump, who was widely known to have been disappointed in Kavanaugh's muted demeanor during the Fox News interview and who himself adopts more aggressive responses when under attack.

"I was surprised, because I think he was ill-advised," said George Priest, Kavanaugh's professor at Yale, of his irascible performance. "That's really not his way of doing things. I think some of the Trump people got to him."

While Kavanaugh's supporters believed the judge was justified in showing some anger, they also bemoaned his critical errors, namely invoking the Clintons and failing to own up to his past as a partier.

"He hurt his credibility a lot by prevaricating over that stuff," said one former colleague. "I don't think it amounts to perjury or an impeachable offense, but it was dumb and unnecessary. I gave him sort of a B minus for the overall performance, and I say that as a friend and someone who was really rooting for him."

Kavanaugh also should have shown more compassion for Ford, the colleague said: "I would have had him watch her testimony. There was a lot of room to be way more gracious than he was, even if you are just being tactical."

The other camp insisted that Kavanaugh's demeanor was that of a man fighting for his personal and professional life. "I would defy anyone not to be angry about that, if they believe the allegations against them were completely false," said Senator Cornyn, adding, "He became very emotional as he choked back tears. But I must say, he wasn't the only one choking back tears during his defense of his good name and his reputation."

Just as people empathized with Ford, many argued, so did they need to put themselves in Kavanaugh's shoes. "How do you want him to respond?" said Randy Berholtz, the Yale Law classmate. "Do you want him to sit there and take it, or do you want him to fight back? Imagine if it were your husband or your father or your brother. People can say anything about anybody and it's very hard to fight it.

"From what I know of him, this guy was a friggin' Boy Scout—he wouldn't strike you as a 'Hey, baby' type of guy," added Berholtz, now general counsel of Innovus Pharmaceuticals. "He struck me as somebody who would be a good dad—somebody who has a sense of service, somebody who has a sense of family, somebody who has a sense of religion and values. Clarence Thomas may have had a creepy side to him, but you're trying to make a sex fiend out of Brett Kavanaugh? So what? He had a few beers."

Some conservative pundits suggested that Kavanaugh also showed immeasurable courage in responding to the committee's questions that day.

"Please, tell us, when falsely accused of gang rape, when your family is facing death threats, and when you know that your political opponents are engineering and timing allegations to inflict maximum damage on you personally," asked the writer David French in *National Review*, "what is the proper amount of anger?"

Rebecca Taibleson, a former Kavanaugh clerk who is now an assistant United States attorney in Milwaukee, said the judge's loss of temper was moving and unfamiliar.

"Yes, I was taken aback by his emotion and anger, but I was also moved by it," she said in an interview later. "If I was falsely accused, I would be like this, too," she said. "If I'm looking at this objectively, to me it seemed like everyone who watched the testimony of Dr. Ford and Judge Kavanaugh saw in there what they wanted to see."

There is a compelling argument to be made that—particularly in the age of #MeToo—a more empathic, enlightened response was called for from Kavanaugh. He perhaps could have acknowledged the possibility that he had been involved in the Ford incident but not remembered it. He could have apologized for any harm done to Ford, condemned sexual assault, and encouraged victims to come forward.

But, particularly in the age of Trump, such a nuanced response would likely have doomed Kavanaugh's nomination. President Trump—whose MO in the face of sexual misconduct charges was to fight them—was looking for a forceful blanket denial. There was no room for ambiguity or nuance; any cracks in the judge's claims of innocence could allow Democrats to frame his words as an admission of guilt. He couldn't be a flawed human being, apologize to people he may have hurt in the past, and vow that he'd grown up and perhaps seen the error of his ways. It had worked for George W. Bush in explaining on the campaign trail his decision to stop drinking at age forty. But in the age of Trump, it was no longer an option.

"The only way this guy could survive was to go full Trump," said Ben Rhodes, Obama's former deputy national security adviser, who is now a writer and political commentator. "Once the bottom fell out, his only lifeline was to become a full-on Trump Republican. I saw that as a metaphor for what's happened to the entire Republican Party: they try to keep their dignity, but when push comes to shove, they have to resort to Trump.

"To see the Republicans not care about the damage they were doing to this institution in pursuit of power was one of the few moments in these last years that I was able to be shocked again," Rhodes continued, referring to the Supreme Court. "It was a pure distillation of the cynicism of their strategy, especially given that they could have just as easily suggested to him that he step aside. They were too far down the track with this guy."

THIRTEEN

Concordia Ordinum

Agreement Among
the Ranks

L ate on the evening of September 27, 2018, Senator Chris
Coons, the Democrat from Delaware, fell asleep with the
lights still on, his contact lenses still in, and his cell phone
under his face.

The balding former lawyer, who holds a master's degree from Yale
Divinity School, had spent the night responding to emails and reading through prep materials for the next morning's vote on whether
to advance Kavanaugh's nomination to the full Senate. Like much of
America, Coons had been shaken by Ford's distressing testimony and
unsettled by Kavanaugh's vitriolic response at the hearing earlier
that day.

Even more than that, Coons had been struck by the realization
that this was a watershed moment for people all over the country who
had experienced sexual assault. Ford's testimony, which he later said

he was hearing "through the ears of whole communities who have been living through comparable painful experiences," was both moving and eye-opening. "That made the contrast to then-Judge Kavanaugh's forceful pushback even sharper," Coons said, "and made me more conscious of the ways in which millions of Americans actually heard this."

When Kavanaugh came out to testify after Ford, Coons expected him to walk the line between expressing empathy and admitting guilt. He presumed Kavanaugh would apologize for the pain Ford had endured, perhaps leaving open the possibility that he had been the assailant she remembered but didn't know it due to his heavy drinking that night.

Instead, Kavanaugh cited his daughters' basketball teammates, his former female clerks, and his mom as a judge, Coons said, effectively using them as shields and portraying himself as the one who had been victimized. "They had laid out this entire case of this good and decent man who has entirely moved past any adolescent misogyny," the senator said. "I was utterly stunned by the forcefulness and aggressiveness of his defense, which was not just a denial but was an attack on Democrats on the committee on a partisan basis."

The morning after the hearing, Friday, September 28, Coons went over the remarks that had been prepared for him by his chief counsel, Erica Songer, a litigator and former federal law clerk. The draft read well. But Coons had woken up believing that the moment called for more. His goal: to articulate—as forcefully as possible—why Kavanaugh should not serve on the Supreme Court.

"I was convinced the committee was on the verge of simply barreling ahead and taking an up-or-down vote and not taking the time to seriously investigate Dr. Ford's allegation," he said. "If I'm trying to persuade my friend Jeff Flake," he said, referencing the moderate

Republican with whom he often shared positions, "I need to make a reasoned, positive, balanced appeal."

Flake was the man Coons most kept in mind as he revised his remarks, because he was one of three crucial swing votes on the Judiciary Committee. Flake was also a friend. Despite their party differences, the two men had been drawn together by shared interests and desire for bipartisanship where possible. Both had spent time in Africa in the 1980s—Coons studying in Kenya and elsewhere in East Africa during college, Flake on a mission for the Mormon Church in southern Africa.

Coons knew he had to appeal to Flake's interest in due process. "Doing things like that—respecting your opponent's key grievance or concern—is a way to move one step in their direction," Coons said, "and hopefully have them hear you."

On his way to the hearing room from his office, Coons ran into three female reporters who had been camped out during the confirmation process. They made small talk about the weekend. Coons mentioned his plan to take his daughter to the Global Citizen Festival, a free concert in New York's Central Park where Cardi B, Janet Jackson, and the Weeknd were to perform. Then one of the reporters showed him an unexpected tweet: Flake intended to vote for Kavanaugh. Coons, shocked, responded with a shower of expletives. Surrounded by the reporters' recording devices and fighting back tears, he then tried without success to formulate a more coherent response.

"I was watching him the whole day before," Coons later said of Flake. "I know him as a husband and a father. And I just couldn't believe that, despite Judge Kavanaugh's pointed rejoinder, that Jeff was still nonetheless going to go ahead and vote for him."

Flake, it turned out, had also endured a sleepless night. He was anxious over a different, though equally nettlesome, question: What

THE EDUCATION OF BRETT KAVANAUGH

precedent would it set if Kavanaugh was not confirmed? Ford's claims, while clear and heartfelt, were unproven. And if unsupported allegations could derail a distinguished public official, Flake feared, it could open the door to a deluge of irreparably damaged lives and careers, maybe due to old grudges or political differences rather than facts.

"That you could have an uncorroborated allegation—thirty-six years ago in this case—would be enough by itself to disqualify someone," Flake later said, "that was too much for me."

Flake had been reared on a cattle ranch in Snowflake, Arizona. He was a fiscal conservative and strict constructionist with an independent streak. During the Trump administration, Flake had been unafraid to break ranks. His 2017 book, *The Conscience of a Conservative*, had criticized the president's temperament as well as his trade policies. That same year, Flake had also announced plans to retire from the Senate amid flagging poll numbers, publicly blaming his party's "complicity" in supporting Trump. Retiring freed Flake from the perennial concerns about popularity and fund-raising that force many members of Congress to vote with the majority. Yet to many, his long, attention-getting farewell, coupled with rumors that he might challenge Trump in the 2020 GOP primary, smacked more of opportunism than true belief.

"Before the allegation came, I was ready to support him," Flake said of Kavanaugh. "I didn't particularly like his performance in the committee, obviously—he was blaming the Clintons, and his exchange with Senator Klobuchar I thought was out of line, but he conceded as much right afterwards."

Flake was in favor of adding a conservative-minded justice to the Supreme Court, and on that score, Kavanaugh was a compelling choice. Flake tried to put himself in Kavanaugh's shoes, to imagine how he would feel if he were similarly accused. He thought back to how the Democratic presidential candidate Michael Dukakis was criticized in 1988 for a lack of emotion when asked if he would support the death penalty should his wife, Kitty, be raped and murdered. (Dukakis said that, as a longtime opponent of capital punishment, he would not.) Now Kavanaugh was under fire for the opposite problem: having too much emotion.

"You got to think, if somebody feels they were unjustly accused, that they would be angry," Flake said in an interview.

Flake was also weighing Kavanaugh's record on the bench and his estimable professional reputation. Flake knew that, despite the previous day's outbursts, many of Kavanaugh's colleagues had praised his equanimity.

These thoughts were on the senator's mind when he stepped into a Hart building elevator that Friday morning. On his way into the elevator, he was accosted by two sexual assault survivors who had come to protest Kavanaugh's confirmation. Together they blocked the door, preventing it from closing as they yelled their protests at the senator. "What you are doing is allowing someone who actually violated a woman to sit on the Supreme Court," said Ana Maria Archila, a community organizer from Queens, New York, while jabbing her finger at Flake. Her voice was emotional; she sounded near tears. "What are you doing, sir?"

Flake, stuck in the corner of the elevator car with a bank of cameras suddenly trained on him, his dirty-blond hair bathed in fluorescent light, looked wretched. He pursed his lips and frowned, at times looking down at the floor while he listened. He poked at the elevator buttons with his right finger.

"I was sexually assaulted and nobody believed me," Maria Galla-gher, another protester, shouted to Flake. "I didn't tell anyone, and you're telling all women that they don't matter."

Urged on by the nearby reporters, one of whom dangled a camera by the elevator doors, Archila grilled Flake about his response to Kavanaugh.

"Senator Flake, do you think Brett Kavanaugh is telling the truth?"

Flake nodded, his eyes glancing at the floor, and appeared to say yes.

"Do you think that he is able to hold the pain of this country and repair it?" asked Archila. "That is the work of justice." She lectured him about the injustice of allowing a man who had harmed a woman to ascend to such a powerful position, still pointing her finger at the downcast Republican. She asked again if Flake believed that Kavanaugh had told the truth. He continued to nod as one of his aides tried to wrap up the conversation by referring Archila to their spokesperson, thanking her for her feedback.

"Saying thank you is not an answer," shouted Archila. "This is about the future of our country, sir!"

After a struggle to either stay inside and close the door or walk out with Archila still blocking the way, Flake began to step forward. "I just issued a statement," he said over the shouting voices and the buzzing of the elevator door, which was trying to close. "I'll be saying more soon."

By the time Flake and Coons entered the committee room, both were unsettled. Convinced that the Republicans were determined to roll forward with Kavanaugh's confirmation, some members of the Judiciary Committee considered a walkout. Klobuchar and Coons, who sat next to each other on the dais, discussed whether to leave or stay and say their piece.

They weren't the only two engaged in doomsaying and last-ditch strategies—either to jettison or cement Kavanaugh's nomination. As the hearing began, Lindsey Graham framed the debate in dire terms. "This has been about delay and destruction, and if we reward this, it is the end of good people wanting to be judges," he argued. "It is the end of any concept of the rule of law. It's the beginning of a process that will tear this country apart."

Having decided to stay, Klobuchar said it was outrageous to proceed and not investigate. "Where is the bravery in this room?" she asked, adding of Kavanaugh, "What is he afraid of if we just spend one week looking at the evidence?"

Then, after Senator Cruz weighed in—"All of us should remember that we're talking about real human beings here. These aren't pawns on a chessboard"—it was Coons's turn.

"You know me—you know I try to be fair to nominees that come before us," he said. He had circles under his eyes and looked grave in his dark suit and American flag lapel pin. "If I were convinced this were nothing more than a partisan hit job designed to take down a good man and hold a position vacant past the election, I would not stand for it."

In light of Ford's testimony and calls he'd personally received from other victims, Coons added, "There is an ocean of pain in this nation, not yet fully heard, not yet fully addressed, not yet appropriately resolved. And I, for one, will not countenance the refrain said by too many in response to these allegations by Dr. Ford that it happened too long ago and that in our nation, boys will be boys. We must do better than that, and we must set a better standard than that for our own families and our future.

"To ask for a week," he concluded, "is not to ask for too much."

Coons's comments were bracing for Flake, who was still processing the encounter he'd just had with Archila and Gallagher. A religious man, Flake appreciated what he later called the "Presbyterian" nature of Coons's speech, in which his colleague had mentioned prayers for Kavanaugh, for Ford, and for the country. Delivered by an ordained minister who occasionally preached in his home state, its tone was measured and humble.

Flake thought a one-week FBI investigation into Ford's claims sounded reasonable. The FBI could work quickly, he knew. And if extending the time frame would make citizens feel better about the Senate's decision, it was worth doing.

The strain of the day was by now showing on Flake's somber face. He stood up and started walking out. Then he tapped Coons on the shoulder and they headed toward the chamber's anteroom.

Standing in that cramped, closet-like space, where the only decorations were a photograph of the Capitol Building lit at night and the beige, red, and green spines of reference volumes on the shelf, Coons expected Flake to try to let him down easy. He'd apologize for their differences, Coons thought, and say he still planned to vote with his caucus.

Instead, Flake was about to change course.

"Look, this is tearing our committee apart, this is tearing our country apart. Can you deliver on what you just said?" Flake asked. He looked almost ill as he spoke.

"Be clear, Jeff," replied Coons. "What are you asking?'"

Flake explained that Coons had made a good argument. He thought it was fair, he said, to pause for further investigation. But not if it was to become a "six-week wild-goose chase," he added.

"I don't speak for the Democratic caucus, I speak for me," Coons said. Still, he added, he was fairly confident that his left-leaning colleagues wouldn't drag out the process for political purposes. They knew even a week was a Republican concession at this point, given that Kavanaugh seemed to have the votes he needed.

Coons acknowledged the political risks of a delay. "Let's be clear: we're going to hold hands and jump off a bridge here," he said. But the two agreed that to move ahead without a fuller investigation would be to disrespect both sexual assault survivors and the American concept of due process.

A short while later, Klobuchar walked in and joined their conversation. Cornyn and Graham followed. Soon almost every committee member had crammed into the anteroom, which was essentially just a carpeted ramp with little more than a small table and a coffeemaker.

They began arguing over Coons and Flake's proposal, with many Republicans objecting to the delay of another investigation. Some argued that the extension would open a Pandora's box, inviting new allegations that couldn't be run down in the time available. It was too much for Democrats to ask, they said.

To gain privacy, Coons and Flake squeezed themselves into the room's telephone booth, containing a narrow desk and a landline phone behind a door marked SENATORS ONLY. The two barely fit inside. After huddling for about fifteen minutes, they called their Republican colleagues Senators Susan Collins of Maine and Lisa Murkowski of Alaska, both of whom had been perturbed by the Ford allegations and were known for consensus building. Flake wanted them to join him in insisting on an FBI investigation so that he could then go to Majority Leader Mitch McConnell and tell him he had three Republican senators who wouldn't vote to move forward on Kavanaugh without the added investigation.

He soon succeeded.

Having secured Collins and Murkowski, Flake tried to get Christopher Wray on the phone, but the FBI director was unreachable in

Alaska. Instead, he received a call back from the deputy attorney general, Rod J. Rosenstein. During that call, George W. Bush tried to reach Flake, having heard from Republicans like Cornyn that Flake was wavering. The former president had been advocating privately for weeks on Kavanaugh's behalf. But Flake, who was at that point tied up on another line with Rosenstein, didn't take Bush's call.

"Kavanaugh had worked for him—he thought a lot of him," Flake said later of Bush. "It was a very intense hour or two back there."

Crucial to Flake was arriving at a bipartisan agreement. In his view, that was the only way the country could begin to heal. "I wanted people to feel better about it," he said. "I didn't know that it would change any votes."

But to those intensely opposed to Kavanaugh, feeling better about it seemed like thin gruel. As the negotiations were taking place, government buildings filled with protesters, some of whom were removed by police officers. The media frantically tried to figure out what was happening with the Senate procedure. After Flake reentered the hearing room, Grassley called on him.

"I think it would be proper to delay the floor vote for up to but not more than one week in order to let the FBI do an investigation, limited in time and scope to the current allegations," Flake said in his remarks. "We ought to do what we can to make sure that we do all due diligence with a nomination this important."

There followed some confusion. "Could we have a description?" Feinstein said.

"What are we voting on?" Patrick Leahy added.

Grassley responded, "We are voting on the motion to report the nomination to the floor. The clerk will call the roll."

Feinstein cut in. "Whoa, that's not my understanding of what—" she said.

Grassley called the vote. Flake voted to advance the nomination to the full Senate with the caveat of a one-week delay, as did all the other Republican senators. Eight Democrats voted against the motion, and two stayed silent in protest.

Because of the narrow 51–49 majority, McConnell was forced to agree to the motion, and Trump in turn ordered the FBI to conduct a limited "supplemental" investigation "in less than a week."

WHILE THE SENATORS deliberated over the need for an additional FBI investigation, Greg Pappajohn, one of Kavanaugh's old friends from Georgetown Prep, was meeting with Don Urgo uptown.

A popular high school football player who had been vice president of the student body as a senior, Pappajohn hadn't attended recent reunions or kept in touch with most of his high school crowd. His email wasn't even included on the blast notes that went out to fellow alums to coordinate events or initiatives, like the letter of support for Kavanaugh. But amid the clamor of September, Pappajohn—now a successful Wall Street investor who had managed a large investment portfolio for the billionaire hedge-fund manager George Soros— resurfaced. He reached out to his friend Don Urgo, and they agreed to meet for lunch.

Sitting in a booth over crab cakes at Clyde's in Chevy Chase, reconnecting after so long, made both Urgo and Pappajohn emotional. Now Pappajohn wanted to know what was going on with their most prominent classmate.

"Look, what's the freaking story here?" he asked Urgo of the Ford allegations. "This is a bunch of BS, correct?"

Urgo, who had attended the highly charged hearing the day before, said yes, there was nothing to Ford's allegations. The two friends discussed the issues that Kavanaugh—and their entire alumni community—were facing.

"This is a big problem," said Pappajohn. "They're going to destroy him, whether it's right or wrong."

Pappajohn argued that both Kavanaugh and Georgetown Prep needed a media strategy, including the hiring of a skilled public-relations professional who could better articulate their stories to the public. Keenly aware of the negative impact of the Kavanaugh accusations, Pappajohn had been composing emails to his own two sons, both young adults, hoping to reassure them that many of the stories emerging about his years at Prep were false.

"The substance of my letter to my sons was, one, don't believe what you are reading. It's nonsense," Pappajohn later said. "One hundred kegs or bust was a rallying cry, but no one ever treated women disrespectfully that I was aware of or saw."

In the middle of the lunch, Urgo's mobile phone rang. He answered.

"You'll never believe who I'm talking to," Urgo said to the caller. Then he handed the phone to Pappajohn.

"It's P. J.," said the caller—the third Georgetown Prep boy Ford had remembered from the gathering where she was assaulted who she thought might have helped her had he heard her cries from the bedroom.

"P. J.," said Pappajohn, who hadn't seen Smyth since their graduation in 1983, "I heard that Ms. Ford thinks you're a really nice guy."

"Pappajohn," Smyth replied, "I gotta tell you something. I've never seen her. I have no idea who this is. This woman is telling the world what a nice guy I am and I have no idea who she is."

AS THE FBI BEGAN ITS WORK, Dr. James Dobson, founder of the conservative advocacy groups Family Talk and Focus on the Family, reported that Ashley Kavanaugh had asked family and friends to pray Psalm 40 for her family and for the nation.

> I waited patiently for the Lord; and he inclined unto me, and
> heard my cry.
> He brought me up also out of a horrible pit, out of the miry
> clay, and set my feet upon a rock, and established my
> goings.
> And he hath put a new song in my mouth, even praise unto
> our God: many shall see it, and fear, and shall trust in
> the Lord.

FOURTEEN

Confirmatio: Sed Quis Custodiet Custodes?

Confirmation: But Who Will Watch the Watchers?

The FBI investigation—which, officially speaking, was merely an extension of the background check that had already been performed on Kavanaugh—was controversial even before it began.

The parameters were the first point of contention. Dictated by the White House, which had the right to direct the due diligence investigations of its own Supreme Court nominee, the initial orders were to limit the scope to parties who had been privy to the events alleged by Ford and Ramirez. Swetnick's allegations were seen as too far-fetched and unsubstantiated to merit serious investigation.

Although there were additional witnesses who might have substantiated the stories beyond the few who had allegedly attended the Ford gathering and those whom Ramirez put in the room when

Kavanaugh allegedly exposed himself, the Republicans felt strongly that the investigation should be contained.

"Anybody with firsthand knowledge or alleged to have firsthand knowledge" were intended to be on the FBI's list, Flake later recalled. "But it wouldn't have to extend to the next level, which would technically [be] hearsay. You know: 'I heard he drank a lot,' or whatever else. Didn't need to go there. But it could expand beyond those if new information came out in those interviews."

The lawyers representing Ford and Ramirez were eager to help buttress their clients' allegations. On Friday, Katz and Bromwich sent a letter to the FBI suggesting a list of thirteen witnesses "who could either attest to Ford's character and honesty or perhaps corroborate her recollections from the 1980s, as well as scores of unnamed potential witnesses who had attended school with Kavanaugh, attended parties with him, or been quoted in recent articles about his drinking and social habits."

Buried in the letter was the allegation regarding Tracy Harmon Joyce, a Yale classmate of Kavanaugh's and close friend of Ramirez's. "We have been advised that while at Yale, Mr. Kavanaugh exposed himself to Ms. Harmon Joyce and forced her to touch his penis," the letter stated. "Witnesses were present and we have been advised that they will be contacting the FBI with their first-hand accounts," it added, using the keyword "first-hand" from the FBI probe's intended parameters. It was the same account that Max Stier, the good-government advocate and classmate of Kavanaugh's, had provided to legislators but not spoken about publicly. How Ford's lawyers had heard about it was not clear.

Right away there was confusion, not just about the scope of the investigation but also about who was running it. Bromwich spent the better part of the evening of Friday the 28th trying to identify the correct recipient of his and Katz's letter, calling the emergency hotline at both the Justice Department and the FBI to request FBI director Wray's email address. He sent the note to an address for Wray, but it bounced back. Finally, Dana Boente, the FBI's general counsel, called Bromwich, suggesting he direct the letter to him.

Coons was having a similar struggle as he sought information on the probe and its restrictions, which struck him as overly narrow from the outset. Nothing had been distributed to him or his colleagues on paper explaining the scope of the inquiry. According to Coons, Mc-Gahn had said it was appropriate for Congress to shape the probe's boundaries. But it soon seemed to Coons that "Congress" in this case meant the majority leaders, namely Grassley and McConnell, without input from the minority senators.

"Majority counsel was already asserting that they spoke for the full committee," Coons said months later. Yet "my recollection is that in every confirmation hearing and in every comparable issue, the majority and the minority worked out the scope of questioning and investigation . . . and that was based on a decades-long precedent."

Together, Coons, Flake, Murkowski, and Collins brainstormed how many witnesses ought to be interviewed, and the number that came to mind was well into the double digits. With enough agents involved, they believed, the interviews could be handled efficiently, rapidly covering a large number of Kavanaugh contemporaries who might shed light on his youthful behavior. Their own offices were getting calls from people who said they could corroborate Ramirez's account, among other tips. But it seemed that the wider outreach those senators envisioned wasn't happening.

On Saturday, President Trump said the FBI agents would have "free rein" over the potential interviewees in the investigation. But *The New York Times* soon reported that just four people—Judge,

Keyser, Smyth, and Ramirez—were scheduled to be interviewed. The White House was calling the shots, though Republican leaders had helped draft the witness list.

By Saturday evening, Trump tweeted that the White House was open to further interviews if the findings of the inquiry demanded them: "I want them to interview whoever they deem appropriate, at their discretion," he said.

On Sunday afternoon, Coons called McGahn on his cell phone. They talked for an hour, during which Coons learned the hard way that there was no rule book to consult in a situation like this, no precedent or standard procedure.

"He was driving his kids to Little League practice or something like that," recalled Coons of McGahn. "He kept insisting that this investigation was going to be done 'by the book.' I had already had the conversation with Flake and Murkowski where it was clear to me that that was important to them. So I said, 'Don, thank you, this is great. Send me the book.'"

McGahn fell silent on the other end of the line.

"Don, can you just have your folks forward to my office the memo, the policy guidance?" asked Coons.

"Well, no," said McGahn.

Coons asked if that was because McGahn found the request inappropriate or because the memo didn't exist. "It's not exactly a book," McGahn said.

So how was the probe being handled? Coons asked.

The way it was normally done, McGahn replied.

By the end of the conversation, "I concluded that there was no book," Coons said. "There was no tightly defined process."

That Sunday, on the national political talk-show circuit, open warfare broke out between angry Democratic senators and Kavanaugh supporters in the White House and Senate. Klobuchar said on CBS's *Face the Nation* that the Republican-mandated boundaries of the late-stage investigation were akin to asking the FBI to "interview the people in their neighborhood on one side of the street." White House counselor Kellyanne Conway fired back at Democrats on CNN, saying that the additional inquiry was necessarily and appropriately circumscribed and "not meant to be a fishing expedition."

Senate Democrats sent the Bureau a list of two dozen suggested witnesses. Ramirez's legal team gave the FBI a list of at least twenty-five individuals who may have had corroborating evidence. Ford, by now back in California but still living in a secure location away from home, put aside some documents the FBI might want to see. They included text threads, emails from the summer discussing her memory of assault, and therapist notes attesting to those memories that she considered private and had not wished to share with the committee staff.

AS THE POLITICAL LEADERSHIP tussled over the Kavanaugh probe, Keyser reported to an FBI field office near her home in Silver Spring, Maryland. She was under the impression that she was the first witness to be interviewed.

For Keyser, Ford's public claims had set in motion a difficult ordeal. The media had hounded her from the moment her name began circulating as the friend who might corroborate Ford's allegations—calling, messaging, and camping out near her home. She thought she was under surveillance, and, with reporters surrounding her house, at times she was. On September 22, about a week after Ford came forward with her claims in *The Washington Post*, Keyser had provided a statement saying that she did not know Kavanaugh and could not recall the incident in question. The following day, September 23, she had told a reporter that although she didn't remember those things, she had been a close friend of Ford's at the time and believed her account to be true.

Over the years, Keyser had remained involved with the friends and institutions of her childhood, if intermittently. She was still a member at the Columbia Country Club, where she married her first husband, the Democratic political consultant Bob Beckel, in 1992, after a three-year courtship marked by golf and partying. "Leland was a very talented golfer," Beckel wrote in his 2015 autobiography of his life, career, and alcoholism. "It also turned out she was a big drinker."

Ford (then Blasey), who had attended a golf tournament in Palm Springs to watch Leland play in 1991, was also a guest at the Beckels' wedding, along with Walter Mondale, the former vice president from Minnesota whose unsuccessful 1984 presidential campaign Beckel had managed. It was one of a number of times the girlfriends would see each other in the decades after high school.

Keyser and Ford had reunited most recently at an East Coast gathering of a half dozen high school friends in April, during a trip Ford had made to celebrate her grandmother's one hundredth birthday. About six months later, after the world had learned Ford's story about Kavanaugh, Keyser expressed concern that she had perhaps failed to come through for her friend at the time of the attack. "I did speak to her, briefly, a couple of times—just 'Are you okay?'" recalled Keyser. "Basically I just wanted to make sure she was okay, and she had not outcried."

Asked what she meant by the word "outcried," Keyser translated it as "cried out."

She explained further. "I was worried when this went down that something had happened that night with those boys," she said, "and I had driven her home or I had helped and she outcried and said she was assaulted and I forgot about it." But Ford assured her, in their conversation after the news frenzy, that, no, she hadn't told Keyser or anyone else about the incident at the time.

Leland eventually divorced Beckel, with whom she'd had two children, and married a man named John Keyser, whom she also later divorced. She had met her lawyer, Howard Walsh, through the Columbia Country Club. A boisterous personality with salt-and-pepper hair who also loved to golf, Walsh was the father of nine and a regular at Blessed Sacrament, the Chevy Chase Catholic church Brett and Ashley Kavanaugh attended.

Walsh handled a range of legal matters for clients from his solo practice in Rockville. One area of focus for him was addiction, and clients who needed advice in navigating the legal problems that could accompany the disease as they attempted to recover. He was also friendly with Ford's brothers.

By the time of the fiery Senate hearing, some of the Holton women who supported Ford had grown frustrated with Keyser. Her comments about the alleged Kavanaugh incident had been too limited, some of them felt, and did not help their friend's case. Surely, given what a close friend Keyser had been, she could say more to substantiate Ford's testimony and general veracity, even if she could not corroborate Ford's more specific memories.

"Let's hope Leland tells the truth this time," said Cheryl Amitay—who had graduated from Holton a year after Ford—in a group text on September 28, a day after the hearing, as the FBI investigation was taking shape. Amitay, who had been treated roughly by boys in high school herself, had quickly become an outspoken supporter of Ford's. She had sat behind Ford during the prior day's testimony and agreed to defend her on television.

"Maybe one of you guys who are friends with her can have a heart to heart," Amitay continued in the text about Keyser. "I don't care, frankly, how fucked up her life is. A lot of us have fucked up lives in one way or another."

One of Ford's classmates, Lulu Gonella, responded that she was planning to meet with Keyser and her lawyer within the hour. Another then cautioned Gonella to be careful in that conversation, given that it would be inappropriate to put pressure on Keyser.

Amitay agreed. "If she changes or amend [*sic*] her statement," she texted, "it needs to hold up."

Another friend—a man who had gone to Landon, Holton's brother school—jumped in with a suggestion on Keyser that read like a veiled reference to her addictive tendencies. "Perhaps it makes sense to let everyone in the public know what her condition is," he said. "Just a thought."

Amitay answered, "Leland is a major stumbling block. Maybe she can attest to being in similar situations with Chrissy that summer, as I'm assuming they both belong to the club and hung out and swim there. . . . She can definitely put out something more supportive is the bottom line. Not looking for fabrication."

The exact details of the meeting at Gonella's house aren't clear. But whatever was actually said there, Keyser later said she felt pressured by both Gonella and Ford's friend Monica McLean to change her story.

"I was told behind the scenes that certain things could be spread about me if I didn't comply," Keyser later said. "So that's where the 'Monica McLean put pressure on me' came from," referring to a *Wall Street Journal* story, published on October 5, stating that McLean had pushed Keyser to "revisit" her story.

Through a lawyer, McLean, a retired FBI agent herself, called the notion that she either pressured Keyser to alter her account or threatened to disclose personal information about Keyser "absolutely false." She added that she "stressed to Ms. Keyser the importance of providing truthful information to the Senate Judiciary Committee." Gonella declined to comment for this book.

Keyser's lawyer, Walsh, sent a letter to the Judiciary Committee on the day Keyser was scheduled to meet with the FBI for the first time. The letter, which quickly leaked to CNN and other news outlets, said that although Keyser had told the press that she believed Ford's account, "the simple and unchangeable truth is that she is unable to corroborate it because she has no recollection of the incident in question."

In the days that followed, Judge and Smyth also met with the FBI. Both had submitted statements on September 18 denying that they had ever attended a gathering like the one Ford described. Now they were asked to contextualize their friendships with Kavanaugh in high school and the social behavior of the 1980s.

Judge, a writer and conservative commentator who had authored two books based on his experience at Georgetown Prep—which he sometimes referred to by the fictionalized name "Loyola Prep"—seemingly had much to contribute. His books talked about himself and his friends through a mix of barely concealed doppelgangers and true facts about Judge's own upbringing and schooling. There were references to excessive drinking, teenage sex, and trashed homes. Judge himself was an alcoholic who had been in recovery for close to thirty years. Before that, he was widely known as funny and clever but also at times as a poorly behaved, blackout drunk. In his book *Wasted*, Judge chronicled his Beach Week adventures in the summer of 1981, right after sophomore year at Prep:

"We lit each other's underwear on fire, had beer fights, and barfed in the sink. A couple of guys took pictures of their penises, and when it became evident that one of the guys had a member that slanted, we called him Slope. . . . There were girls in and out constantly. . . . Most of the time everyone, including the girls, was drunk. If you could breathe and walk at the same time, you could hook up with someone. This did not mean going all the way for the most part . . . but after a year spent in school without girls, heavy petting was virtually an orgy."

Kavanaugh, obliquely featured in *Wasted* as the puking "Bart O'Kavanaugh," was not happy about the book's publication. At his fifteenth Georgetown Prep reunion, Kavanaugh—then working for the law firm Kirkland & Ellis—told a classmate that he had threatened Judge, saying, "If you use my name, I'll sue you." Nobody was surprised. ("In all fairness," the classmate to whom Kavanaugh made the statement said, "I think the rest of the class would have told Mark that, too.")

Judge had spent much of September 2018 dodging journalists, hiding away in the Bethany Beach, Delaware, home of family friends from Potomac. On September 24, a *Washington Post* reporter tracked him down there, spotting a car parked in the house's driveway containing "piles of clothing, a collection of Superman comics and a package addressed to Judge at the Potomac home where he lived three years ago." The newspaper ran a photo of Judge on his cell phone in a red T-shirt and baseball cap. Before declining further comment, Judge asked the *Post* reporter, "How'd you find me?"

In fact, Judge had often been itinerant since his family home in Potomac was sold a few years earlier, amid his mother's declining health. (His father had died of cancer years earlier.) Since then, Judge had frequently relied on the spare rooms or homes of friends and family. In the run-up to the Kavanaugh hearings, Judge had chatted on the phone with reporters, reliving fond memories from his

Georgetown Prep days in a way that was supportive of the judge. But as the Ford allegations surfaced in September—allegations upon which only Judge could shed light, as the one alleged eyewitness—Judge, who had always been so expansive about his high school years, suddenly clammed up.

"I think a couple hours with the FBI will sober up even the most recalcitrant drunk," said Michael Judge, Mark's estranged older brother, in a later interview. "The paranoia of being interrogated by the feds, I'm sure it scared the hell out of [him]."

Patrick Smyth—the Prep buddy with whom Kavanaugh had stayed in closer touch than he had with Judge—had his FBI interview around the same time as Judge. Smyth later told friends at the Georgetown Prep reunion that Ford's claims were a dead end because there was nothing to them. He also said that he had agreed to the FBI meeting as a way to proactively help Kavanaugh rather than wait for a subpoena.

On September 30, Ramirez went to her lawyer John Clune's Boulder conference room to be interviewed by two Colorado-based FBI agents: Kevin P. Hoyland and Amy Howard.

Ramirez's lawyer Stan Garnett, also present, was pleased that the supervisory special agent was Todd Sandstedt, having worked closely with him when he was district attorney. "He's career FBI through and through—very professional, very appropriate," Garnett said. "I said, 'Make sure you bring in people who know how to do trauma-informed interviewing.' He said, 'I've got two good people who will do a really good job with this,' and they did do a really good job."

The night before the interview, Ramirez finally had her first good night's sleep in weeks. "I thought, 'They're going to listen and put it all together and spend time,'" she said. "I was very hopeful, and the agents were very nice."

During the meeting, which lasted about two hours, the agents asked Ramirez many questions. At one point, she took a break to stretch her legs. At the end, as the agents were on their way out, one said something to the effect of "We find you credible."

"They made that comment," Clune said. "And they said, 'Look, we'll do whatever we are authorized to do and we'll do it as well as we can, I can promise you that.'"

Yet Bill Pittard, another Ramirez lawyer, said the agents also made clear that their hands were tied, explaining, "'We have to wait to get authorization to do anything else,'" he recalled. "It was almost a little apologetic."

WHILE THE FBI was interviewing its top four witnesses, others who believed they had relevant information were trying to contact the agency. One of them was Kavanaugh's college classmate Kerry Berchem, now a senior attorney at the prominent law firm Akin Gump Strauss Hauer & Feld, in Manhattan. After watching Ford's testimony, Berchem notified the office of her home senator, Democratic Richard Blumenthal of Connecticut, of her belief that certain texts she'd exchanged with classmate and close friend Karen Yarasavage raised questions as to whether Kavanaugh and his friends or representatives had been trying to influence events as far back as July.

Berchem's exchanges with Yarasavage had started with seemingly innocent social contacts, but—in the context of the Ford and Ramirez allegations—they had taken on importance as potentially relevant material to show the FBI.

On August 30, Yarasavage was one of ten women from Kavanaugh's class who signed a letter to the Senate Judiciary Committee, expressing "admiration and respect for our friend, Brett," and prais-ing him as "immensely generous, intelligent, and warm."

Nearly a month later, on September 23, when the *New Yorker* story about Ramirez's encounter with Kavanaugh came out, Yarasavage texted Berchem in reference to the alleged party during freshman year: "I don't know if I was there. My story is that we were such close friends who shared many intimate details with each other and I never heard a word of this."

Yarasavage suggested that Ramirez had confused Kavanaugh with another Yale classmate who had "pulled his unit out."

"Could she be so wildly mistaken??" she said of Ramirez.

Berchem cautioned Yarasavage against casting aspersions on Ramirez, warning that it "will kill your friendship" and defending Ramirez as "the opposite of manipulative."

Yarasavage was dismissive. "What friendship?" she asked, alluding to the fact that Ramirez had recently distanced herself. "I haven't spo-ken to her in 10 years." She added that Ramirez was her daughter's godmother but had "basically abandoned that ship."

Berchem was upset by Yarasavage's callous response to Ramirez's potential trauma.

"Karen I am not trying to tell you what to do," Berchem wrote. "Who am I to do so. But is there a reason that she fell off the grid? And if in fact this happened do you want to be part of hurting her even further?"

Later that day, Yarasavage texted Berchem that she had received a call from "Brett's guy," adding later, "Brett asked me to go on record and now *New Yorker* aren't answering their phones!"

Kavanaugh was questioned about the Yarasavage-Genda wedding during a private Judiciary Committee interview on September 25.

Asked if he had interacted with Ramirez at the wedding, Kavanaugh replied, "I'm sure I saw her, because it wasn't a huge wedding. And at any wedding, you would see the people that you went to school with. But I don't have a specific recollection."

Kavanaugh was also asked whether, prior to the publication of the *New Yorker* piece, he had ever "discussed or heard discussion about the incident" Ramirez described in *The New Yorker*. He answered, "No."

On September 27, Senator Orrin Hatch asked Kavanaugh during the hearings, "When did you first hear of Ms. Ramirez's allegations against you?"

Kavanaugh answered, "In the last—in the period since then, the *New Yorker* story."

Bob Bauer, former White House counsel for President Obama, subsequently remarked to NBC News: "It would be surprising, and it would certainly be highly imprudent, if at any point Judge Kavanaugh directly contacted an individual believed to have information about allegations like this."

Berchem sent a summary of her text history with Kavanaugh (including an attachment of the messages, with some names redacted) to Senators Blumenthal, Murkowski, Flake, and Collins on Friday, September 28. To Berchem, these texts suggested that Kavanaugh had anticipated the Ramirez allegations before they surfaced in *The New Yorker* for the first time.

But the texts were not given to the FBI by the Republican committee staff. "After we were made to jump through several hoops that delayed our moving forward, it became clear that the majority committee staff had not turned this summary over to the FBI and, in fact, had no intention of turning it over to the FBI," a spokeswoman for Senator Blumenthal told NBC News. "With our assistance, Kerry submitted her summary to the FBI herself."

George Hartmann, a Grassley spokesman, responded that Berchem's texts "do not appear relevant or contradictory to Judge Kavanaugh's testimony."

"This appears to be another last-ditch effort to derail the nomination with baseless innuendo by Democrats who have already decided to vote no," Hartmann said.

Between September 30 and October 3, Berchem made three submissions to the FBI's online portal, spoke with three people answering phones for the FBI, and had several email exchanges with an FBI agent.

Other Kavanaugh classmates also went to great lengths to connect with the FBI. Mark Krasberg wanted to share the names of people he believed would corroborate the Ramirez claims. Between Friday, September 28, and Thursday, October 4, Krasberg contacted three different Senate offices, an FBI field office, and the Senate Judiciary Committee in order to convey his information, but he was passed around, cut short, or ignored until the final hours of the inquiry on October 5.

Ken Appold, another Yale classmate, had a similar experience. After being passed around from email to an 800 number to an online form, he wondered whether the FBI or other decision makers were taking Kavanaugh tips seriously.

Later, he noted that none of the people Ramirez said were in the room—Genda, Dave Todd, and Dave White—"came forward and said, 'I was there and this didn't happen.'"

Instead, Appold added, they all said, "'I have no recollection.'"

Appold himself never heard from the FBI. "I wasn't surprised; the investigative powers of the FBI were too limited," he said. "It wasn't part of their mandate to do more than was absolutely necessary."

"If they had interviewed me," he added, "I would have been happy to cooperate."

Yale classmate Kathleen Charlton also tried in vain to reach the FBI.

Todd, Genda, and White did not respond to interview requests for this book.

In 2019, sitting on her favorite couch in the modest but comfortable three-level house she shares with her husband in Boulder, Colorado, Ramirez now looked very different from the bright-eyed, smiley young woman who came to Yale in 1983 prepared to assume the best in people. The cute bangs, plump cheeks, and high-waisted jeans had been replaced by straight hair, lean features, and a world-weariness. Instead of the buoyancy many of her classmates remember, Ramirez had grown decidedly earthbound.

She choked up as she talked about friends like Dave Todd failing to speak up on her behalf. Indeed, it was hard for Ramirez to talk about anything associated with the incident without crying. She could be on another topic entirely, but as soon as the conversation landed on that night at Yale, Ramirez struggled to get the words out. The woman who seemed so strong a moment ago suddenly seemed breakable.

ON WEDNESDAY, OCTOBER 3, Keyser initiated a second meeting with FBI agents. She had had second thoughts since her initial interview four days earlier, when she'd recounted being friends with Ford, attending parties together, and often being the designated driver because Ford didn't have her license. But she couldn't recall the event Ford described.

Between Saturday, September 29, and Tuesday, October 2, Keyser mulled over the memories Ford had shared with the Senate. She had dated Judge and been close to Blasey, then known as "Chrissy." But she couldn't shake the fact that, as she looked through old photographs of Kavanaugh now in circulation, he didn't look at all familiar. How could that possibly be, Keyser wondered, given that Ford had dated Kavanaugh's good friend Chris Garrett and she herself had gone out once or twice with his other good friend, Mark Judge? The more Keyser thought about it, the more dubious she was about Ford's account.

In part, Keyser thought Ford's account rang false because Ford had usually spent the entire summer in Rehoboth Beach, not in the greater Washington area, where the assault was said to have occurred. But Ford noted that in 1982, her Rehoboth vacation had lasted just two or three weeks.

Late Tuesday night, Keyser called her lawyer, Walsh. "I said, 'You know what, I don't feel good about something,'" she said in recounting the moment later. The facts that troubled her were both logistical and character-driven. "It would be impossible for me to be the only girl at a get-together with three guys, have her leave, and then not figure out how she's going to get home," said Keyser, adding that it would have been hard for Ford to get from Chevy Chase, where the party was widely assumed to have taken place, to her home in Potomac.

"I've been thinking about who I was at sixteen rather than who Chrissy was at sixteen," Keyser said. Despite her own history with drugs and alcohol, Keyser said she was not a heavy drinker at that point in high school.

"That's when I changed," added Keyser, referring to her overall posture toward Ford's account. "I just really didn't have confidence in the story."

She talked about the aspects of Ford's account that didn't ring true to her. For one thing, she said, the party Ford described did not square with Keyser's memory of typical gatherings from that period.

"I remember get-togethers," Keyser said, reiterating what she had told the FBI, "not that small. And I don't remember hanging out with

Georgetown Prep people as much as my friends think." Finally, she reiterated her conviction—bolstered by days of reviewing pictures and maps—that she did not know Kavanaugh.

Keyser said she gave investigators "my whole history of using," adding, "because I've had a couple of relapses, but not with opioids.

"I told the FBI about myself," she added, "basically everything I've ever done in my life.

"And the second thing was just sort of the conversation I had had with people that wanted me to remember something different," Keyser added, referring to her interactions with McLean and Gonella, which McLean strongly denies, "so I let the FBI know that, too."

Keyser believes something bad happened to her friend along the lines that she described. "I do," she said. "I think something happened, but I don't know what. And I haven't been close enough to her over the years to know that something went down. I haven't seen her in a long, long time. I do think that something happened to her, and that maybe she is a victim of some sort of trauma."

Still, she holds firm to her lack of confidence in the specifics of the Kavanaugh account: "Those facts together I don't recollect, and it just didn't make any sense."

Looking back, Keyser's role in casting doubt on the Ford story seems odd, even to her. "It was totally against my alignment, what went down," Keyser said. "I'm a Democrat. I own a political podcast with Bob [Beckel] that's very Democratic."

But when it comes to Kavanaugh, Keyser said, "the guy has a very impressive record . . . he has a really impressive record. So the bottom line is, you just don't screw with the processes here, I don't think. That's my belief."

At least one senator's office learned of Ford's supposition that Keyser had driven her home on the night of the gathering. But whatever credibility that detail might have lent to Ford's account risked being undermined by Keyser herself, whose history of addiction made her a problematic witness to put on national television.

Months after Kavanaugh was already sitting on the court, a copy of a *National Review* article on his confirmation hung, framed, in Keyser's downstairs bathroom. Dated October 8, 2018, it bore the headline "Was Leland Keyser the Hero of the Kavanaugh Controversy?"

FORD AND KAVANAUGH themselves were never interviewed by the FBI. On October 2, Ford's attorneys Bromwich and Katz sent a letter to FBI director Christopher Wray and FBI general counsel Dana Boente saying they had yet to hear from the FBI about interviewing Ford.

"We have repeatedly asked you to identify the Supervisory Special Agent responsible for this investigation, so that we could contact him or her directly. We have received no response," the letter said. "It is inconceivable that the FBI could conduct a thorough investigation of Dr. Ford's allegations without interviewing her, Judge Kavanaugh, or the witnesses we have identified in our letters to you."

Senator Feinstein said later, "Dr. Ford requested to be interviewed by the FBI, but that request was denied, reportedly with the approval of the White House and Senate Republicans. It was critical that Brett Kavanaugh be interviewed as well, since senators were only given five minutes to ask Brett Kavanaugh questions and he frequently refused to answer the questions asked."

Several senators expressed skepticism that the FBI investigation would be conducted in good faith and in earnest. "My mantra is distrust but verify," Senator Blumenthal told MSNBC. "I believe that Jeff Flake truly wants a real investigation, not a check-the-box sham. And that's what the FBI ought to be doing." Blumenthal described the deadline as "tight and arbitrary . . . too accelerated and too artificial to really get the job done."

In retrospect, however, many believed Flake was merely acting in the interest of self-preservation, perhaps to preserve his possible presidential ambitions—that he called for a supplemental FBI investigation to appear sympathetic to victims of sexual assault but then accepted its limited scope, in keeping with the Republican base.

Trump had held his fire during the confirmation process, but at a rally in Mississippi for Senator Cindy Hyde-Smith, the gloves came off. He defended young men falsely accused and brazenly mocked Ford. "'I had one beer,'" he said, mimicking her testimony. "'How did you get home?' 'I don't remember.' 'How'd you get there?' 'I don't remember.' 'Where is the place?' 'I don't remember.' 'How many years ago was it?' 'I don't know.'"

Senators on both sides of the aisle quickly condemned the remarks. Flake called them "appalling" on NBC's *Today* show. "There is no time and no place for remarks like that," he said, "but to discuss something this sensitive at a political rally is just not right."

Kavanaugh's liberal opponents made political hay of Trump's comments, turning them into an internet ad to pressure senators to vote no. Murkowski told reporters, "The president's comments yesterday mocking Dr. Ford were wholly inappropriate and in my view unacceptable." Even Grassley took to Twitter to "plead w. all" to stop attacks and "destruction of" Ford. But notwithstanding their poor taste, Trump's comments helped the Republican cause. "He showed he had skin in the game for Kavanaugh," one GOP staffer said.

In a *Washington Post* op-ed, Coons hammered away at what he saw as a toothless FBI investigation: "I remain very concerned that we might not get the prompt but thorough investigation that these serious allegations warrant and that the Senate and the American people deserve."

One day later, Democratic senators on the Judiciary Committee sent Grassley a letter expressing their concern about the majority's "mischaracterizing or selectively disclosing information regarding the allegations of sexual misconduct by Judge Kavanaugh."

McConnell took to the Senate floor to decry what he called intimidation from those on the "far left."

"They've tried to bully and intimidate us," McConnell said. "We'll not be intimidated by these people. There is no chance in the world they're going to scare us out of doing our duty."

Ben Rhodes, Obama's former deputy national security adviser, said it struck him as "totally bizarre" that the White House could so circumscribe an FBI's investigation. "In eight years, I can't think of a similar situation in which an FBI is being tightly scripted out of the White House," he said. "I couldn't understand why the FBI would agree to that. That to me is one of the unknown questions of this whole thing."

Some suggested it may have been because the deputy attorney general, Rosenstein—who had worked with Kavanaugh under independent counsel Ken Starr—had spent all his political capital on the Mueller investigation. Just as the Ford allegations were coming to light, Rosenstein was dealing with reports that he had secretly recorded President Trump in the White House in order to expose the chaos of his administration. He reportedly discussed recruiting cabinet members to invoke the 25th Amendment to remove Trump as unfit.

Others wondered whether FBI director Wray may have been loyal to Kavanaugh, having followed two years behind him at Yale College and Yale Law School and overlapped with him in the Bush White House, where he oversaw the Justice Department's Criminal Division.

The investigation was concluded on October 4. On that day, a twenty-eight-year friend of Ramirez's signed a sworn affidavit—her name was subsequently redacted—in which she said that in the early nineties, "Ramirez told me of an incident that happened to her while she was a freshman at Yale University.

"At this time, Ms. Ramirez specifically mentioned that a male classmate exposed his penis to her without her consent," the friend wrote. "I have been, and remain willing to go on the record with the FBI to discuss the above conversation. . . . As of the signing of this Affidavit, I have yet to be contacted by any FBI agents."

Just as attorneys and supporters for Ramirez and Ford were bemoaning the limitations of the FBI investigation, there appeared to be opposition research going on at their expense. Jen Klaus, one of Ramirez's former roommates, told NBC News that committee staff members had called her on October 4, put her on speakerphone, and asked about Ramirez's drinking habits, the party culture at Yale, and whether there was a student there known for "dropping his pants." She said, "they suggested Ramirez's allegation was a case of mistaken identity."

"It just gave me the impression they were suggesting perhaps it was [another classmate] who threw his penis in her face instead of Brett," said Klaus. "Why would they be asking me this?"

George Hartmann, the committee's press secretary, responded in a statement to NBC News that "no suggestion of mistaken identity was made. The committee has received numerous tips and asked Ms. Klaus for information she could provide one way or the other."

There were mistaken-identity theories circling around Ford, too. In the days before the September 27 hearing, at least two men had come forward to share stories of how they had "kissed" or "made out" with a young girl in the 1980s whom they now believed to be Ford. One of them said she had been wearing a bathing suit under her clothes at the time of the hookup and that "the kissing ended when a friend jumped on them as a joke."

The committee had also heard from Ford's graduate school boyfriend, Brian Merrick, now a real estate agent in Malibu, California. In a signed affidavit to the Judiciary Committee in which his name was redacted, Merrick stated that during his six years of dating Ford, she had "never indicated a fear of flying," "never brought up anything regarding her experience as a victim of sexual assault," and "never mentioned Brett Kavanaugh." Those facts, particularly the statement about Ford's fear of flying, sparked doubts in the minds of Republicans about Ford's authenticity.

Yet according to Merrick, both in the affidavit and in a later interview, he never doubted her truthfulness. "I think she's an honest person," he said. "She always was honest.

"I think she does believe something happened to her," he continued, adding of Kavanaugh, "Whether or not it was him I have no knowledge."

WHEN THE FBI'S INVESTIGATION was completed, McConnell announced that its results would not be made publicly available; the White House would loan the FBI report to Congress for just twenty-four hours, starting on October 4, and senators would have to view it in a special soundproof reading room in the Senate building known as a sensitive compartmented information facility, or SCIF.

To enter the SCIF, senators had to go past a guard through a set of heavy metal double doors requiring punched access codes. The viewing began at 8 a.m., with Grassley getting the first look, followed by Feinstein at 9 a.m. Then, at ten, Senate Judiciary Republicans were invited in, followed by the committee's Democrats at eleven, and so on in alternating intervals. The legislators were not allowed to take notes on paper or to bring in any personal electronic devices. They were not provided copies. They could not bring in staffers. They could not relay any of the findings.

Tim Kaine, the former vice presidential candidate and senator from Virginia, tweeted, "The 'report' is available for Senators to review in a secure office but get this—there's only ONE copy! That means Senators have to sign up for hour-long slots between now and the expected vote. There may not even be time for all 100 of us to read it before our first vote!"

Inside the SCIF, said Flake, senators were sharing single pages of the FBI's summary report, at times reading key passages aloud to one another. Coons noted banker's boxes stacked up in one area, containing the paperwork associated with all six of Kavanaugh's prior background checks—a volume of material he and his colleagues couldn't possibly sift through during the time allotted.

The North Dakota Republican Heidi Heitkamp said in an interview, "You can't make this up. I've been here six years and we've never had to go into a secured room to review documents on a judicial appointment.

"I'm a former attorney general who has dealt a lot with criminal investigations," she continued, adding that the FBI's report was woefully incomplete. "I would have sent it back and said, 'Do better.'"

Whitehouse said the Republicans had used the confidentiality of the report to their own advantage. "We've played this game before: you basically say, 'There's nothing in there,' and we can't say, 'Yes, here's what's in there,' because that would be violating the confidentiality of the report," he said. "Republicans used the confidentiality against the truth."

Reactions to the report split, perhaps predictably, along partisan lines; Republicans said they were satisfied that the FBI investigation had produced nothing new. Democrats said it raised more questions than answers.

Grassley: "There's nothing in it that we didn't already know."

Eshoo: "A travesty."

Whitehouse: "Bogus."

"They couldn't refuse to take information, although they tried very hard," Whitehouse added. "I've been a former state attorney general, a U.S. attorney, and spent twelve years on the Judiciary Committee—I've never seen a situation where the FBI more diligently tried to fend off information as the clock ran out.

"The confidentiality of it was not particularly unusual; what was unusual was all the ways in which there had been intrusions into standard operating procedure in order to avoid getting things into the record," he continued. "I would view the Ramirez allegations as not having been even remotely investigated. I would view the repeated statements by Republicans that Ford's were uncorroborated as legal and factual falsehoods by any reasonable definition of corroboration."

Flake, however, was largely satisfied with the investigation. "I would have preferred, obviously, that this be done a lot sooner, and that it would be a lot broader," he said in an interview later. "But it was thorough in terms of the primary witnesses, those who were there."

While he could not discuss the specifics of the report, Flake said, "there was nothing that came out of those interviews that corroborated the initial allegation. And I felt that that was sufficient for me."

On October 5, the Senate voted to advance Kavanaugh's nomination to a final vote, scheduled for October 6, 2018.

That same day, NBC News said Ramirez had identified to the FBI the "eyewitnesses who were in the room during the alleged incident": Dave Todd, Kevin Genda, and Dave White. The report attracted little to no attention.

Also on October 5, Grassley released his executive summary of the FBI's investigation, issuing a concise conclusion. "The Supplemental Background Investigation confirms what the Senate Judiciary Committee concluded after its investigation," it stated, and then added in bold: "**There is no corroboration of the allegations made by Dr. Ford or Ms. Ramirez.**"

In statements prepared for this book, Feinstein said neither this summary nor the Republicans' later memo about the investigation regarding individuals they interviewed had been made available to the minority. "A number of individuals who made salacious allegations against Dr. Ford were not identified and were 'anonymous sources,'" Feinstein said. "And both documents included information about Dr. Ford's past relationships (something that is prohibited under rape shield laws passed by Congress). All of those individuals should have been interviewed and questioned under oath.

"The Trump White House limited the scope of what the FBI could review," Feinstein continued. "The FBI review ignored a number of witnesses, and was rushed to completion. This was not a legitimate investigation."

One key senator, however, had heard all she needed to hear. And that senator was arguably the one who mattered most in the end. Once Murkowski decided to vote against confirmation, that left only Susan Collins as the one remaining pro-choice Republican who could determine Kavanaugh's fate. And she came down on his side, taking to the Senate floor on October 5 to make the case in a forty-five-minute speech that earned her the wrath of the left and the hosannas of the right.

"We must always remember that it is when passions are most inflamed that fairness is most in jeopardy," Collins said in her remarks. "The presumption of innocence is relevant to the advice and consent function when an accusation departs from a nominee's otherwise exemplary record. I worry that departing from this presumption could lead to a lack of public faith in the judiciary and would be hugely damaging to the confirmation process moving forward."

On Saturday, October 6, 2018, mothers and fathers of Yale students descended on the campus for the annual Family Weekend. As evening fell and the sky darkened, parents headed off to various activities—an improv performance in a basement theater at Pierson residential college, an a cappella concert at Dwight Chapel, one of the famous clam pies at Frank Pepe Pizzeria Napoletana.

Families strolling past the majestic Sterling Memorial Library, at the center of campus, passed the 1993 fountain sculpture designed by architect Maya Lin, a Yale alumna, which pays tribute to women at the school. On this particular weekend, the elliptical installation had been turned into a makeshift shrine in honor of Ford and Ramirez. All around the granite surface, individual flowers were laid out, stem by stem—yellow, white, pink, and red. And on the ground, in colorful block chalk letters: SOLIDARITY WITH SURVIVORS.

Meanwhile, about three hundred miles away, in Washington, D.C., Vice President Mike Pence firmly tapped the traditional ivory gavel in the Senate chamber on Capitol Hill. His repeated attempts to have the clerk call the roll were continually interrupted by screaming protesters. "I do not consent. I do not consent," shouted one. "Where is my representation?"

Pence calmly kept insisting, "The sergeant at arms will restore order in the gallery."

Finally, after successfully quieting the outbursts, Pence concluded the session. Brett M. Kavanaugh had been confirmed by the closest vote for a Supreme Court justice in more than 150 years: "The ayes are fifty," Pence said. "The nays are forty-eight."

Hamartia

Missing the Mark

Years ago, when she was practicing her closing arguments at the family dinner table, Martha Kavanaugh often returned to her signature line as a state prosecutor. "Use your common sense," she'd say. "What rings true? What rings false?"

Those words made a strong impression on her young son, Brett. They also made a strong impression on us as the authors of this book. In reviewing our findings, we looked at them in two ways: through the prism of reporting and through the lens of common sense.

As women, we know that sexual assaults often aren't corroborated. They often happen without witnesses, and many victims avoid reporting them out of shame or fear. But as reporters, we need evidence; we rely on the facts. Without corroboration, Ford's and Ramirez's claims would be hard to accept.

As women, we could not help but be moved by the accounts of Ford and Ramirez, and understand why they made such a lasting impact. As reporters, we had a responsibility to test those predilections. We had to offer Kavanaugh the benefit of the doubt, venturing to empathize with his suffering if he was falsely accused.

As mothers of daughters, we were prone to believe and support the women who spoke up. As mothers of sons, we had to imagine what it would be like if the men we loved were wrongly charged with these offenses.

As people, our gut reaction was that the allegations of Ford and Ramirez from the past rang true. As reporters, we uncovered nothing to suggest that Kavanaugh has mistreated women in the years since.

Ultimately, we combined our notebooks with our common sense and came to believe an utterly human narrative: that Ford and Ramirez were mistreated by Kavanaugh as a teenager, and that Kavanaugh over the next thirty-five years became a better person.

We come to this complicated, seemingly contradictory, and perhaps unsatisfying conclusion based on the facts as we found them.

In the course of our ten-month investigation, we conducted hundreds of interviews with principal players in Kavanaugh's education, career, and confirmation. We read thousands of documents. We reviewed hours of television interviews, along with reams of newspaper, magazine, and digital coverage. We studied maps of Montgomery County as well as housing renovation plans and court records. We watched Kavanaugh's confirmation hearings multiple times.

Unproven as it is, the account of Christine Blasey Ford—to use Martha's phrase—"rings true." Ford's social circle overlapped with that of Kavanaugh as a high school student. She dated his good friend Chris Garrett. Her good friend Leland Keyser dated Mark Judge. Judge and Kavanaugh, whom Ford recalled being together in the room where she was assaulted, were close friends. They were often seen together at parties, and their tendency to drink beer, sometimes to excess, was well known.

None of that means that Ford was, in fact, assaulted by Kavanaugh. But it does mean that she has a baseline level of credibility as an accuser.

Her credibility is affirmed in other ways, too. We have seen no evidence of Ford fabricating stories, either recently or historically. Multiple people attest to her honesty. Last August, she passed a polygraph test focused on her Kavanaugh memories. Her former boyfriend Brian Merrick said in a sworn affidavit to the Senate Judiciary Committee that he hadn't known of her fear of flying or of tight spaces when they dated in the 1990s, raising questions for Republicans about the anxiety issues Ford has attributed in part to the alleged assault. But Merrick also said in the affidavit and in a later interview that he never doubted Ford's truthfulness.

Experts on both memory and sex crimes say that Ford's spotty recollections of the alleged assault are in line with those of a typical victim: clear on the basic elements of the violation and its perpetrator (especially given that, in this case, that person was alleged to be an acquaintance), hazy on ancillary elements like the exact location and the transportation that got her there and back. Victims also often keep their experiences to themselves.

"She was one of the most competent, credible, and believable witnesses I have ever seen in over a decade of prosecuting cases," said Allison Leotta, who spent twelve years as a federal prosecutor in Washington, focusing on sex crimes, domestic violence, and child abuse. "What she described was a very bread-and-butter acquaintance sexual assault."

Using Martha's common-sense standard, there is no reason Ford would have come forward with her account if she didn't believe it.

Ford has led a quiet life for many years. She has no love of the spotlight, and she pleaded with lawmakers and *The Washington Post* for weeks to preserve her privacy. It was only when Ford believed she was on the brink of being exposed that she identified herself publicly. After that, she endured a terrifying series of death threats and other harassment, forcing her family to separate at times and to relocate. The time it took to testify and secure herself and her family forced Ford to take time away from her teaching job.

Moreover, we have seen no evidence that she was influenced by anyone, other than the family and friends from whom she sought counsel, the California congresswoman and senator she contacted for help, and the lawyers she handpicked from a list of suggestions. To date, Ford has enjoyed no apparent financial gain as a result of coming forward. Her lawyers and public relations advisers donated their time. Her transportation to Washington was covered, to keep her safe and comfortable before and after her testimony. Her security costs were handled by a crowdsourced GoFundMe account. The money left over once her expenses were paid has been designated for trauma survivors.

Other leads we pursued neither indicted nor exonerated Kavanaugh.

We located Judge, who declined to elaborate much beyond his statement to the public and to the FBI, which was that he didn't remember the incident. We reached out, repeatedly, to Smyth, the third boy who allegedly attended the party but did not witness the assault. Smyth did not answer our calls and emails, but he has consistently said to friends as well as to the FBI that he has no memory of the event or of Ford. We spoke multiple times to Keyser, who also said that she didn't recall that get-together or any others like it. In fact, she challenged Ford's accuracy. "I don't have any confidence in the story," she said.

But Keyser's skepticism was structured on some erroneous or

irrelevant tent poles. Keyser thought the whole setup Ford described—the Columbia Country Club, followed by a gathering with boys at a local home—sounded wrong, given that Keyser was working at the Congressional Country Club that summer. But Keyser acknowledged that she was a member of the Columbia club, and that she might have stopped by to watch Ford dive and they decided to go to a party. (Ford also said not to assume that the gathering had originated at the club, guessing that it might have been arranged by Keyser and Judge by phone or in person elsewhere.)

Keyser said she didn't recognize Kavanaugh from high school photos. She did recognize and remember Judge, whom she said she had dated once or twice and bumped into at a recovery meeting in Potomac in the mid-aughts. It is possible that Ford's account is wrong and that Keyser's lack of recollection is proof of that. But experts say that memories of insignificant people and places in our lives often aren't stored. And Keyser's memory might be affected by her struggles with alcohol and other substances. In the months after the confirmation battle, she continued to appear perturbed by her unexpected role in it, indicating in a text message to one of the authors late in March that she believed she was being surveilled at home, possibly by people related to the Kavanaugh matter.

We looked for the house, which Ford said was located somewhere between hers, in Potomac, and the Columbia Country Club. She had described the layout: barely furnished, containing an upstairs level, and, perhaps most critically, featuring a narrow set of stairs with walls on both sides. She said that Judge in particular seemed possessive of the place, suggesting that it belonged to him, a friend, or a relation.

Working with those parameters, we looked for family members whose house Judge might have accessed, with or without its inhabitants' permission. We ruled out his older siblings, who, according to his brother, Michael, were not living in the area in question at that time. We also ruled out his grandmother, who had lived on the Washington side of Chevy Chase, with her adult daughter, Anita—Mark and Michael's aunt. The two women rarely went out in those days, according to Michael. (The layout of that house, which was sold years ago and was recently rented by Mike Pence before he became vice president, also didn't match.)

Eventually, we generated a short list of two possibilities, one belonging to a Judge family friend in Potomac and the other to a Georgetown Prep classmate in Bethesda. Both houses have been renovated, and floor plans and other housing documents in Montgomery County from before 1986 are scarce. Ultimately, since the houses' layouts from 1982 couldn't be firmly established, Ford could not make clear determinations on whether either resembled the one she remembered.

According to Martha's common-sense test, the claims of Deborah Ramirez, while not proven by witnesses, also ring true. Ramirez, who was a Yale classmate of Kavanaugh's, said he thrust his penis at her during a drunken party in their freshman-year dormitory, Lawrance Hall. The people who allegedly witnessed the event—Kavanaugh's friends Kevin Genda, David Todd, and David White—have kept mum about it. Kavanaugh has denied it. If such an incident had occurred, Kavanaugh said, it would have been "the talk of campus."

Our reporting suggests that, in fact, it was. At least five people have a strong recollection of hearing about the alleged incident with Ramirez long before Kavanaugh was a federal judge. Yale classmates Kenneth Appold and Richard Oh recall hearing about it immediately after it happened. Ramirez's mother, Mary Ann LeBlanc, recalls being told about it by her daughter—without specifics—during college. Michael Wetstone, a graduate school classmate of Appold in religious studies, recalls being told about the incident by Appold within a few years of when it allegedly happened. A fifth person—an unidentified friend of Ramirez's who said in a recent affidavit that she heard about the incident in the 1990s—remembers being told about it within a decade of its alleged occurrence. And two other people from Kavanaugh and Ramirez's Yale class, Chad Ludington and James Roche, vaguely remember hearing about something happening to Ramirez during freshman year.

Of course, given the lack of eyewitness corroboration, Ramirez could be misremembering the situation, perhaps due to inebriation. She has said she doesn't remember telling anyone what happened in the immediate aftermath of the alleged event. But since the story got around campus anyway, either Ramirez is mistaken in that, or some other witness to the event repeated the account and spread the story to others. Like Ford, Ramirez has no apparent personal or political motivation to bring down Kavanaugh. It did not even occur to her to tell her story publicly; she was contacted about it by *The New Yorker*, which was following up on a tip it had received from another source. Many friends and former classmates have described Ramirez as both honest and guileless.

Next to the two credible witnesses—Ford and Ramirez—are a number of less convincing ones. The most notable of them is Julie Swetnick, who claimed to have been gang-raped by a group of un-identified boys at a 1982 party where Kavanaugh and Judge were present. Swetnick also said she had attended more than ten parties with Kavanaugh and Judge, and that she had seen the two participate in "trains" of boys waiting to have sex with incapacitated girls at "many" of those parties.

Kavanaugh called those allegations "outrageous." Swetnick's law-yer, Michael Avenatti, never made himself or his client available for questions for this book, despite multiple requests. Numerous George-town Prep alumni from that era—including some who were support-ive of Ford—cast doubt upon aspects of Swetnick's account. Generally speaking, they said that, while isolated incidents of assault might have occurred without their knowledge, there would have been no way that repeated gang rapes could have taken place without a larger group of them being aware of it, especially if they involved Kava-naugh and Judge, who were very social.

"What I was thinking, and what kind of was reflected in the con-versations I had with others, was 'Did you ever hear anything about this? No? No, nothing?'" said Tom Downey, one of Kavanaugh's Prep classmates, in an interview. "I never saw it. And, boy oh boy, if it had happened ten times, eight times, we all would've known about it."

Using Martha's common-sense test, the Swetnick allegations, at least as they pertain to Kavanaugh and Judge, "ring false." The same can be said of an account that the two men sexually assaulted a woman on a Rhode Island boat in 1985. It can also be said about yet another account that Kavanaugh groped, assaulted, and raped a woman in the backseat of a car at a date and place that were not identified.

Even with these questionable or admittedly false accounts of sex-ual assault, however, there exists a through line with the more sub-stantiated ones: heavy drinking. Kavanaugh's alcohol use as a young man seems to have led to both bad behavior and, very possibly, bad memory. Scores of friends and former classmates have attested to Ka-vanaugh's penchant for beer and for excessive drinking during his high school and college years. Kavanaugh himself said, repeatedly, "Sometimes I had too many beers."

He denied that he ever forgot what happened during a night of heavy alcohol consumption. But friends and former classmates say that his slurring, stumbling reactions to alcohol in college—which led in one case to damaging a car and in another to helping provoke a bar fight—suggest otherwise. And the probability that Kavanaugh experienced memory loss when drunk—even if he can't, or won't, acknowledge it—means there is at least some possibility that he mistreated the women in question but truly doesn't remember it.

We considered the theory that Kavanaugh had lied—about the Ford assault, the Ramirez incident, or even the fact that he'd never blacked out from drinking. According to Martha's common-sense test, Kavanaugh had an incentive to beat back any blot on his moral character while under consideration for one of the most trusted positions in our democracy. Such potential taints, of course, would include sexual assault, boorish behavior in general, and irresponsible drinking. Prior Supreme Court nominations have been scuttled over far less. Judge Douglas H. Ginsburg, for example, was forced to withdraw his nomination to the Supreme Court in 1987 after admitting that he had smoked marijuana, an issue that would not likely trouble many senators today.

Based on our reporting, Kavanaugh's testimony contained a number of inaccurate or misleading assertions: that the references to Renate in the yearbook were innocent homages, for example, or that he was not indeed the character named Bart O'Kavanaugh in Judge's book. Multiple classmates from Georgetown Prep recall the sexually themed boasts that Kavanaugh and his friends made about a young Renate, and the fact that Kavanaugh's nickname was Bart was so well established that during his confirmation hearings it was used in group emails involving him and his classmates.

But in his testimony, Kavanaugh put a glossier sheen on the Renate matter—calling it a "clumsily intended" reference meant to "show affection." He essentially evaded the O'Kavanaugh question (having threatened to sue Judge in 1997 if he used his real name in the book).

"You'd have to ask him," Kavanaugh told Senator Leahy when asked whether Judge had been referring to him with the name O'Kavanaugh.

These dodges and others like them, while certainly artful and perhaps disingenuous, may not technically amount to lying—particularly since Kavanaugh, as an experienced lawyer, knows well the perils of doing so under oath. Kavanaugh instead could have offered up incomplete versions of the truth, or representations of his past behaviors that were kinder than the perceptions of other people—who were also there and had the benefit of greater objectivity. Without knowing what memories lay in Kavanaugh's head when he spoke, however, it is hard for us to separate lies from bad or manipulated facts.

We considered Kavanaugh's discussions of his drinking and sexual history. During the hearings, he frequently made only the most grudging admissions of excessive boozing—for example, using "Sometimes I had too many beers" to cover years of what at times appears to have been binge drinking. Still, he was acknowledging the behavior, even if his former classmates found that acknowledgment inadequate. He was less elliptical about the sexual assault accusations, categorically denying that he had ever sexually assaulted anyone, ever. He denied the Ford and Ramirez claims specifically. He asserted that he was a virgin through high school and for "many years" afterward, even though his virginity was at best a contextual detail, rather than evidence disproving that he sexually assaulted women.

By allowing no possibility that he had ever assaulted anyone, including Ford, or exposed his penis to Ramirez, Kavanaugh may have boxed himself into a lie. But that's the case only if he knowingly uttered a falsehood by denying events he actually did remember. If he genuinely has no recollection of them, and no document, friend, or other evidence surfaced, he was not consciously being dishonest.

Some have offered the position that Kavanaugh was a blackout drinker who lost portions of his memory and simply wasn't aware of it. That notion sounds plausible. In a blackout state—a complex neurological condition—portions of memory may be lost without a person's realizing it. Only later evidence of what happened in the lost moments can demonstrate the lapse.

Sarah Hepola, author of the bestseller *Blackout: Remembering the Things I Drank to Forget*, wrote in an opinion column last year, "Blackouts are like a philosophical riddle inside a legal conundrum: If you can't remember a thing, how do you know it happened?"

Of all the fraught moments at the September 27 hearing, the questioning about blacking out seemed to exercise Kavanaugh most. During a back-and-forth with Senator Klobuchar in which she shared the fact of her own father's alcoholism, Kavanaugh grew so rude and disrespectful that he later felt obligated to apologize. During an exchange with the prosecutor Rachel Mitchell about whether he had ever blacked out, passed out, or otherwise lost memory during a period of copious drinking, Kavanaugh bristled, stammered, and seemed to scoff. A third exchange with Senator Whitehouse, about the "Ralph Club" and other references to excessive drinking from Kavanaugh's yearbook, was venomous. But because it appears unlikely we'll find evidence either to prove the 1982 allegations or to discover exactly what was in Kavanaugh's head during those hearings thirty-six years later, the blackout theory—at least as it pertains to Ford—is probably destined to be no more than that.

Above and beyond the accusations of misdeeds, the charges of telling falsehoods, and the theme of heavy drinking sits another, more encompassing, dilemma: Kavanaugh's temperament. Despite superlative marks from the American Bar Association and many associates, Kavanaugh's usual evenness was absent from the September 27 hearing.

His furious, indignant exchanges with senators during the testimony were searing. They caused retired justice John Paul Stevens, who had once praised Kavanaugh's jurisprudence, to say the judge was unfit for the high court. More than 2,400 law professors and many Americans agreed. The Bar Association called for an FBI investigation. Given that the hearings had technically been a job interview and not a criminal proceeding, several pundits argued that Kavanaugh blew it.

On October 4, Kavanaugh realized his mistake and tried to make amends. His performance the prior week, he wrote in an op-ed, "reflected my overwhelming frustration at being wrongly accused, without corroboration, of horrible conduct completely contrary to my record and character. My statement and answers also reflected my deep distress at the unfairness of how this allegation has been handled. . . . I might have been too emotional at times. I know that my tone was sharp, and I said a few things I should not have said. I hope everyone can understand that I was there as a son, husband and dad. I testified with five people foremost in my mind: my mom, my dad, my wife, and most of all my daughters." He promised Americans that he would return to the equilibrium and fair-mindedness he had long demonstrated.

Temperament was not a central focus of our investigation. But it is worth noting that our reporting showed Kavanaugh's to be historically courteous. Young lawyers were struck by his interest in their careers, how Kavanaugh would chat for hours after Federalist Society gatherings or—in bumping into them on the D.C. Metro—inquire about their work in a way that reflected how closely he'd listened in the past.

Former colleagues described him as unassuming and unpretentious— "a Bud Light kind of guy," in the words of Richard Re, an assistant professor at UCLA School of Law, who clerked for Kavanaugh on the federal appeals court.

A journalist who covered Kavanaugh's circuit court saw him often in the cafeteria line, talking baseball with the staff as he ordered his sandwich. Dozens of former clerks, many of them women, cited his mentorship, his warmth, his eagerness to help advance their professional prospects, and his willingness to support their personal lives, including raising families. Many said they had never seen Kavanaugh as inflamed as he had been on September 27—neither before nor since.

None of this is an excuse for what many regarded as an offensive and potentially prejudicial performance. But it provides some context.

As reporters, it's not for us to opine on whether Kavanaugh's youthful misdeeds or angry testimony should have blocked him from the Supreme Court. That question was left to the president, who supported Kavanaugh's confirmation; the Senate, which voted to approve him; and, ultimately, American voters, who showed their feelings at the ballot box and in impeachment petitions. Some thought the mere possibility that Kavanaugh had assaulted Ford and others—allegations that, they felt, were bolstered by the stories of heavy drinking and chauvinistic yearbook boasts—meant Kavanaugh should have been replaced. Others point out that our juvenile-justice system is built on the long-held belief that a young person's bad decisions shouldn't haunt them for years to come. That is why most juvenile records and many juvenile court proceedings are kept largely confidential.

The country was deeply and bitterly divided on Kavanaugh. In the days after the polarizing hearings, 48 percent of Americans opposed his confirmation, and about 42 percent supported it, according to a Quinnipiac poll. Arguments about Ford's motivations and Kavanaugh's performance split families and friends. Those standoffs spilled into the halls of Capitol Hill, where longtime staffers found themselves in the most poisonous environment they could remember, with colleagues taking their disagreements over the confirmation process personally. "I can't believe you guys are really doing this," one aide to a senior Democratic senator remembers hearing from a Republican staffer.

Since the contentious confirmation hearings, the gulf separating Kavanaugh's admirers and his detractors has only widened. In late December, most voters polled by the research firm PerryUndem believed Kavanaugh had lied about his teenage years. Forty-nine percent had a largely unfavorable impression of him, as compared with the 29 percent who had a favorable one. Thirty-five percent said the Senate did the right thing in confirming him; a close 41 percent disagreed. (By contrast, an overwhelming 58 percent of Americans polled after the Clarence Thomas confirmation supported him, with 30 percent opposed.) Fifty-five percent of voters believed Ford over Kavanaugh—a sixteen-point margin of favor.

The Kavanaugh confirmation stirred painful discussion about gender dynamics and who is empowered in our country. Parents had tough conversations with their children about consent and abuse. Grown men—including classmates of Kavanaugh's at Yale and Georgetown Prep—contacted old girlfriends and apologized for pushy sexual behavior. Others hardened their belief that women are more likely than ever to interpret innocuous touches and comments as sexual assault or harassment, evidence of a #MeToo movement gone too far. Women thought hard about their underrepresentation in politics and in other professions.

On Tuesday, October 9, Kavanaugh reported to the Supreme Court for his first day on the bench. He heard oral arguments from two cases involving state sentencing practices for criminals with prior violent offenses, asking questions and deferentially apologizing for interrupting at one point. Despite female protesters outside the building, Kavanaugh was welcomed warmly by Chief Justice John Roberts and, at the end of the public session, shook hands with Justice Elena Kagan, who had hired him to teach at Harvard when she was dean of the law school. Ashley, Margaret, Liza, and his parents watched the proceedings.

Ford had a very different autumn. On leave from teaching because of the strain of the Kavanaugh hearings, she continued to receive devastating threats and online attacks. She and her family moved in and out of hotels and at least one borrowed house. Her video endorsement of Rachael Denhollander, the former gymnast who went public about the sexual abuse she'd endured from the physician Larry Nassar, was greeted with a spiteful backlash that left her emotionally reeling.

Over the months that followed, Ford would consider writing a book of her own or meeting with television producers. But the stress of reliving a past trauma, something she'd done at great length already, and the risk of pulling loved ones back into the klieg lights kept stopping her. She focused on how best to show her appreciation to the tens of thousands of letters of support she'd received, many from sexual assault survivors. She also became involved with the Project on Institutional Courage, which approaches problems of sexual violence through social science research.

Kavanaugh's former classmates looked at their educational years in a new light. To some, the casual misogyny they remembered suddenly seemed more sinister and threatening. They bemoaned the ugliness of the confirmation process.

"Had it been in a different venue—privately, and without so much on the line as it relates to the political direction of this very country—then perhaps both of them could have been more genuine in terms of why they were there and why they were speaking about this incident," said Joe Conaghan, a Prep classmate who signed a letter of support for Ford but nonetheless backed Kavanaugh's confirmation.

"And if I'm right. about what I suspect was true, which is that she was telling the truth," Conaghan added, "then perhaps Brett would have been able to render an apology to her that might have helped her heal in a real, genuine way. But as it stands in my mind, neither one was healed by the incident, because it was so politicized."

Polls show that the Kavanaugh confirmation had a direct impact on the midterm elections, in which Democrats took control of the House of Representatives and lost two seats in the Senate. Among the casualties were Democrats Heidi Heitkamp, Joe Donnelly, and Claire McCaskill, who lost their red-state Senate seats after voting against Kavanaugh; Joe Manchin may well have preserved his by voting for Kavanaugh. Some Democrats pledged to pursue impeachment proceedings against the newly seated justice.

Republican leaders fought back. Grassley referred Michael Avenatti, Swetnick's attorney, for criminal investigation, along with the tipsters attached to the fallacious accounts of the Rhode Island assault and the backseat rape, as well as Swetnick herself. On November 2, committee Republicans issued a 414-page memo summarizing their actions during the Kavanaugh confirmation process, with related affidavits and interview transcripts attached. Since the memo, which contained a number of misleading or incomplete assertions—many of them unfavorable to Ford—was never approved by committee Democrats, it could not, technically, be considered an official report.

Some senators have capitalized on public profiles that were enhanced by the hearings, namely Senators Kamala Harris, Cory Booker, and Amy Klobuchar, who announced their candidacies for president in 2020, and Coons and Flake, who went on talk shows together to discuss their bipartisan efforts. Joe Biden, the former vice president and longtime senator who had chaired the Judiciary Committee during the Clarence Thomas confirmation, apologized to Anita Hill for the way he handled those hearings. (She did not accept.)

The hyperbolic rhetoric that had governed the process persisted. President Trump said that "it's a very scary time for young men in America." Senate Majority Leader Mitch McConnell, who received a standing ovation when he entered the East Room for Kavanaugh's swearing-in, said the confirmation was "the single most important thing I've been involved in in my career." Senator Lindsey Graham called the hearings "the low point of my time in the Senate." Mike Davis, the powerful aide to the Judiciary Committee whose aggressive efforts helped pull Kavanaugh across the finish line, called the way the judge had been attacked "un-American."

Senator Dianne Feinstein issued a statement saying that Kavanaugh's confirmation had put "women's reproductive rights, civil rights, environmental protections, worker's rights, the ability to implement gun safety rules and the ability to hold presidents accountable at risk for a generation.

"Today is a sad day," she added. "Tomorrow we must pick ourselves up and keep fighting."

Eshoo also described herself as "enormously sad."

"I was left with the feeling that he got away with something again," she said in an interview. "Life is not a straight line—many times we wish it were. You take steps forward and you want to keep taking more steps in order to make progress, but there are always setbacks along the way."

Deborah Ramirez continued to page through the many supportive notes she had saved. One contained a poem called "What Is Justice," which made Ramirez think about what that concept meant for her.

"You can't look at justice as just the confirmation vote," she said. "There is so much good that came out of it. There is so much more good to come."

Christine Blasey Ford was selected as one of the Time 100, the magazine's annual list of the year's most influential people—as was Kavanaugh. She considered attending the April 23 ceremony in New York City, where celebrity honorees like Glenn Close, Martha Stewart, and Dwayne "the Rock" Johnson walked the red carpet and Taylor Swift performed hits like "Delicate" and "Shake It Off" at Frederick P. Rose Hall. In the end, however, Ford stayed home.

At the time of this writing, Kavanaugh has just completed his first term on the court. Whether he'll prove a centrist and occasional swing voter, in the mold of his mentor Justice Anthony Kennedy, or a more reliable conservative, like his onetime schoolmate Justice Neil Gorsuch, remains to be seen. How Kavanaugh—and indeed the country— has been shaped by his confirmation will take time to understand. Painful as it seems now, the process had much to teach. As Virgil wrote in book one of *The Aeneid*, "Someday it will be helpful to have recalled even these events."

Robin Pogrebin and Kate Kelly
July 2019

NOTES

PROLOGUE. *NOSTOS*: HOMECOMING

xxii **The next day, about four hundred:** Kate Kelly, "Back at Georgetown Prep, Kavanaugh Is Hailed as a Hero," *The New York Times*, October 28, 2018, https://www.nytimes.com/2018/10/28/us/politics/kavanaugh-georgetown -prep.html.

xxii **During the years when it was still part:** Stephen J. Ochs, *Academy on the Patowmack: Georgetown Preparatory School, 1789–1927* (Rockville, MD: George-town Preparatory School, 1989), 48, 51. See also Georgetown University, "What's a Hoya?," accessed June 29, 2019, https://alumni.georgetown.edu /news/fast-facts-hoyas-should-know.

xxii **about six since the devastating accusation:** Emma Brown, "California Professor, Writer of Confidential Brett Kavanaugh Letter, Speaks Out About Her Allegation of Sexual Assault," *Washington Post*, September 16, 2018, https://www.washingtonpost.com/investigations/california-professor -writer-of-confidential-brett-kavanaugh-letter-speaks-out-about-her-alle gation-of-sexual-assault/2018/09/16/46982194-b846-11e8-94e b-3bd52dfe917b _story.html?utm_term=.9603d597e1e3.

xxii **"live on the sunrise side of the mountain":** "Judge Brett M. Kavanaugh to Students: Love Your Friends, Live on the Sunrise Side of the Mountain, and

Stay Humble," accessed June 29, 2019, https://www.law.edu/news-and-events/2018/05/2018-0529-Commencement2018.html.

xxii **his wife had been targeted:** Emily Birnbaum, "CNN: Kavanaugh and His Family Getting Threats," *The Hill*, September 20, 2018, https://thehill.com/homenews/senate/407673-cnn-kavanaugh-and-his-family-getting-threats.

xxii **Nearly two hundred had signed:** Letter to Majority Leader Mitch McConnell et al., Senate Judiciary Committee, July 9, 2018, https://www.judiciary.senate.gov/download/kavanaughs-georgetown-prep-classmates.

xxiv **describing Tobin Finizio:** Kavanaugh hearing transcript, Testimony before the Senate Judiciary Committee, September 27, 2018, https://www.washingtonpost.com/news/national/wp/2018/09/27/kavanaugh-hearing-transcript/?utm_term=.c2541dcc5f2b.

CHAPTER 1. *ALEA IACTA EST*: THE DIE HAS BEEN CAST

1 **At nine o'clock on the evening:** Transcript and video of President Trump's Kavanaugh nomination announcement, *The New York Times*, July 9, 2018, https://www.nytimes.com/2018/07/09/us/politics/trump-supreme-court-announcement-transcript.html.

3 **her "'oh, shit' moment":** Michael Barbaro, "Senator Claire McCaskill on Losing Missouri and the Politics of Purity," December 20, 2018, in *The Daily*, produced by Lynsea Garrison, podcast, https://www.nytimes.com/2018/12/20/podcasts/the-daily-senator-claire-mccaskill-missouri-interview.html.

4 **"supremely qualified by the objective characteristics":** "Bush-Appointed DC Circ. Judge Vouches for Garland," *Law360*, April 1, 2016, https://www.law360.com/articles/779549/bush-appointed-dc-circ-judge-vouches-for-garland+&cd=4&hl=en&ct=clnk&gl=us.

5 **had voted with him 93 percent of the time:** Alex Swoyer, "Kavanaugh, Garland Voted Together 93 Percent of the Time," *The Washington Times*, September 5, 2018, https://www.washingtontimes.com/news/2018/sep/5/kavanaugh-garland-voted-together-93-pct-time/.

5 **Kavanaugh only grudgingly made the short list:** Clark L. Hildabrand, "Here's Which People on Trump's List Are Most Likely to Replace Anthony Kennedy," *The Federalist*, June 29, 2018, https://thefederalist.com/2018/06/29/heres-people-trumps-list-likely-replace-kennedy/.

5 **He had disappointed them with his 2011 opinion:** Joan Biskupic, "Kavanaugh's Obamacare Rulings Under Microscope as He Meets Manchin," CNN, July 30, 2018, https://www.cnn.com/2018/07/30/politics/brett-kavanaugh-obamacare-joe-manchin/index.html.

5 **The Federalist Society list was long:** Hildabrand, "Here's Which People on Trump's List Are Most Likely to Replace Anthony Kennedy," June 29, 2018.

6 **"Bushy. Swampy. Chiefy":** Authors' own reporting, but first published in Jake Sherman and Anna Palmer, *The Hill to Die On* (New York: Crown, 2019), p. 303.

7 **relatively low initial support:** Harry Enten, "Brett Kavanaugh is the Least Popular Supreme Court Nominee in 30 Years," CNN, September 20, 2018, https://www.cnn.com/2018/09/22/politics/brett-kavanaugh-least-popular/index.html.

8 **"a land in which women":** NCC staff, "On This Day: Senate Rejects Robert Bork for the Supreme Court," National Constitution Center, October 23, 2018, https://constitutioncenter.org/blog/on-this-day-senate-rejects-robert-bork-for-the-supreme-court/.

8 **In Kavanaugh's last two rounds . . . basis for such an investigation:** David A. Graham, "How Kavanaugh's Last Confirmation Hearing Could Haunt Him," *The Atlantic*, July 17, 2018, https://www.theatlantic.com/politics/archive/2018/07/how-kavanaughs-last-confirmation-hearing-could-haunt-him/565304/.

9 **the Washington-area country club crowd:** Authors' own reporting, but first published in Sherman and Palmer, *The Hill to Die On*, p. 303.

9 **had retired after six women accused him:** Matt Zapotosky, "Prominent Appeals Court Judge Alex Kozinski Accused of Sexual Misconduct," *Washington Post*, December 8, 2017, https://www.washingtonpost.com/world/national-security/prominent-appeals-court-judge-alex-kozinski-accused-of-sexual-misconduct/2017/12/08/1763e2b8-d913-11e7-a841-2066faf731ef_story.html?ut m_term=.5f084cca7801. See also Niraj Chokshi, "Federal Judge Alex Kozinski Retires Abruptly After Sexual Harassment Allegations," *The New York Times*, December 18, 2017, https://www.nytimes.com/2017/12/18/us/alex-kozinski-retires.html.

10 **Kentuckian initially argued for his own pick:** Maggie Haberman and Jonathan Martin, "McConnell Tries to Nudge Trump Toward Two Supreme Court Options," *The New York Times*, July 7, 2018, https://www.nytimes.com/2018/07/07/us/politics/trump-mcconnell-supreme-court.html.

10 **Among Barrett's skeptics, there was concern:** Laurie Goodstein, "Some Worry About Judicial Nominee's Ties to a Religious Group," *The New York Times,* September 28, 2017, https://www.nytimes.com/2017/09/28/us/amy-coney-barrett-nominee-religion.html. See also Amy Coney Barrett and John H. Garvey, "Catholic Judges in Capital Cases," *Marquette Law Review* 303, vol. 81 (1997–1998), https://scholarship.law.nd.edu/cgi/viewcontent.cgi?article=1523&context=law_faculty_scholarship.

12 **on July 2, when Kavanaugh was interviewed:** Christopher Catelago, Nancy Cook, and Andrew Restuccia, "How a Private Meeting with Kennedy Helped Trump Get to 'Yes' on Kavanaugh," *Politico,* July 7, 2018, https://www.politico .com/story/2018/07/09/brett-kavanaugh-trump-private-meeting-706137.

12 **when the judge met with Vice President Mike Pence:** Amy Howe, "Kavanaugh Returns Questionnaire," *SCOTUSblog,* July 25, 2018, https://www .scotusblog.com/2018/07/kavanaugh-returns-questionnaire/.

12 **Kavanaugh spoke again with Trump:** Seung Min Kim, Ann E. Marimow, Robert Barnes, and Elise Viebeck, "Supreme Court Nominee Brett Kavanaugh Won't Commit to Removing Himself from Cases Directly Affecting Trump," *Washington Post,* September 5, 2018, https://www.washingtonpost .com/powerpost/kavanaugh-hearing-trumps-supreme-court-nominee-fac es-senate-grilling/2018/09/05/97fda1ac-b081-11e8-9a6a-565d92a3585d _story.html?utm_term=.525648ec4791.

13 **Team Kavanaugh had another force . . . Trump's son Donald Jr.:** Catelago, Cook, and Restuccia, "How a Private Meeting." See also Carl Hulse, *Confirmation Bias* (New York: HarperCollins, 2019), p. 208, and Adam Liptak and Maggie Haberman, "Inside the White House's Quiet Campaign to Create a Supreme Court Opening," *The New York Times,* June 28, 2018, https:// www.nytimes.com/2018/06/28/us/politics/trump-anthony-kennedy-retire ment.html?hp& action=click&pgtype=Homepage&clickSource=story-heading &module=first-column-region&r egion=top-news&WT.nav=top-news.

14 **Kavanaugh had spent just a few years total . . . Monica Lewinsky scandal:** Senate Judiciary Committee, "Questionnaire for Nominee to the Supreme Court," accessed June 29, 2019, https://www.judiciary.senate.gov/imo /media/doc/Brett%20M.%20Kavanaugh%20SJQ%20(PUBLIC).pdf.

15 **"His judicial record spans":** J. D. Vance, "The Case for Brett Kavanaugh," *The Wall Street Journal,* July 2, 2018, https://www.wsj.com/articles/the-case -for-brett-kavanaugh-1530572358.

CHAPTER 2. *HOYA SAXA*: WHAT ROCKS

17 *Hoya Saxa*: The Georgetown Preparatory School motto derived from Georgetown University's motto. The date of first usage is not entirely clear but is estimated as 1840, when the university and the preparatory school was part of the same institution. See Stephen J. Ochs, *Academy on the Patowmack: Georgetown Preparatory School, 1789–1927* (Rockville, MD: Georgetown Preparatory School, 1989), 51. See also Georgetown University, "What's a Hoya?,"

accessed June 29, 2019, https://alumni.georgetown.edu/news/fast-facts-hoyas-should-know.

17 **a letter signed by nearly two hundred:** Michael J. Bidwill et al. to Mitch McConnell et al., letter from Brett Kavanaugh's Georgetown classmates, July 9, 2018, accessed at Senate Judiciary Committee site, https://www.judiciary.senate.gov/download/kavanaughs-georgetown-prep-classmates.

17 **An elite Jesuit boys' school:** Details in this chapter on Georgetown Preparatory School are informed by the authors' reporting, often from interviews with alumni from the late 1970s and early and mid-1980s, as well as from readings from *The Little Hoya*, yearbooks, and other contemporaneous writings. For background on the founding of the school, see Ochs, *Academy on the Patowmack*; see also Mark Gavreau Judge, *God and Man at Georgetown Prep: How I Became a Catholic Despite 20 Years of Catholic Schooling* (New York: The Crossroad Publishing Company, 2005); see also "Prep History at a Glance" and "Notable Alumni" among other pages on the Georgetown Preparatory School website, https://www.gprep.org/about/prep-history-at-a-glance.

18 **his father, Edward, started working:** Scott Shane, Steve Eder, Rebecca R. Ruiz, Adam Liptak, Charlie Savage, and Ben Protess, "Influential Judge, Loyal Friend, Conservative Warrior—and D.C. Insider," *The New York Times*, July 14, 2018, https://www.nytimes.com/2018/07/14/us/politics/judge-brett-kavanaugh.html; see also "Pamela G. Bailey to Be New President of the Cosmetic, Toiletry, and Fragrance Association," BusinessWire, March 5, 2005, https://www.businesswire.com/news/home/20050314006114/en/Pamela-G.-Bailey-New-President-Cosmetic-Toiletry.

18 **Brett would still remember:** Brett Kavanaugh hearing Senate Judiciary Committee opening statement transcript, September 4, 2018, https://www.politico.com/story/2018/09/04/full-text-brett-kavanaugh-confirmation-hearing-opening-statements-806420.

18 **Kavanaugh's mother, Martha:** Brett Kavanaugh Senate Judiciary Committee hearing opening statement transcript; see also Paul Schwartzman and Michelle Boorstein, "The Elite World of Brett Kavanaugh," *Washington Post*, July 11, 2018, https://www.washingtonpost.com/local/dc-politics/the-elite-world-of-brett-kavanaugh/2018/07/11/504d945e-8492-11e8-8f6c-46cb43e3f306_story.html.

18 **Partway through Brett's years . . . she would become a judge:** Schwartzman and Boorstein, "The Elite World of Brett Kavanaugh."

19 **won the prestigious Headmaster's Award:** Shane, Eder, et al., "Influential Judge," *The New York Times*, July 14, 2018; see also Michael Walsh, "How Brett

Kavanaugh's Religious Upbringing Shaped His Thinking," Yahoo News, July 12, 2018, https://www.yahoo.com/news/brett-kavanaughs-religious-upbringing -shaped-thinking-131552610.html.

21 **Brett didn't have a car:** Brett Kavanaugh Senate Judiciary Committee hearing transcript, September 27, 2018, https://www.washingtonpost.com/news /national/wp/2018/09/27/kavanaugh-hearing-transcript/?utm_term= .5043560df7e8.

22 **A military-style social hierarchy:** Authors' reporting, but see also Evgenia Peretz, "Men for Others, My Ass: After Kavanaugh, Inside Georgetown Prep's Culture of Omerta," *Vanity Fair*, December 17, 2018, https://www.vanityfair .com/news/2018/12/inside-georgetown-prep-culture-of-omerta-scandal.

26 **His extracurricular activities:** See Brett Kavanaugh's 1982 summer calendar, provided to the Senate Judiciary Committee in September 2018, https:// www.washingtonpost.com/apps/g/page/politics/brett-kavanaughs-calendar -from-1982/2332/; Kavanaugh hearing transcript from September 27, 2018; authors' reporting.

26 **But when drinking beer or palling around:** Authors' reporting; see also Marc Fisher, Anne Marimow, and Michael Kranish, "The Rise and the Reckoning: Inside Brett Kavanaugh's Elite Circles of Influence," *Washington Post*, October 4, 2018, https://www.washingtonpost.com/politics/the-rise-and -the-reckoning-inside-brett-kavanaughs-circles-of-influence/2018/10/04 /bd8dcf4e-c677-11e8-b1ed-1d2d65b86d0c_story.html?utm_term=.dcaa2407 80b4; see also declaration of Paul Rendón to Senate Judiciary Committee, October 1, 2018, https://www.judiciary.senate.gov/download/paul-rendon -declaration_-kavanaugh-nomination.

26 **On Monday mornings before class:** Authors' reporting; see also declaration of Paul Rendón to Senate Judiciary Committee.

27 **has called the boasts "horrible, hurtful":** Kate Kelly and David Enrich, "Kavanaugh's Yearbook Page Is 'Horrible, Hurtful' to a Woman It Named," *The New York Times*, September 24, 2018, https://www.nytimes.com/2018 /09/24/business/brett-kavanaugh-yearbook-renate.html.

28 **the parents also left town from time to time:** Authors' reporting; see also Peretz, "Men for Others, My Ass"; Mark Gavreau Judge, *Wasted: Tales of a Gen X Drunk* (Center City, MN: Hazelden, 1997).

28–29 **As a junior . . . sent everybody home:** Judge, *Wasted*, pp. 74–79.

34 **Some criticized Bidwill:** Seth Cox, "Reactions and Thoughts on the Michael Bidwill Situation," SBNation, July 11, 2018, https://www.revengeofthebirds .com/2018/7/11/17559066/reactions-and-thoughts-on-the-michael-bidwill -situation-arizona-cardinals-brett-kavanaugh.

CHAPTER 3. *INVENIAM VIAM AUT FACIAM:*
I WILL FIND A WAY OR MAKE ONE

35 *Inveniam Viam aut Faciam:* The Holton-Arms School's motto.

36 **Kavanaugh, who had turned seventeen . . . Anne Dougherty, and Chris Garrett:** Authors' reporting including interviews and excerpts of *The Little Hoya*, Georgetown Preparatory School's official newspaper, from 1982 as well as Kavanaugh's 1982 summer calendar, provided to the Senate Judiciary Committee in September 2018, https://www.washingtonpost.com/apps/g/page /politics/brett-kavanaughs-calendar-from-1982/2332/. See also Brett Kavanaugh Senate Judiciary Committee hearing transcript, September 27, 2018, https://www.washingtonpost.com/news/national/wp/2018/09/27/kavanaugh -hearing-transcript/?utm_term=.c2541dcc5f2b.

37 **"Because we were going to be seniors":** Mark Gavreau Judge, *Wasted: Tales of a Gen X Drunk* (Center City, MN: Hazelden, 1997), p. 92.

37 **show up hungover:** Judge, *Wasted*, p. 93.

37 **"When I was in town":** Kavanaugh Senate Judiciary Committee hearing transcript, September 27, 2018.

38–39 **Founded by two Washington women . . . light of knowledge:** Kathy Orton, "Kalorama Condominiums Were Once the Holton-Arms School for Girls," *Washington Post*, February 1, 2019, https://www.washingtonpost.com/realestate /kalorama-condominiums-were-once-the-holton-arms-school-for-girls/201 9/01/31/297f16da-20e2-11e9-8e21-59a09ff1e2a1_story.html?noredirect =on&utm_term=.78b0ade12fd8; see also "First Lady Biography: Jackie Kennedy," *National First Ladies' Library*, accessed July 16, 2019, http://www.firstladies .org/biographies/firstladies.aspx?biography=36; and also "Holton-Arms History," Holton-Arms school site, accessed July 16, 2019, https://www.holton-arms .edu/about/history-of-holton-arms.

40 **"In class, she always contributed":** Jessica Contrera, Ian Shapira, Emma Brown, and Steve Hendrix, "Kavanaugh Accuser Christine Blasey Ford Moved 3,000 Miles to Reinvent Her Life. It Wasn't Far Enough," *Washington Post*, September 27, 2018, https://www.washingtonpost.com/local/christine -blasey-ford-wanted-to-flee-the-us-to-avoid-brett-kavanaugh-now-she-may -testify-against-him/2018/09/22/db942340-bdb1-11e8-8792-78719177250f _story.html?utm_term=.7915d422d455.

41 **Tuition was in line with Prep's:** Eric Pianin and *Washington Post* staff writer, "Private Schools Widely Oppose D.C. Tax Credit," *Washington Post*, October 24, 1981, https://www.washingtonpost.com/archive/local/1981/10/24/private -schools-widely-oppose-dc-tax-credit/d31dab9a-4532-49ea-9595-331a385a6200 /?utm_term=.dcc6fcfe932a.

42 **Blasey accompanied Garrett to several:** Christine Blasey Ford Senate Judiciary Committee hearing transcript, September 27, 2018, https://www.washingtonpost.com/news/national/wp/2018/09/27/kavanaugh-hearing-transcript/?utm_term=.5043560df7e8.

42 **swimming and practicing diving:** Blasey Ford Senate Judiciary Committee hearing transcript, September 27, 2018.

44 **One evening after a day:** Blasey Ford Senate Judiciary Committee hearing transcript, September 27, 2018.

44 **She does have a visual memory:** Blasey Ford Senate Judiciary Committee hearing transcript, September 27, 2018, and also authors' reporting.

45 **she went upstairs to use the bathroom:** Blasey Ford Senate Judiciary Committee hearing transcript, September 27, 2018, and also authors' reporting.

45 **Here is how she describes it:** Blasey Ford Senate Judiciary Committee hearing transcript, September 27, 2018, and also authors' reporting.

45–46 **He urged Kavanaugh on . . . as they descended:** Blasey Ford Senate Judiciary Committee hearing transcript, September 27, 2018, and also authors' reporting.

46 **She remembers getting a D:** Contrera, Shapira, Brown, and Hendrix, "Kavanaugh Accuser Christine Blasey Ford Moved 3,000 Miles to Reinvent Her Life"; authors' reporting on additional details.

47 **California agreed with Blasey:** Contrera, Shapira, Brown, and Hendrix, "Kavanaugh Accuser Christine Blasey Ford Moved 3,000 Miles to Reinvent Her Life"; authors' reporting on additional details; Christine Blasey résumé, accessed in Senate Judiciary Committee memorandum on November 2, 2018, https://www.judiciary.senate.gov/imo/media/doc/2018-11-02%20Kavanaugh%20Report.pdf.

48 **In 2012, she shared the broad contours:** Russell Ford declaration to the Senate Judiciary Committee, September 25, 2018.

48 **At one point the Fords argued . . . a few of her friends in Palo Alto:** Christine Blasey Ford Senate Judiciary Committee hearing transcript, September 27, 2018; declarations to Senate Judiciary Committee of Keith Koegler, Adela Gildo-Mazzon, September 24, 2018, and Rebecca White, September 25, 2018.

48 **Over a pizza dinner:** Declaration of Adela Gildo-Mazzon, September 24, 2018; authors' reporting.

49 **The topic arose again three years later:** Declaration of Keith Koegler, September 24, 2018; authors' reporting.

49 **One evening the following year:** Declaration of Rebecca White, September 25, 2018.

52 **That same morning, Ford followed:** Christine Blasey Ford WhatsApp texts, Friday, July 6, 2018, accessed through Senate Judiciary Committee report on November 2, 2018.

53 **Four days after that:** Christine Blasey Ford WhatsApp text, Friday July 10, 2018, accessed through Senate Judiciary Committee report on November 2, 2018.

CHAPTER 4. *LUX ET VERITAS*: LIGHT AND TRUTH

55 *Lux et Veritas*: The Yale University motto.

60 **"We had basketball every day":** Brett Kavanaugh interview with Senate Judiciary Committee, Sept. 25, 2018, https://www.judiciary.senate.gov/download /092518-bmk-interview-transcript-redacted.

61 **writing about sports for the *Yale Daily News*:** Brett Kavanaugh, "Lackluster Yale Needs a Boost," *Yale Daily News*, January 15, 1986.

61 **Rusty Sullivan, another sportswriter:** Alanna Durkin Richer and Jennifer Peltz, "At Yale, Kavanaugh Stayed Out of Debates at a Time of Many," August 28, 2018, https://apnews.com/ce93f04d0594441ebe14f7cfb2442f11.

62 **Delta Kappa Epsilon fraternity, or DKE:** John Davenport, "Fraternities Are No Laughing Matter," *Yale Daily News*, January 31, 1986.

62 **Lynne Brookes, who was captain:** Aaron C. Davis, Emma Brown, and Joe Heim, "Kavanaugh's 'Choir Boy' Image on Fox Interview Rankles Former Yale Classmates," *Washington Post*, September 25, 2018, https://www.washingtonpost .com/investigations/2018/09/25/ea5e50d4-c0eb-11e8-9005-5104e9616c21 _story.html.

63 **after attending a UB40 concert:** Emily Bazelon and Ben Protess, "Kavanaugh Was Questioned by Police After Bar Fight in 1985," *The New York Times*, October 2, 2018, https://www.nytimes.com/2018/10/01/us/politics/kavanaugh -bar-fight.html.

65 *Washington Post Magazine* **article about redecorating:** Jura Koncius, "Making Sense of a Many Splendored Collection," *Washington Post*, May 5, 1985, https://www.washingtonpost.com/archive/lifestyle/magazine/1985/05/05 /making-sense-of-a-many-splendored-collection/acc781f1-80ed-4666 -a875-2c5419b6c653/.

65 **Ramirez said the guys kept picking her:** Authors' own reporting, but first published in Ronan Farrow and Jane Mayer, "Senate Democrats Investigate a New Allegation of Sexual Misconduct, from Brett Kavanaugh's College Years," *The New Yorker*, September 23, 2018, https://www.newyorker.com

/news/news-desk/senate-democrats-investigate-a-new-allegation-of-sexual
-misconduct-from-the-supreme-court-nominee-brett-kavanaughs-college
-years-deborah-ramirez.

67 **Michael Wetstone, another classmate:** Jane Mayer and Ronan Farrow, "The
F.B.I. Probe Ignored Testimonies from Former Classmates of Kavanaugh," *The
New Yorker*, October 3, 2018, https://www.newyorker.com/news/news-desk
/will-the-fbi-ignore-testimonies-from-kavanaughs-former-classmates.

CHAPTER 5. *ONUS PROBANDI*: THE BURDEN OF PROOF

71 **She had participated in a local Women's March:** Julia Prodis Sulek,
"Christine Blasey Ford Feared an Avalanche of Attacks if She Went Public
About Kavanaugh, Friends Say," *The Mercury News*, September 17, 2018,
https://www.mercurynews.com/2018/09/17/metoo-spurred-christine-blasey
-ford-to-open-up-about-alleged-attack-year-before-kavanaugh-nomination
-friends-say/.

71 **Her political donations in recent years:** Federal Election Commission individual contribution records, accessed June 30, 2019.

72 **"Brett Kavanaugh physically and sexually":** "Read Christine Blasey Ford's
Initial Letter to Dianne Feinstein," *Axios*, September 23, 2018, https://www
.axios.com/brett-kavanaugh-christine-blasey-ford-feinstein-letter-9337f417
-1078-4334-8a81-c2b4fc051f99.html.

75 **She had no intention of telling:** Christine Blasey Ford Senate Judiciary
Committee hearing transcript, September 27, 2018; authors' reporting.

77 **On August 7, a former FBI agent:** Jeremiah Hanafin, Christine Blasey Ford
polygraph examination report, August 10, 2018, in Senate Judiciary Committee memo; authors' reporting.

77 **Ford filled a legal-pad page:** Christine Blasey Ford, handwritten account of
alleged assault, August 7, 2018, in Senate Judiciary Committee memo.

77 **The examination rested:** Jeremiah Hanafin, Blasey Ford polygraph report,
August 10, 2018; see also photograph of Christine Blasey Ford taken during
August 7, 2018, polygraph test, https://www.usatoday.com/story/news
/politics/2018/09/26/christine-blasey-fords-polygraph-test-brett-kavana
ugh-sexual-assault-allegations/1434270002/.

CHAPTER 6. *AMBITIO*: AMBITION, OR COURTING THE VOTE

80 **his accumulated debt:** Amy Brittain, "Supreme Court Nominee Brett Kavanaugh Piled Up Credit Card Debt by Purchasing Nationals Tickets, White

House Says," *Washington Post*, July 11, 2018, https://www.washingtonpost
.com/investigations/supreme-court-nominee-brett-kavanaugh-piled-up
-credit-card-debt-by-purchasing-nationals-tickets-white-house-says/2018
/07/11/8e3ad7d6-8460-11e8-9e80-403a221946a7_story.html.

80 **Also in the mix was Bill Shine:** Katherine Krueger, "Ex-Fox News Exec
Who Allegedly Helped Cover Up Harassment Is Helping Prep Brett Kavanaugh," *Splinter News*, September 19, 2018, https://splinternews.com/ex-fox
-news-exec-who-allegedly-helped-cover-up-harassme-1829175692.

80 **Even Senators Orrin Hatch and Lindsey Graham:** Seung Min Kim, "Republicans Drill Kavanaugh in Mock Hearings in Preparation for Real Questioning," *Washington Post*, August 30, 2018, https://www.washingtonpost.com/politics
/republicans-drill-kavanaugh-in-mock-hearings-in-preparation-for-real
-questioning/2018/08/30/dd4b853c-ac9c-11e8-8f4b-aee063e14538_story.html.

81 **Nevertheless, Kavanaugh achieved a strong enough record:** Brett Kavanaugh Supreme Court Questionnaire, 2018, https://www.judiciary.senate
.gov/imo/media/doc/Brett%20M.%20Kavanaugh%20SJQ%20(PUBLIC).pdf.

82 **"He had one of the most impressive résumés":** Judge Walter K. Stapleton
statement at Kavanaugh confirmation hearing for D.C. Circuit, C-SPAN
video, May 6, 2006, 00:22:45, https://www.c-span.org/video/?192420-1/brett
-kavanaugh-testifies-dc-circuit-confirmation-hearing-2006.

82 **In a 1991 *Yale Law Journal* article:** Alex Kozinski, "Confessions of a Bad
Apple," *Yale Law Journal*, 1991, https://digitalcommons.law.yale.edu/cgi/view
content.cgi?article=7349&context=ylj.

82 **"my good friend":** Judge Alex Kozinski statement at Kavanaugh confirmation hearing for D.C. Circuit, C-SPAN video, May 6, 2006, 00:31:43, https://
www.c-span.org/video/?192420-1/brett-kavanaugh-testifies-dc-circuit-con
firmation-hearing-2006.

83 **"Learned from the master" . . . "being a judge means":** Alex Kozinski and
Brett Kavanaugh on panel, *Life on the Bench*, video, National Lawyers Convention, November 14, 2015, https://fedsoc.org/commentary/videos/life-on-the
-bench-event-audio-video.

83 **"was a gut punch for me":** Brett Kavanaugh testimony, Senate Judiciary
Committee hearing, September 5, 2018, C-SPAN video, 1:22:24, https://
www.c-span.org/video/?449705-1/supreme-court-nominee-brett-kavanaugh
-confirmati on-hearing-day-2-part-1&playEvent&start=4897.

84 **video of naked women skydiving:** Emily Peck, "Brett Kavanaugh and the
Men Who Say Nothing," *Huffington Post*, September 25, 2018, https://www
.huffpost.com/entry/kavanaugh-kozinski-harassment-silence_n_5baa8151e4
b0f101d38375ab.

84 **"This last response leaves me wondering"**: Heidi Bond, "I Received Some of Kozinski's Infamous Gag List Emails. I'm Baffled by Kavanaugh's Responses to Questions About Them," *Slate*, September 14, 2018, https://slate .com/news-and-politics/2018/09/kavanaugh-kozinski-gag-list-emails-senate -hearings.html.

84 **"McCarthyism, pure and simple"**: Steven Calabresi, "Brett Kavanaugh and His Association with Alex Kozinski," *The Hill*, August 12, 2018, https:// thehill.com/opinion/judiciary/401468-brett-kavanaugh-and-his-association -with-alex-kozinski.

85 **Kavanaugh later described his phone call from Priest**: Ryan J. Foley and Curt Anderson, "Kavanaugh's Ties to Disgraced Mentor Loom Over Confirmation," Associated Press, August 29, 2018, https://apnews.com/e37ba9b c11014b72a5db6f926f80eb42.

85 **"that often meant, in the Yale Law School environment"**: Brett Kavanaugh speech to American Enterprise Institute, "From the Bench: Judge Brett Kavanaugh on the Constitutional Statesmanship of Chief Justice William Rehnquist," September 18, 2017, https://www.aei.org/wp-content/uploads/2017 /08/from-the-bench.pdf.

86 **"none of us can say that Judge Kavanaugh stood out"**: Letter to Judiciary Committee, August 27, 2018, https://www.judiciary.senate.gov/download/23 -classmates-from-yale-law-school-class-of-1990-to-grassley-feinstein _-kavanaugh-nomination.

87 **"'What happens on the bus stays on the bus'"**: Pema Levy, "Brett Kavanaugh Gave a Speech About Binge Drinking in Law School," *Mother Jones*, September 17, 2018, https://www.motherjones.com/politics/2018/09/brett-kavanaugh -gave-a-speech-about-binge-drinking-in-law-school/.

88 **"limited dance moves"**: Hailey Fuchs and Adelaide Feibel, "A Sports Junkie Who Ate Pasta with Ketchup: Law School Friends Reflect on Kavanaugh's Time at YLS," *Yale Daily News*, July 12, 2018, https://yaledailynews.com /blog/2018/07/12/a-sports-junkie-who-ate-pasta-with-ketchup-law-school -friends-reflect-on-kavanaughs-time-at-yls/.

89 **Kenneth Christmas . . . during the confirmation hearings**: Statement of Kenneth C. Christmas, Jr., before the Senate Committee on the Judiciary, September 7, 2018 https://www.judiciary.senate.gov/imo/media/doc/Christ mas%20Testimony.pdf.

89 **Kavanaugh named as the tenth an employment discrimination case**: Brett Kavanaugh Supreme Court Questionnaire, 2018, https://www.judiciary.senate .gov/imo/media/doc/Brett%20M.%20Kavanaugh%20SJQ%20(PUBLIC).pdf.

89 **As a law student:** Brett M. Kavanaugh, "Defense Presence and Participation: A Procedural Minimum for Batson v. Kentucky Hearings," *Yale Law Journal*, 1989, https://digitalcommons.law.yale.edu/cgi/viewcontent.cgi?article=7241&context=ylj.

90 **"a criminal trial free of racial discrimination in the jury selection process":** Adam Liptak, "Excluding Black Jurors in Curtis Flowers Case Violated Constitution, Supreme Court Rules," *The New York Times*, June 21, 2019, https://www.nytimes.com/2019/06/21/us/politics/curtis-flowers-supreme-court-in-the-dark-podcast.html.

90 **he'd scribble on a whiteboard the pros and cons of a given case:** Nina Totenberg, "Examining What Justice Anthony Kennedy's Retirement Means," NPR, June 28, 2018, https://www.npr.org/2018/06/28/624165381/examining-what-justice-anthony-kennedy-s-retirement-means.

91 **"I am strongly opposed to giving the President any 'break' in the questioning":** Brett Kavanaugh memo to the Independent Counsel Kenneth Starr, 1998, https://www.archives.gov/files/research/kavanaugh/releases/kavanaugh8.15.98.pdf.

92 **"It makes no sense at all to have":** Brett Kavanaugh, "Independent Counsel Statute Future" speech at Georgetown University Law Center, C-SPAN video, February 19, 1998, https://www.c-span.org/video/?101056-1/independent-counsel-statute-future.

92 **"a scenario whereby the President and the independent counsel are adversaries":** Brett Kavanaugh, "The President and the Independent Counsel," *Georgetown Law Journal*, 1998, https://www.justsecurity.org/wp-content/uploads/2018/06/BrettMKavanaughThePreside.pdf.

92 **"if President Clinton could have focused on Osama bin Laden":** Brett Kavanaugh, "Separation of Powers During the Forty-Fourth Presidency and Beyond," *Minnesota Law Review*, 2009, http://www.minnesotalawreview.org/wp-content/uploads/2012/01/Kavanaugh_MLR.pdf.

94 **"sweet" and "the All-American girl":** Greg Jaklewicz and Timothy Chipp, "Abilenians Fondly Regard Ashley Estes, Wife of Trump Supreme Court Nominee Brett Kavanaugh," *Abilene Reporter-News*, July 13, 2018, https://www.reporternews.com/story/news/local/2018/07/13/abilene-tx-love-wife-trump-supreme-court-nominee-ashley-estes-kavanaugh/778674002/.

94 **President Bush and the first lady hosted a sit-down dinner:** Marc Fisher, Ann E. Marimow, and Michael Kranish, "The Rise and the Reckoning: Inside Brett Kavanaugh's Circles of Influence," *Washington Post*, October 4, 2018, https://www.washingtonpost.com/politics/the-rise-and-the-reckoning-inside

-brett-kavanaughs-circles-of-influence/2018/10/04/bd8dcf4e-c677
-11e8-b1ed-1d2d65b86d0c_story.html.

94 **"the first lifetime appointment" he'd arranged for Kavanaugh:** White House Office of the Press Secretary, "President Attends Swearing-In Ceremony for Brett Kavanaugh to the U.S. Court of Appeals for the District of Columbia Circuit," June 1, 2006, https://georgewbush-whitehouse.archives .gov/news/releases/2006/06/20060601-4.html.

94 **"a more partisan record than any single nominee":** Remarks from Senator Chuck Schumer, "Confirmation Hearing on the Nomination of Brett M. Kavanaugh to Be Circuit Judge for the District of Columbia Circuit," April 27, 2004, https://www.congress.gov/108/chrg/shrg24853/CHRG-108shrg24853 .htm.

95 **a pragmatic approach to the bench:** Edith Roberts, "Potential Nominee Profile: Brett Kavanaugh," *SCOTUSblog,* June 28, 2018, https://www.scotus blog.com/2018/06/potential-nominee-profile-brett-kavanaugh/.

95 **the so-called "Eureka dinners":** Stephanie Kirchgaessner, "Dining Club Emails Reveal Kavanaugh's Close Ties to Trump's Solicitor General," *The Guardian,* October 25, 2018, https://www.theguardian.com/us-news/2018/oct /25/brett-kavanaugh-eureka-club-noel-francisco-emails.

96 **Even the ACLU recognized that Kavanaugh had been sympathetic:** ACLU, "Report of the American Civil Liberties Union on the Nomination of Judge Brett M. Kavanaugh to Be Associate Justice of the United States Supreme Court," August 15, 2018, https://www.aclu.org/sites/default/files /field_document/final_aclu_report_on_judge_brett_m_kavanaugh.pdf.

96 **an expert on battered women's syndrome:** Brett Kavanaugh opinion in *U.S. v. NWOYE,* June 10, 2016, https://www.leagle.com/decision/infco20160610132.

96 **"He wrote a primer essentially on the defense of battered women's syndrome for lawyers":** Remarks from A. J. Kramer, "Senate Judiciary Committee Hearing on the Nomination of Brett Kavanaugh to Be an Associate Justice of the Supreme Court, Day 4, Part 2," September 7, 2018, https://www.judiciary .senate.gov/download/09-04-2018-kramer-testimony.

96 **"I myself do not know what his views are on the political issues of the day":** Remarks from Rebecca Taibleson, "Senate Judiciary Committee Hearing on the Nomination of Brett Kavanaugh to Be an Associate Justice of the Supreme Court, Day 4, Part 2," September 7, 2018, https://www.judiciary .senate.gov/download/taibleson-testimony.

97 **"sudden drop" in female law clerks on the Supreme Court:** Linda Greenhouse, "Women Suddenly Scarce Among Justices' Clerks," *The New York*

Times, August 30, 2006, https://www.nytimes.com/2006/08/30/washington
/30scotus.html.

97 **"He said, 'You're a mom coming to clerk'":** Remarks from Sarah Pitlyk at
Heritage Foundation panel, "Who Is Brett Kavanaugh?—A Closer Look at
Trump's Supreme Court Nominee," August 9, 2018, https://www.heritage
.org/courts/event/who-brett-kavanaugh-closer-look-trumps-supreme
-court-nominee.

97 **The judge himself demonstrated:** Schwartzman and Boorstein, "The Elite
World of Brett Kavanaugh."

98 **"opening these doors for a new generation of women lawyers":** Remarks
from Maureen E. Mahoney, "Senate Judiciary Committee Hearing On the
Nomination of Brett Kavanaugh to Be an Associate Justice of the Supreme
Court, Day 4, Part 2," September 7, 2018, https://www.judiciary.senate.gov
/download/mahoney-testimony.

98 **Kavanaugh liked his clerks to have a "certain look":** Emily Peck, "Brett
Kavanaugh Liked Female Clerks Who Looked a 'Certain Way,' Yale Student
Was Told," *Huffington Post*, September 19, 2018, https://www.huffpost.com
/entry/yale-student-brett-kavanaugh-clerkship-look_n_5ba2f051e4b0181540
d9e2bb. See also: Stephanie Kirchgaessner and Jessica Glenza, "'No Accident'
Brett Kavanaugh's Female Law Clerks 'Looked Like Models,' Yale Professor
Told Students," *The Guardian*, September 20, 2018, https://www.theguardian
.com/us-news/2018/sep/20/brett-kavanaugh-supreme-court-yale-amy-chua.

CHAPTER 7. *VIDES STYGIAM PALUDEM*:
YOU ARE GAZING AT THE STYGIAN SWAMP

103 **nearly three-quarters of the votes:** Santa Clara County Registrar of Voters
Post-Election Report for November 8, 2016, presidential general election, ac-
cessed June 30, 2019, https://www.sccgov.org/sites/rov/Resources/Documents
/Statistics/ROV%20Post-Election%20Report%20Oct%202017%20Rev.-%20
November%208%202016%20Presidential%20General%20Election.pdf.

103 **Late in August, after Ford began:** Christine Blasey Ford Senate Judiciary
Committee hearing transcript, September 27, 2018, https://www.washing
tonpost.com/news/national/wp/2018/09/27/kavanaugh-hearing-transcript
/?utm_term=.5043560df7e8.

105 **The Republicans maintained that the volume:** Manu Raju and Lauren
Fox, "Republicans Won't Budge on Kavanaugh Documents Amid Dem Accusations of Hiding Records," CNN, August 2, 2018, https://www.cnn

.com/2018/08/02/politics/brett-kavanaugh-documents-republican-not
-budging/index.html.

106 **ushered out by Ashley:** Jim Daly, "Kavanaugh's Daughters Should Not Have
to Watch Their Dad Being Bullied—When Is All of This Going to Stop?,"
Fox News, September 5, 2018, https://www.foxnews.com/opinion/kavanaughs
-daughters-should-not-have-to-watch-their-dad-being-bullied-when-is-all
-of-this-going-to-stop.

108 **At 5:24 p.m. on Wednesday:** Ryan Grim, "Dianne Feinstein Withholding
Brett Kavanaugh Document from Fellow Judiciary Committee Members,"
The Intercept, September 12, 2018, https://theintercept.com/2018/09/12/brett
-kavanaugh-confirmation-dianne-feinstein/.

109 **Feinstein publicly acknowledged:** Seung Min Kim, Twitter, September 13,
2018, https://twitter.com/seungminkim/status/1040283042202443776.

109 **"Two officials familiar with the matter":** Nicholas Fandos and Catie Ed-
monson, "Dianne Feinstein Refers a Kavanaugh Matter to Federal Investigators," *The New York Times*, September 13, 2018, https://www.nytimes.com
/2018/09/13/us/politics/brett-kavanaugh-dianne-feinstein.html.

110 **"Upon receipt of the information":** Kristina Peterson and Jess Bravin,
"Feinstein Relays Allegation About Kavanaugh to FBI," *The Wall Street Journal*, September 13, 2018, https://www.wsj.com/articles/kavanaugh-discussed
-solicitor-generals-post-with-trump-transition-team-1536859134.

110 **saw a story on the website *ThinkProgress*:** Ian Millhiser, "Brett Kavanaugh
Has a Mysterious #MeToo Problem," *ThinkProgress*, September 13, 2018,
https://thinkprogress.org/brett-kavanaugh-has-a-mysterious-metoo-problem
-5a24b572d72d/.

111 **On September 14, the Ford allegations surfaced:** Ronan Farrow and Jane
Mayer, "A Sexual-Misconduct Allegation Against the Supreme Court Nominee Brett Kavanaugh Stirs Tension Among Democrats in Congress," *The New
Yorker*, September 14, 2018, https://www.newyorker.com/news/news-desk/a
-sexual-misconduct-allegation-against-the-supreme-court-nominee-brett
-kavanaugh-stirs-tension-among-democrats-in-congress.

112 **Working quickly through a network:** Chris Geidner, Tarini Parti, and Zoe
Tillman, "Here's How that Letter from 65 Women Supporting Brett Kavanaugh Came Together So Quickly," *BuzzFeed News*, September 14, 2018, https
://www.buzzfeednews.com/article/chrisgeidner/brett-kavanaugh-allegations
-women-letter-chuck-grassley.

112 **"Through the more than 35 years":** Jennifer Slye Aniskovich et al., Letter
to Charles Grassley and Dianne Feinstein about Brett Kavanaugh, September

14, 2018, https://www.judiciary.senate.gov/download/2018-09-14-65-women
-who-know-kavanaugh-from-high-school_-kavanaugh-nomination.

CHAPTER 8. *IUDICANS IUDICEM*: JUDGING THE JUDGE

115 **On September 16, the world learned:** Emma Brown, "California Professor,
Writer of Confidential Brett Kavanaugh Letter, Speaks Out About Her Allegation of Sexual Assault," *Washington Post*, September 16, 2018, https://www
.washingtonpost.com/investigations/california-professor-writer-of-confi
dential-brett-kavanaugh-letter-speaks-out-about-her-allegation-of-sexual
-assault/2018/09/16/46982194-b846-11e8-94eb-3bd52dfe917b_story.html
?utm_term=.b1e0b23bf5c9.

115 **was pressuring Feinstein to brief:** Ryan Grim, *We've Got People: From Jesse
Jackson to Alexandria Ocasio-Cortez, the End of Big Money and the Rise of a Movement* (Washington, D.C.: Strong Arm Press, 2019), 372; authors' reporting.

115 **Early in the week of September 10:** Authors' reporting; see also Brian Stel-
ter, "Post Reporter Says Kavanaugh Accuser 'Was Terrified of Going Public,'" CNN Business, September 17, 2018, https://money.cnn.com/2018/09/16
/media/reliable-sources-09-16-18/index.html.

116 **Russell, driving one of their sons:** Jessica Contrera, Ian Shapira, Emma
Brown, and Steve Hendrix, "Kavanaugh Accuser Christine Blasey Ford
Moved 3,000 Miles to Reinvent Her Life. It Wasn't Far Enough," *Washington
Post*, September 27, 2018, https://www.washingtonpost.com/local/christine
-blasey-ford-wanted-to-flee-the-us-to-avoid-brett-kavanaugh-now-she-may
-testify-against-him/2018/09/22/db942340-bdb1-11e8-8792-78719177250f
_story.html.

117 **would end up spending about $22 million:** Chris Walker, "Conservative
'Dark Money' Group Spent $22 Million to Promote Brett Kavanaugh," *Hill
Reporter*, May 19, 2019, https://hillreporter.com/conservative-dark-money
-group-spent-22-million-to-promote-brett-kavanaugh-36289.

117 **The National Rifle Association also spent large sums:** "NRA-ILA
Launches Major Advertising Campaign Urging Confirmation of Brett Kavanaugh," August 7, 2018, https://www.nraila.org/articles/20180807/nra-ila
-launches-major-advertising-campaign-urging-confirmation-of-judge
-brett-kavanaugh.

117 **accused her of wanting to "assist":** Nicholas Fandos, "Dianne Feinstein
Rode One Court Fight to the Senate. Another Has Left Her Under Siege,"
The New York Times, September 16, 2018, https://www.nytimes.com/2018

/09/21/us/politics/dianne-feinstein-brett-kavanaugh-sexual-misconduct
.html.

118 **he unequivocally denied:** Brett Kavanaugh interview with the Senate Judiciary Committee, September 17, 2018, https://www.judiciary.senate.gov/imo
/media/doc/09.17.18%20BMK%20Interview%20Transcript%20(Re
dacted).pdf.

118 **Susanna Jones, its head of school:** Valerie Strauss, "High School Attended
by Kavanaugh's Accuser Says It Is 'Proud' of Her for Speaking Up," *Washington Post*, September 17, 2018, https://www.washingtonpost.com/education
/2018/09/17/high-school-attended-by-kavanaughs-accuser-comes-out-sup
port-her/.

118 **Twenty-three members of Ford's 1984 class:** Allyson Abrams Bergman
et al., Letter to Congress on Christine Blasey Ford, September 17, 2018, https://
static1.squarespace.com/static/5ba01d0c3917ee078e3c3da8/t/5ba106b86d2a7
39e1b8b15d7/1537279672511/Letter+to+Congress+-+Holton+Class+of
+1984.pdf.

119 **More than six hundred Holton alumnae:** Sarah Burgess et al., "We Stand
with Dr. Christine Blasey Ford," accessed June 30, 2019, https://www.stand
withblaseyford.com/.

119 **"her worst fears have materialized":** Debra S. Katz and Lisa J. Banks, Letter
to Charles Grassley, September 18, 2018, https://www.judiciary.senate.gov
/imo/media/doc/2018-09-25%20Ford%20Document%20Production.pdf.

119 **Ford had been targeted ... the lawyers argued:** Katz and Banks, Letter to
Charles Grassley.

119 **"I do not recall the party":** Barbara "Biz" Van Gelder, Letter to Charles
Grassley and Dianne Feinstein regarding Brett Kavanaugh confirmation,
September 18, 2018, https://twitter.com/seungminkim/status/1042146479073
374209/photo/1.

119 **"I have no knowledge of the party":** Eric B. Bruce, Letter to Charles Grassley and Dianne Feinstein regarding confirmation hearing of Brett Kavanaugh, September 18, 2018, accessed via Senate Judiciary Committee November
2, 2018, https://www.judiciary.senate.gov/download/2018-09-18-smyth-to
-judiciary-committee_--ford-allegations.

120 **The GoFundMe campaign:** "Help Christine Blasey Ford," GoFundMe.com,
initiated September 18, 2018, https://www.gofundme.com/help-christine-blasey
-ford.

120 **The Palo Alto community also showed its support:** Bay Area News Group,
"Supporters of Christine Blasey Ford Rally on the Ground, in the Air—'Her
Story Is Our Story,'" *The Mercury News*, September 20, 2018, https://www

.mercurynews.com/2018/09/20/photos-palo-alto-moms-rally-in-support
-of-christine-blasey-ford/; see also George Kelly, "Hundreds Attend Vigil in
Palo Alto to Support Christine Blasey Ford," *The Mercury News*, September
23, 2018, https://www.mercurynews.com/2018/09/23/thousands-attend-vigil
-in-palo-alto-to-support-blasey-ford/.

120 **Mike Davis, Grassley's lieutenant, trumpeted on Twitter:** Todd Ruger,
"Judiciary Staffer's Tweets Fuel Fight Over Kavanaugh Accuser," *Roll Call*,
September 20, 2018, https://www.rollcall.com/news/politics/staffers-tweets
-fuel-fight-kavanaugh-accuser.

122 **Then Edward Whelan, a friend of Kavanaugh's:** Morgan Sung, "Man
Tries to Use Zillow to Prove Kavanaugh's Innocence and Ends Up Owning
Himself," *Mashable*, September 20, 2018, https://mashable.com/article/ed
-whelan-uses-zillow-kavanaugh-innocence-conspiracy-theory/.

122–23 **Steve Schmidt, a longtime Republican:** Zack Beauchamp, "Ed Whelan's
Tweets Have Created a Second Kavanaugh Scandal," *Vox*, September 21, 2018,
https://www.vox.com/policy-and-politics/2018/9/21/17886430/brett-kavanaugh
-news-ed-whelan-trump.

123 **"mistaken identity" argument:** Seung Min Kim, Josh Dawsey, and Emma
Brown, "Kavanaugh Accuser Won't Testify Monday but Open to Doing so
Later Next Week," *Washington Post*, September 21, 2018, https://www.wash
ingtonpost.com/politics/gop-vows-to-move-ahead-with-kavanaugh-vote-if
-his-accuser-doesnt-testify-monday/2018/09/20/a7132ee8-bcf5-11e8-8792
-78719177250f_story.html?noredire ct=on&utm_term=.91ecea8c2aae.

123 **Whelan . . . later apologized:** Ed Whelan, Twitter, September 21, 2018,
https://twitter.com/EdWhelanEPPC/status/1043117304152817664.

128 **"no recollection of ever being at a party":** Burgess Everett, "Woman Denies Attending Party Where Alleged Kavanaugh Assault Occurred," *Politico*,
September 22, 2018, https://www.politico.com/story/2018/09/22/kavanaugh
-ford-woman-party-letter-836913.

128 **The following day, Keyser told:** Kim, Dawsey, and Brown, "Kavanaugh Accuser Won't Testify Monday."

128 **she had parlayed her athletic talent:** "Women's Golfers Say Goodbye to
Their First-Ever Head Coach," *The Hoya*, October 21, 2005, https://www.the
hoya.com/womens-golfers-say-goodbye-to-their-first-ever-head-coach/;
see also, "Women's Golf Head Coach Leland Keyser Resigns," Georgetown
Athletics, October 12, 2005, http://www.guhoyas.com/news/2005/10/12
/Women_s_Golf_Head_Coach_Leland_Keyser_resigns.aspx.

129 **She had lost a boyfriend after a diving accident:** *Leakas v. Columbia Country
Club*, civil case filed in U.S. District Court for the District of Maryland, July

9, 1993, https://law.justia.com/cases/federal/district-courts/FSupp/831/1231
/1802366/.

129 **captured on film by** *Daily Mail* **reporters:** Laura Collins, "'Christine Ford
Threw Her Under the Bus.' . . ." *Daily Mail*, October 3, 2018, https://www
.dailymail.co.uk/news/article-6235463/Christine-Fords-high-school-friend
-blindsided-named-corroborating-witness.html.

129 **"Okay. So we're on the same page":** Brett Kavanaugh interview with Senate
Judiciary Committee, September 25, 2018, https://www.judiciary.senate.gov
/imo/media/doc/09.25.18%20BMK%20Interview%20Transcript%20
(Redacted).pdf.

130 **appeared on** *PBS NewsHour***:** Video and transcript of Travis Lenkner interview, *PBS NewsHour*, September 25, 2015, https://www.pbs.org/newshour
/show/kavanaugh-supporter-we-have-all-the-information-we-need-on
-yale-allegation.

CHAPTER 9. *INNOCENS*: THE INNOCENT

139 **"I cannot imagine her making this up":** Ronan Farrow and Jane Mayer,
"Senate Democrats Investigate a New Allegation of Sexual Misconduct, from
Brett Kavanaugh's College Years," *The New Yorker*, September 23, 2018,
https://www.newyorker.com/news/news-desk/senate-democrats-investigate
-a-new-allegation-of-sexual-misconduct-from-the-supreme-court-nominee
-brett-kavanaughs-college-years-deborah-ramirez.

141 **Garry, now a high school teacher and coach:** Louisa Garry, "Senate Judiciary Committee Hearing on the Nomination of Brett Kavanaugh to Be an
Associate Justice on the Supreme Court, Day 4, Part 1," C-SPAN video, September 7, 2018, https://www.c-span.org/video/?c4750840/louisa-garry.

143 *The Washington Times* **then published an article:** Victor Morton, "Kavanaugh Accuser Deborah Ramirez Refuses to Talk to Congress: 'Read the *New
Yorker*,'" *Washington Times*, September 25, 2018, https://www.washingtontimes
.com/news/2018/sep/25/deborah-ramirez-brett-kavanaugh-accuser-wont
-testi/.

145 **"Neither** *The New Yorker* **nor** *The New York Times*":** Stephanie Saul, Robin
Pogrebin, Mike Mcintire, and Ben Protess, "In a Culture of Privilege and
Alcohol at Yale, Her World Converged with Kavanaugh's," *The New York
Times*, September 25, 2018, https://www.nytimes.com/2018/09/25/us/politics
/deborah-ramirez-brett-kavanaugh-allegations.html.

146 **Kavanaugh . . . cited the** *Times***'s decision not to publish:** Brett Kavanaugh
interview with Senate Judiciary Committee, September 25, 2018, https://

www.judiciary.senate.gov/imo/media/doc/09.25.18%20BMK%20Interview
%20Transcript%20(Redacted).pdf.

146 **Julie Swetnick came forward with her own alarming accusations:** Declaration of Julie Swetnick, September 25, 2018, http://fm.cnbc.com/applications
/cnbc.com/resources/editorialfiles/2018/09/26/swetnickstatement.pdf.

151 **three thousand Yale women signed an open letter:** "Open Letter from
Women of Yale in Support of Deborah Ramirez," September 24, 2018, https://
medium.com/@yalewomenforwomen/open-letter-from-women-of-yale-in
-support-of-deborah-r amirez-685bf4bb84f0.

151 **More than fifteen hundred Yale men issued a similar letter:** "An Open
Letter from Men of Yale in Support of Deborah Ramirez, Christine Blasey
Ford and others," September 25, 2018, https://medium.com/@yalemen80s
/an-open-letter-from-men-of-yale-in-support-of-deborah-ramirez-c hristine
-blasey-ford-and-others-ffc878fd600a.

CHAPTER 10. *LEGE DURA VIVUNT MULIERES*:
WOMEN LIVE UNDER A HARSH LAW

154 **On September 24, Koegler:** Declaration of Keith Koegler declaration on
Christine Blasey Ford, September 24, 2018, Senate Judiciary Committee
memo, https://www.judiciary.senate.gov/imo/media/doc/2018-11-02%20Kava
naugh%20Report.pdf.

155 **Ford's husband, Russell, along with her close friends:** Declarations of
Russell Ford, Adela Gildo-Mazzon, and Rebecca White on Christine Blasey
Ford, September 24, 2018 and September 25, 2018, Senate Judiciary Committee memo, https://www.judiciary.senate.gov/imo/media/doc/2018-11-02%
20Kavanaugh%20Report.pdf.

156 **Hoffman said later:** Reid Hoffman's full statement on the matter, provided
May 25, 2019 to authors: "As Dr. Blasey Ford was preparing to testify before
Congress, Mark Pincus and I received word that she needed assistance in getting to Washington in as safe a way as possible, and we were asked to help. At
that point, it was widely known that she was receiving serious violent threats.
In order to serve the public interest, Dr. Blasey Ford was clearly taking a huge
personal risk. So, we agreed to help provide transportation so she could she
could give her sworn testimony. We did so because we believed then, as we do
now, that it is important to take seriously accusations of violence against
women." In a subsequent statement, provided June 17, 2019, to authors, Mark
Pincus said: "My motivation to do this, in addition to what Reid said already,
was that I wanted to make sure that she had a chance to be heard."

158 **in the wake of the** *Washington Post* **story:** Emma Brown, "California Professor, Writer of Confidential Brett Kavanaugh Letter, Speaks Out About Her Allegation of Sexual Assault," *Washington Post*, September 16, 2018, https://www.washingtonpost.com/investigations/california-professor-writer-of-confidential-brett-kavanaugh-letter-speaks-out-about-her-allegation-of-sexual-assault/2018/09/16/46982194-b846-11e8-94eb-3bd52dfe917b_story.html.

158 **"categorically"** . . . **"a hearing as soon as possible":** Lisa Mascaro, "Kavanaugh Denies Allegation of Sexual Misconduct in School," Associated Press, September 14, 2018, https://www.apnews.com/ee8c3ce45bd5427a8830c6eb6ff42e1f; see also Kasie Hunt and Rebecca Shabad, "Kavanaugh: I Will Attend Monday Hearing 'So That I Can Clear My Name,'" NBC News, September 20, 2018, https://www.nbcnews.com/politics/congress/kavanaugh-preps-senate-testimony-assault-allegations-n911441.

159 **White House could decide Kavanaugh wasn't worth:** Gabriel Sherman, "'The Strategy Was to Try and Do Something Really Big': Trump Wanted to Nuke Rosenstein to Save Kavanaugh's Bacon," *Vanity Fair*, September 24, 2018, https://www.vanityfair.com/news/2018/09/trump-wanted-to-nuke-rosenstein-to-save-kavanaughs-bacon; see also Christina Wilkie, "Trump: 'I Could Be Persuaded' to Change Mind on Kavanaugh after Hearing," CNBC, September 26, 2018, https://www.cnbc.com/2018/09/26/trump-i-could-be-persuaded-to-change-mind-on-kavanaugh-after-hearing.html.

159 **a group of Democratic Senators sent a letter:** Statement from Amy Klobuchar et al., September 20, 2018, https://www.klobuchar.senate.gov/public/index.cfm/2018/9/klobuchar-harris-other-senators-who-served-as-prosecutors-and-attorneys-general-urge-the-president-to-direct-the-federal-bureau-of-investigation-to-reopen-its-background-investigation-into-judge-brett-kavanaugh.

160 **an NBC/***Wall Street Journal* **poll:** Janet Hook, "Opposition to Kavanaugh Nomination Grows Among Voters, New Poll Shows," *The Wall Street Journal*, September 20, 2018, https://www.wsj.com/articles/opposition-to-kavanaugh-nomination-grows-among-voters-new-poll-shows-1537477360.

160 **Kavanaugh's wife, Ashley, received death threats:** Kristina Peterson, Peter Nicholas, and Natalie Andrews, "Kavanaugh Accuser Open to Negotiations to Testify Before Senate Panel," *The Wall Street Journal*, September 20, 2018, https://www.wsj.com/articles/senators-in-standoff-over-handling-of-kavanaugh-sexual-assault-allegations-1537451055; see also Nicole Darrah, "Brett Kavanaugh, Wife, and Christine Blasey Ford All Receiving Death Threats," Fox News, September 21, 2018, https://www.foxnews.com/politics/brett-kavanaugh-wife-and-christine-blasey-ford-all-receiving-death-threats-graphic-language.

160 **He worked with Beth Wilkinson:** Ariane de Vogue and Eli Watkins, "Brett Kavanaugh, Christine Blasey Ford to Testify on Assault Allegations in Public Monday," CNN, September 17, 2018, https://www.cnn.com/2018/09/17/politics /brett-kavanaugh-testimony/index.html.

160 **He and his wife tried to explain:** Brett and Ashley Kavanaugh interview with Martha MacCallum, Fox News, September 24, 2018, https://www .foxnews.com/transcript/kavanaugh-i-never-sexually-assaulted-anyone.

161 **"I've never sexually assaulted anyone":** And other details from Fox News interview, Brett and Ashley Kavanaugh interview with Martha MacCallum, Fox News.

162 **reports . . . that Ramirez had been calling around:** Saul et al., "In a Culture of Privilege and Alcohol at Yale, Her World Converged with Kavanaugh's," *The New York Times*, September 25, 2018, https://www.nytimes.com/2018/09/25 /us/politics/deborah-ramirez-brett-kavanaugh-allegations.html.

162 **Swetnick's claims that he and Mark Judge:** Declaration of Julie Swetnick, September 25, 2018, http://fm.cnbc.com/applications/cnbc.com/resources /editorialfiles/2018/09/26/swetnickstatement.pdf.

163 **"We had numerous conversations":** Peter Baker and Nicholas Fandos, "Show How You Feel, Kavanaugh Was Told, and a Nomination Was Saved," *The New York Times*, October 6, 2018, https://www.nytimes.com/2018/10/06 /us/politics/kavanaugh-vote-confirmation-process.html.

163 **"I'm stronger than mule piss":** Baker and Fandos, "Show How You Feel, Kavanaugh Was Told, and a Nomination Was Saved."

164 **Kavanaugh and his close high school friends:** Kate Kelly and David Enrich, "Kavanaugh's Yearbook Page Is 'Horrible, Hurtful' to a Woman It Named," *The New York Times*, September 24, 2018, https://www.nytimes.com /2018/09/24/business/brett-kavanaugh-yearbook-renate.html.

165 **Kavanaugh denied having boasted . . . any of the Prep boys:** Kelly and Enrich, "Kavanaugh's Yearbook Page Is 'Horrible, Hurtful' to a Woman It Named."

167 **Tiverton, Rhode Island, man named Jeffrey Catalan:** See Senate Judiciary Committee memo, November 2, 2018, https://www.judiciary.senate .gov/imo/media/doc/2018-11-02%20Kavanaugh%20Report.pdf; see also Janine Weisman, "Crank Calls Directed at Kavanaugh Accuser Bombard Newport Woman Overnight," *The Newport Daily News*, September 27, 2018, https ://www.providencejournal.com/news/20180927/crank-calls-directed-at-kavanaugh-accuser-bombard-newport-woman-overnight/1.

168 **tip sent to Senator Kamala Harris's San Diego office:** Senate Judiciary Committee memo, November 2, 2018.

168 **Judy Munro-Leighton later claimed credit:** Letter from Charles Grassley to Jeff Sessions and Christopher Wray on "fabricated allegations," November 2, 2018, https://www.judiciary.senate.gov/download/grassley-to-justice-dept-fbi_-munro-leighton-referral-.

171 **Ford's testimony played out like a master class in authenticity and simplicity:** Christine Blasey Ford Senate Judiciary Committee hearing, September 27, 2018, https://www.washingtonpost.com/news/national/wp/2018/09/27/kavanaugh-hearing-transcript/?utm_term=.28ec87d58caf; see also video of hearing, C-SPAN video, September 27, 2018, https://www.c-span.org/video/?451895-1/professor-blasey-ford-testifies-sexual-assault-allegations-part-1&playEvent.

CHAPTER 11. *INDE IRA ET LACRIMAE*: THEN ANGER AND TEARS

178 **calls jumped 147 percent:** Abigail Abrams, "National Sexual Assault Hotline Spiked 147% During Christine Blasey Ford Hearing," *Time*, September 27, 2018, https://time.com/5409239/national-sexual-assault-hotline-spike-christine-blasey-ford-hearing/.

178 **Ashley Judd, Ellen DeGeneres:** Nicholas Hautman, "Ellen DeGeneres, Mariska Hargitay and More Stars Support Christine Blasey Ford During Brett Kavanaugh Hearing," *Us*, September 27, 2018, https://www.usmagazine.com/celebrity-news/news/stars-support-christine-blasey-ford-during-brett-kavanaugh-hearing/.

178 **Emmy Rossum, and other prominent celebrities:** Natasha Penrose, "Women Are Thanking Dr. Ford for Her Bravery on Twitter," *Elle*, September 27, 2018, https://www.elle.com/culture/career-politics/a23493387/twitter-reactions-christine-ford-kavanaugh-hearing/.

178 **Sally Field:** Sally Field, Twitter, September 27, 2018, https://twitter.com/sally_field/status/1045354845660635136.

178 **Charlie Baker, the Republican governor of Massachusetts:** Spencer Buell, "Charlie Baker: Kavanaugh Accusations 'Are Sickening and Deserve an Independent Investigation,'" *Boston Magazine*, September 27, 2018, https://www.bostonmagazine.com/news/2018/09/27/baker-kavanaugh-sickening/.

178 **"I thought her testimony was very compelling":** NBC News Tweet of Trump comments, Twitter, September 28, 2018, https://twitter.com/NBCNews/status/1045740388663873536.

179 **Chris Wallace pronounced Ford's testimony a "disaster":** German Lopez, "Fox News's Chris Wallace on the Kavanaugh Hearing: 'This Is a Disaster for the Republicans,'" September 27, 2018, https://www.vox.com/policy-and

-politics/2018/9/27/17910490/christine-blasey-ford-kavanaugh-senate-hearing
-fox-news-chris-wallace.

179 **Mike Cernovich wrote on Twitter:** Jenna Amatulli, "Conservatives, Right-Wing Media Respond to Christine Blasey Ford's Testimony," *Huffington Post*, September 27, 2018, https://www.huffpost.com/entry/fox-news-christine -blasey-ford-testimony-kavanaugh-hearing_n_5bacfc7ee4b0425e3c2123e6.

179 **"Heartbreaking, credible, and compelling":** Elizabeth Warren, Twitter, September 7, 2018, https://twitter.com/SenWarren/status/1045357573724151811.

179 **Graham told the press scrum that Ford was "a nice lady":** Paul McLeod, "Lindsey Graham Says Christine Blasey Ford Hasn't Convinced Him to Oppose Kavanaugh," *BuzzFeed News*, September 27, 2018, https://www.buzzfeed news.com/article/paulmcleod/lindsey-graham-lashed-out-ford -allegations-political.

179 **Louisiana senator Bill Cassidy:** Meghan Keneally, "Mixed Reactions to Kavanaugh and Ford's Differing Testimony," ABC News, September 27, 2018, https://abcnews.go.com/US/heartbreaking-credible-compelling-reactions -christine-blasey-fords-testimony/story?id=58126112.

179–80 **Rachel Mitchell would say in her final report:** Rachel Mitchell memorandum to Senate Republicans, September 30, 2018, https://static.politico.com /28/7f/80157df74b96bb352b10f8b7aa66/09-30-18-mitchell-memo-ford-allega tions.pdf.

180 **The closest Ford could come:** In an interview with Michael Judge, Mark Judge's older brother, author was told that Mark did, in fact, work at the Potomac Village Safeway during the summer of 1982. Mark writes about the job, without identifying the store, on p. 98 of his book *Wasted*: "I spent a few weeks working as a bag boy at a local supermarket."

180 **Louellen Welsch:** "How Americans Across the Country Are Reacting to Christine Blasey Ford's Testimony," *The New York Times*, September 27, 2018, https://www.nytimes.com/2018/09/27/us/dr-ford-kavanaugh-reaction.html.

181 **Ralph's public comments:** Jessica Contrera and Ian Shapira, "Christine Blasey Ford's Family Has Been Nearly Silent Amid Outpouring of Support," *Washington Post*, September 27, 2018, https://www.washingtonpost.com/local /christine-blasey-fords-own-family-has-been-nearly-silent-amid-outpouring -of-support/2018/09/26/49a3f4a6-c0d6-11e8-be77-516336a26305_story .html?utm_term=.667cf7d28236.

182 **1996 foreclosure case:** Kyra Haas, "Fact-checking False Link Between Foreclosure Case, Brett Kavanaugh Sexual Assault Allegations," Politifact, September 20, 2018, https://www.politifact.com/facebook-fact-checks/statements/2018 /sep/20/blog-posting/kavanaughs-mother-dismissed-foreclosure-case/.

182 **Burning Tree Golf Club:** Ben Schreckinger and Daniel Lippman, "Power Elite of Suburban Washington Split over Kavanaugh Allegations," *Politico*, September 17, 2018, https://www.politico.com/story/2018/09/17/power-elite -of-suburban-washington-split-over-kavanaugh-allegations-826318.

182 **Senator Schumer and his colleagues:** Authors' reporting; see also Ryan Grim, *We've Got People: From Jesse Jackson to Alexandria Ocasio-Cortez, the End of Big Money and the Rise of a Movement* (Washington, D.C.: Strong Arm Press, 2019), pp. 374–375.

182 **Just before noon, as the judge was escorted:** AP News, Video of Brett Kavanaugh's departure from Chevy Chase home, September 27, 2018, accessed on YouTube, https://www.youtube.com/watch?v=vBV3hhzI02s.

183 **"You need to reboot the room":** Carl Hulse, *Confirmation Bias: Inside Washington's War over the Supreme Court, From Scalia's Death to Justice Kavanaugh* (New York: HarperCollins, 2019), p. 253.

184 **"Less than two weeks ago, Dr. Ford publicly accused":** Brett Kavanaugh Opening Statement, September 27, 2018, https://www.cnn.com/videos/poli tics/2018/09/27/brett-kavanaugh-opening-statement-senate-hearing-vpx .cnn. For full hearing transcript of Brett Kavanaugh's September 27, 2018, hearing, see: https://www.washingtonpost.com/news/national/wp/2018/09 /27/kavanaugh-hearing-transcript/?utm_term=.ced0255926ca.

187 **Twitter posts to mock and degrade almost anyone:** Michael D. Shear and Eileen Sullivan, "Trump Calls Omarosa Manigault Newman 'That Dog' in His Latest Insult," *The New York Times*, August 14, 2018, https://www.nytimes .com/2018/08/14/us/politics/trump-omarosa-dog.html; see also Christina Caron, "Trump Mocks LeBron James's Intelligence and Calls Don Lemon 'Dumbest Man' on TV," *The New York Times*, August 4, 2018, https://www .nytimes.com/2018/08/04/sports/donald-trump-lebron-james-twitter.html.

199 **"The Judge as Umpire":** Brett M. Kavanaugh, "The Judge as Umpire: Ten Principles," *Catholic University Law Review*, June 22, 2016, https://scholarship .law.edu/cgi/viewcontent.cgi?referer=https://www.google.com/&httpsredir =1&article=3383&context=lawreview.

CHAPTER 12. *FALSUS IN UNO, FALSUS IN OMNIBUS?:* FALSE IN ONE THING, FALSE IN ALL THINGS?

205 **"Brett stood up there and lied about who he was":** Lynne Brookes, "Kavanaugh 'Lied' in Interview, Drank to Excess, Classmate from Yale Says," *Good Morning America* video, ABC News, https://abcnews.go.com/GMA/News /video/kavanaugh-lied-interview-drank-excess-classmate-yale-58146577.

206 **"It wasn't drunk to the point of having trouble getting up every month or two"**: James Roche, CNN video, https://www.realclearpolitics.com/video/2018/10/03/kavanaugh_freshman_roommate_i_saw_him_do_stuff_he_said_under_oath_he_didnt_do.html.

206 **"So angry, so disgusted, so sad"**: Mike McIntire, Linda Qiu, Steve Eder, and Kate Kelly, "At Times, Kavanaugh's Defense Misleads or Veers off Point," *The New York Times*, September 28, 2018, https://www.nytimes.com/2018/09/28/us/politics/brett-kavanaugh-fact-check.html.

206 **"It's the twilight zone"**: Brett Kavanaugh interview with Senate Judiciary Committee, September 25, 2018, https://www.judiciary.senate.gov/imo/media/doc/09.25.18%20BMK%20Interview%20Transcript%20(Redacted).pdf.

206 **Dan Murphy and Chris Dudley**: Brian Reis et al., "Two More Yale Classmates Release Statements on Kavanaugh," CNN, October 1, 2018, https://www.cnn.com/politics/live-news/kavanaugh-fbi-investigation-oct-18/h_3d80c164e1cc62a398f3dd1d37ac41d8.

207 **"To the day I die, I'll believe that he did not do this"**: Tom Kane interview on CNN, Twitter, https://twitter.com/NewDay/status/1045639045588475906.

208 **"assuming that there are any lines anymore"**: Benjamin Wittes, "I Know Brett Kavanaugh, but I Wouldn't Confirm Him," *The Atlantic*, October 2, 2018, https://www.theatlantic.com/ideas/archive/2018/10/why-i-wouldnt-confirm-brett-kavanaugh/571936/.

208 **"a howl of rage"**: Wittes, "I Know Brett Kavanaugh, but I Wouldn't Confirm Him."

209 **More than 2,400 law professors**: "The Senate Should Not Confirm Kavanaugh," *The New York Times*, October 3, 2018, https://www.nytimes.com/interactive/2018/10/03/opinion/kavanaugh-law-professors-letter.html.

209 **One of the most stinging critiques**: Adam Liptak, "Retired Justice John Paul Stevens Says Kavanaugh Is Not Fit for Supreme Court," *The New York Times*, October 4, 2018, https://www.nytimes.com/2018/10/04/us/politics/john-paul-stevens-brett-kavanaugh.html.

209 **Mark Osler and Michael Proctor**: Michael Proctor and Mark Osler, Letter to Charles Grassley and Dianne Feinstein, October 2, 2018, https://www.scribd.com/document/389979642/Kavanaugh-classmates-withdraw-support#from_embed?campaign=SkimbitLtd&ad_group=38395X1559799Xd4612ee955477affac51b7fd6c9e2950&keywo rd=660149026&source=hp_aff iliate&medium=affiliate.

211 **"I would defy anyone not to be angry about that"**: Sheryl Gay Stolberg, "A New Front in the Kavanaugh Wars: Temperament and Honesty," *The New*

York Times, October 1, 2018, https://www.nytimes.com/2018/10/01/us/politics/brett-kavanaugh-temperament-honesty.html.

212 **"what is the proper amount of anger"**: David French, "The Complete Case for Kavanaugh," *National Review*, October 5, 2018, https://www.nationalreview.com/2018/10/kavanaugh-case-for-confirmation-allegations-explained/.

CHAPTER 13. *CONCORDIA ORDINUM*: AGREEMENT AMONG THE RANKS

217 **Both had spent time in Africa:** Mary Clare Jalonick, "From Africa to the Anteroom: Flake, Coons Forge Rare Bond," Associated Press, October 2, 2018, https://www.apnews.com/31b4e77aa91549e9a1a34b39777ecb75.

217 **Flake intended to vote for Kavanaugh:** Jordain Carney, "Flake Says He Will Vote to Confirm Kavanaugh," *The Hill*, September 28, 2018, https://thehill.com/homenews/senate/408914-flake-says-he-will-vote-to-confirm-kavanaugh.

219 **Michael Dukakis was criticized in 1988 for a lack of emotion:** "Dukakis' Deadly Response," *Time*, http://content.time.com/time/specials/packages/article/0,28804,1844704_1844706_1844712,00.html.

219 **On his way into the elevator:** Video of the confrontation at https://www.youtube.com/watch?v=bshgOZ8QQxU.

221 **"All of us should remember"**: Remarks by Ted Cruz at Senate Judiciary Committee hearing, September 28, 2018, C-SPAN video, https://www.c-span.org/video/?452084-1/senator-flake-calls-delaying-kavanaugh-vote-fbi-background-check-reopen&live.

221 **"You know me—you know I try to be fair"**: Remarks by Chris Coons at Senate Judiciary Committee hearing, September 28, 2018, CNN, September 28, 2018, http://transcripts.cnn.com/TRANSCRIPTS/1809/28/ip.01.html.

227 **Ashley Kavanaugh had asked family and friends to pray Psalm 40:** Benjamin Gill, "What Dr. Dobson and Ashley Kavanaugh Are Praying for the Kavanaugh Family & America," Christian Broadcasting Network News, October 1, 2018, https://www1.cbn.com/cbnnews/us/2018/october/what-dr-dobson-and-ashley-kavanaugh-are-praying-for-the-kavanaugh-family-and-america.

CHAPTER 14. *CONFIRMATIO—SED QUIS CUSTODIET CUSTODES?*: CONFIRMATION—BUT WHO WILL WATCH THE WATCHERS?

231 **President Trump said the FBI agents would have "free rein"**: Remarks by President Trump, C-SPAN video, September 29, 2018, https://www.c-span

.org/video/?452287-2/president-trump-fbi-investigation-kavanaugh-blessing-disguise.

232 **"I want them to interview whoever they deem appropriate, at their discretion"**: Donald Trump, Twitter, September 29, 2018, https://twitter.com/realdonaldtrump/status/1046230634103025664?lang=en.

233 **Klobuchar said on CBS's *Face the Nation***: Amy Klobuchar on CBS *Face the Nation*, September 30, 2018, https://www.cbsnews.com/news/transcript-sen-amy-klobuchar-on-face-the-nation-sept-30-2018/.

233 **Kellyanne Conway fired back**: Remarks by Kellyanne Conway on CNN's *State of the Union*, September 30, 2018, https://www.cnn.com/2018/09/30/politics/kellyanne-conway-kavanaugh-fbi-cnntv/index.html.

233 **Keyser had provided a statement**: Leland Keyser statement to Judiciary Committee, September 22, 2018, https://www.judiciary.senate.gov/imo/media/doc/2018-09-22%20Keyser%20to%20Committee%20Investigators%20-%20Ford%20Allegations.pdf.

236 **Through a lawyer, McLean**: Monica McLean's full statement—a statement provided to the *Wall Street Journal* during the confirmation process, as well as a new statement provided for the publication of this book—is as follows: "Any notion or claim that Ms. McLean pressured Leland Keyser to alter Ms. Keyser's account of what she recalled concerning the alleged incident between Dr. Ford and Brett Kavanaugh is absolutely false. Also false is any notion or claim that Ms. McLean, either directly or indirectly, threatened to disclose personal information about Ms. Keyser. To the contrary, Ms. McLean stressed to Ms. Keyser the importance of providing truthful information to the Senate Judiciary Committee and urged her to obtain counsel from her attorney."

237 **"the simple and unchangeable truth"**: Grace Segers, "Christine Blasey Ford's Friend Clarifies Statement About Alleged Assault by Brett Kavanaugh," CBS News, September 29, 2018, https://www.cbsnews.com/news/christine-blasey-ford-friend-leland-keyser-clarifies-statement-about-alleged-assault-by-brett-kavanaugh/.

237 **Judge and Smyth also met with the FBI**: P. J. Smyth statement to Senate Judiciary Committee, September 18, 2018, https://www.judiciary.senate.gov/download/2018-09-18-smyth-to-judiciary-committee_--ford-allegations; see also Mark Judge statement to Senate Judiciary Committee, September 18, 2018, https://www.judiciary.senate.gov/imo/media/doc/2018-09-18%20Judge%20to%20Grassley,%20Feinstein%20(Kavanaugh%20Nomination).pdf.

237 **"We lit each other's underwear on fire"**: Mark Gavreau Judge, *Wasted: Tales of a Gen X Drunk* (Center City, MN: Hazelden, 1997), p. 56.

238 **hiding away in the Bethany Beach, Delaware, home:** Gabriel Pogrund, Carol D. Leonnig, and Aaron C. Davis, "'How'd you find me?': Mark Judge Has Been Holed Up in a Beach House in Delaware amid a Media Firestorm," *Washington Post*, September 24, 2018, https://www.washingtonpost.com /investigations/howd-you-find-me-mark-judge-has-been-holed-up-in-a -beach-house-in-delaware-amid-a-media-firestorm/2018/09/24/9d4829aa -c041-11e8-be77-516336a26305_story.html?utm_term=.4df6f2bd4c6a.

240 **Yarasavage was one of ten women from Kavanaugh's class who signed a letter:** Yale College women letter to Senate Judiciary Committee, August 30, 2018, https://www.whitehouse.gov/wp-content/uploads/2018/09/2018-08-30 -Yale-College-Women-in-Support-of-Kavanaugh-FINAL.pdf.

242 **Kavanaugh was also asked:** Brett Kavanaugh interview with Senate Judiciary Committee, September 25, 2018, https://www.judiciary.senate.gov /imo/media/doc/09.25.18%20BMK%20Interview%20Transcript%20 (Redacted).pdf.

242 **Senator Orrin Hatch asked:** Brett Kavanaugh Senate Judiciary Committee hearing transcript, September 27, 2018, https://www.washingtonpost.com /news/national/wp/2018/09/27/kavanaugh-hearing-transcript/?utm_term =.c3fa18cd4e28.

242 **Bob Bauer . . . remarked to NBC News:** Heidi Przybyla and Leigh Ann Caldwell, "Text Messages Suggest Kavanaugh Wanted to Refute Accuser's Claim Before It Became Public," October 1, 2018, NBC News, https://www .nbcnews.com/politics/supreme-court/mutual-friend-ramirez-kavanaugh -anxious-come-forward-evidence-n915566.

242 **"After we were made to jump through several hoops":** Przybyla and Caldwell, "Text Messages Suggest Kavanaugh Wanted to Refute Accuser's Claim Before It Became Public."

243 **George Hartmann, a Grassley spokesman:** Przybyla and Caldwell, "Text Messages Suggest Kavanaugh Wanted to Refute Accuser's Claim Before It Became Public."

247 *National Review* **article on his confirmation:** Rich Lowry, "Was Leland Keyser the Hero of the Kavanaugh Controversy?," *National Review*, October 8, 2018, https://www.nationalreview.com/corner/was-leland-keyser-the-hero -of-the-kavanaugh-controversy/.

247 **Bromwich and Katz sent a letter to FBI director:** Brett Samuels, "Attorneys for Ford Say They Haven't Heard from FBI about Kavanaugh Investigation," *The Hill*, October 2, 2018, https://thehill.com/regulation/court -battles/409552-attorneys-for-ford-say-they-havent-heard-from-fbi-in -investigation.

247 **"My mantra is distrust but verify"**: Ian Schwartz, "Sen. Blumenthal on Kavanaugh Investigation, 'Distrust But Verify,'" RealClear Politics, October 1, 2018, https://www.realclearpolitics.com/video/2018/10/01/blumenthal_on _kavanaugh_investigation_distrust_but_verify.html.

248 **"I had one beer'"**: "Trump Mocks Dr. Christine Blasey Ford's Testimony at Mississippi Rally," CBS News, October 2, 2018, https://www.cbsnews.com /news/donald-trump-mocks-christine-blasey-ford-testimony-make-america -great-again-rally-mississippi-landers-center-2018-10-02/.

248 **Flake called them "appalling"**: Jonathan Allen, "Trump Mocks Kavanaugh Accuser Christine Blasey Ford at Campaign Rally," NBC News, October 2, 2018, https://www.nbcnews.com/politics/politics-news/trump-mocks-chris tine-blasey-ford-mississippi-campaign-rally-n916061?fbclid=IwAR2rHfS5u LeOu0F0-sl_Z35L2wGmIO3zGD5Kh57YdOlYkYaHhwcC87PzSaE.

248 **Murkowski told reporters:** Kristina Peterson, "Murkowski: Trump Comments 'Absolutely, Wholly Unacceptable,'" October 3, 2018, https://www.wsj .com/livecoverage/kavanaugh/card/1538584273.

248 **Even Grassley took to Twitter:** Chuck Grassley, Twitter, October 3, 2018, https://twitter.com/ChuckGrassley/status/1047516105567363073.

248 **In a *Washington Post* op-ed, Coons:** Senator Chris Coons, "We Need the Facts on Kavanaugh. Here's How the FBI Can Get Them," *The Wall Street Journal*, October 2, 2018, https://www.washingtonpost.com/opinions/heres -what-the-fbi-investigation-into-the-kavanaugh-allegations-should-look -like/2018/10/02/8709d4e8-c65b-11e8-9158-09630a6d8725_story.html?utm _term=.69b77c320bce.

249 **Democratic senators on the Judiciary Committee sent Grassley a letter:** Richard Durbin et al., Letter to the Senate Judiciary Committee, October 3, 2018, https://www.durbin.senate.gov/imo/media/doc/Letter%20to%20Ch airman%20Grassley%20-%20October%203,%202018.pdf.

249 **McConnell took to the Senate floor:** Jordain Carney, "McConnell Slams Anti-Kavanaugh Protests, 'Intimidation Tactics,'" *The Hill*, October 3, 2018, https://thehill.com/blogs/floor-action/senate/409654-mcconnell-slams -anti-kavanaugh-protests-intimidation-tactics.

249 **Rosenstein was dealing with reports that he had secretly recorded President Trump:** Adam Goldman and Michael S. Schmidt, "Rod Rosenstein Suggested Secretly Recording Trump and Discussed 25th Amendment," *The New York Times*, September 21, 2018, https://www.nytimes.com/2018/09/21 /us/politics/rod-rosenstein-wear-wire-25th-amendment.html.

250 **a twenty-eight-year friend of Ramirez's signed a sworn affidavit:** Madeline St. Amour, "Another Witness Who Offered to Speak with FBI Comes

Forward in Deborah Ramirez Case," *Daily Camera*, October 4, 2018, https://
www.dailycamera.com/2018/10/04/another-witness-who-offered-to-speak
-with-fbi-comes-forward-in-deborah-ramirez-case/.

250 **Jen Klaus, one of Ramirez's former roommates:** Heidi Przybyla, "The
Battle over Accusations Goes on as Kavanaugh Nomination Advances," NBC
News, October 5, 2018, https://www.nbcnews.com/politics/supreme-court
/battle-over-accusations-goes-kavanaugh-nomination-advances-n917136.

250 **"no suggestion of mistaken identity was made":** Heidi Przybyla, "The
Battle over Accusations Goes on as Kavanaugh Nomination Advances."

251 **The committee had also heard from Ford's graduate school boyfriend,
Brian Merrick:** Senate Judiciary Report, November 2, 2018, https://www.ju
diciary.senate.gov/imo/media/doc/2018-11-02%20Kavanaugh%20Report.pdf.

251 **McConnell announced that its results would not be made publicly available:** Igor Bobic and Arthur Delaney, "Mitch McConnell Says FBI's Kavanaugh Report Won't Be Made Public," *Huffington Post*, October 2, 2018,
https://www.huffpost.com/entry/mitch-mcconnell-fbi-kavanaugh-report
-public_n_5bb3c909e4b0876eda992325.

251 **a special soundproof reading room:** "How Senators Read the FBI Report
on Kavanaugh: 5 Fast Facts You Need to Know" *The Heavy*, October 4, 2018,
https://heavy.com/news/2018/10/fbi-report-kavanaugh-senate-scif/.

251–52 **The viewing began at 8 a.m.:** Daniel Chaitin, "Here Is the Schedule for
Senators to View the FBI's Kavanaugh Investigation Report on Thursday,"
Washington Examiner, October 3, 2018, https://www.washingtonexaminer
.com/news/here-is-the-schedule-for-senators-to-view-the-fbis-kavanaugh
-investigation-report-on-thursday.

252 **Tim Kaine . . . tweeted:** Tim Kaine, Twitter, October 4, 2018, https://twitter
.com/timkaine/status/1047887516387479552.

253 **"There's nothing in it that we didn't already know":** Jack Crowe, "Grassley:
Nothing in FBI Report 'We Didn't Already Know,'" *National Review*, October
4, 2018, https://www.nationalreview.com/news/chuck-grassley-nothing-new
-fbi-brett-kavanaugh-report/.

253 **On October 5, the Senate voted to advance Kavanaugh's nomination to
a final vote:** Annie Daniel, Jasmine C. Lee, and Sarah Simon, "How Every
Senator Voted on Advancing Kavanaugh's Confirmation," *The New York
Times*, October 5, 2018, https://www.nytimes.com/interactive/2018/10/05/us
/politics/kavanaugh-live-vote-procedural.html.

254 **Ramirez had identified to the FBI the "eyewitnesses":** Heidi Przybyla,
"The Battle over Accusations Goes On as Kavanaugh Nomination Advances."

254–55 **a forty-five-minute speech:** Transcript of Susan Collins's speech, *The New York Times*, October 5, 2018, https://www.nytimes.com/2018/10/05/us/politics /susan-collins-speech-brett-kavanaugh.html.

255 **the traditional ivory gavel:** "The Senate's New Gavel," U.S. Senate website, https://www.senate.gov/artandhistory/history/minute/The_Senates_New _Gavel.htm.

256 **"I do not consent. I do not consent":** Gina Martinez, "'I Do Not Consent.' Kavanaugh's Confirmation Vote Was Interrupted Multiple Times by Screaming Protesters," *Time*, October 6, 2018, https://time.com/5417844/i-do-not -consent-kavanaughs-confirmation-vote-was-interrupted- multiple-times-by -screaming-protesters/.

256 **"The ayes are fifty," Pence said. "The nays are forty-eight":** *The Guardian*, YouTube video, October 6, 2018, https://www.youtube.com/watch?v =L0uqdwjiUbo.

EPILOGUE. *HAMARTIA*: MISSING THE MARK

267 **"Blackouts are like a philosophical riddle":** Sarah Hepola, "Kavanaugh and the Blackout Theory," *The New York Times*, September 29, 2018, https:// www.nytimes.com/2018/09/29/opinion/sunday/brett-kavanaugh-drinking -blackouts.html.

268 **he wrote in an op-ed:** Brett Kavanaugh, "I Am an Independent, Impartial Judge," *The Wall Street Journal*, October 4, 2018, https://www.wsj.com/articles /i-am-an-independent-impartial-judge-1538695822.

269 **Quinnipiac poll:** "More U.S. Voters Say Don't Confirm Kavanaugh, Quinnipiac University National Poll Finds; More Voters Believe Ford Than Kavanaugh," October 1, 2018, https://poll.qu.edu/national/release-detail?Release ID=2574.